WomenPreneurs

WomenPreneurs: 21st Century Success Strategies brings together some three decades of research and writing to provide readers with a map for recognizing problems that many will encounter in organizational and entrepreneurial environments, the reasons these conditions exist and solutions that have worked for numerous successful women.

Dorothy Perrin Moore, Ph.D. is an Emeritus Professor of Business Administration at The Citadel, Charleston, South Carolina, U.S.A., where she held the title of Distinguished Professor of Entrepreneurship. She is the author of *Careerpreneurs—Lessons From Leading Women Entrepreneurs on Building A Career Without Boundaries,* which received the *ForeWord Magazine* Book of the Year Gold Award in the field of Business and the co-author of *Women Entrepreneurs—Moving Beyond the Glass Ceiling.*

WomenPreneurs

21st Century Success Strategies

Dorothy Perrin Moore

NEW YORK AND LONDON

First published 2012
by Routledge
711 Third Avenue, New York, NY 10017

Simultaneously published in the UK
by Routledge
2 Park Square, Milton Park, Abingdon, Oxon OX14 4RN

Routledge is an imprint of the Taylor & Francis Group, an informa business

Library of Congress Cataloging in Publication Data
Moore, Dorothy P.
Womenpreneurs: 21st century success strategies / Dorothy Perrin Moore.
p. cm.
Includes index.
1. Self-employed women—United States. 2. Women-owned business enterprises—United States. 3. Businesswomen—United States.
4. Entrepreneurship—United States. I. Title.
HD6072.6.U5M663 2012
658.4'012082—dc23

2011035494

ISBN: 978-0-415-89684-9 (hbk)
ISBN: 978-0-415-89685-6 (pbk)
ISBN: 978-0-203-12668-4 (ebk)

Typeset in Baskerville
by RefineCatch Limited, Bungay, Suffolk, UK

Printed and bound in the United States of America
by Edwards Brothers, Inc.

DEDICATION

This book is dedicated to the full engagement of the entrepreneurial spirit in all women and men who want to move our economy forward and to compete on a level playing field in today's diverse, global, technological and competitive market.

There is a special dedication to each of the women who provided profile cases for this book to enable readers to understand that there is not just one path to a bright and successful career but many, and it is with determination, drive, and the willingness to take the risk, to take a path less travelled, to invest in your continued education, health, and physical fitness and in building the right alliances that will serve you in good stead on your route. Seldom is success a straight line—it is through your decisive actions that others will follow and be inspired.

This book is also dedicated to my four precious grandchildren, who are inspirations to me but who have a way to go before they take their places in the world of work, whatever they decide those places are: James, Daniel, Justin and Dylan Moore.

PARTICIPANT PROFILE INDEX

1. The New Work Landscape
   Gail K. Naughton, Founder, Chairman and CEO, Histogen
   Nikki Hardin, Founder and Publisher Skirt!® Magazine
   Denise L. Devine, Founder, CEO and President, Nutripharm, Inc. and Froose® Brands, LLC
   Eleanor Tabi Haller-Jorden, General Manager, Catalyst Europe AG

2. Organizations: Leadership and Management
   Rebecca Smith, Founder and President, A. D. Morgan Corporation
   Maria L. Maccecchini, Ph.D., President and CEO, QR Pharma, Inc.
   Shabnam Rezaei, President, Big Bad Boo
   Judith V. Moore, Founder and CEO, Charleston Cookie Company, LLC

3. Work, Life and Career Strategies
   Ruth Ann Menutis, Founder, The Grove and Branded Works
   Suzy Spafford, Founder and CEO, Suzy's Zoo
   Aliza Sherman, Founder, Cybergrrl, Conversify and Mediaegg
   Kay Koplovitz, Founder and CEO, Koplovitz & Company

4. On the Road to Enterpreneurship
   Deborah Szekely, Founder, The Golden Door; Co-Founder (with Edmond Szekely), Rancho La Puerta

CONTENTS

PREFACE

This book began with the suggestion that I update the newspaper columns and other writings I have done over the years to provide a set of essays of contemporary value to three groups of potential readers. The first consists of higher education faculty teaching courses in management, human resource management, entrepreneurship, women's studies, and gender and diversity, and directors of professional development workshops interested in acquiring supplemental readings on the topics. The second consists of women in the workplace, those contemplating entry or seeking jobs, parents who want to provide daughters with guidance (as well as sons) and significant others who want those they love to have a safer journey navigating the rapid changes and twisting paths in advancing their careers. The third group includes entrepreneurial women in all stages of venture development, ranging from the nascents, through those identified in the "missing middle" to the more seasoned business owner. For all these people, I hope the book will serve as a valuable resource and guide.

When I first began writing columns for the Charleston *Post and Courier*, I brought with me the ethic of peer-reviewed academic writing that if you say something you must present the sources and evidence. From the beginning, so readers would know they were not just getting the author's opinion, my columns have been full of phrases like "According to XYZ's recent study" or "Data from the Bureau of Labor Statistics suggest" or "As the recent report issued by MNO says." As time passes, older data are replaced by new, fresh research findings appear and must be considered along with their predecessors, and people address different questions. Consequently, nearly all of the essays in this volume have been rigorously updated, evolving from the original core article to one that speaks to the present and the future. For this reason, I have included at the end of each chapter a complete list of sources and other works consulted for each essay.

As my work proceeded, I realized that the book would benefit if the themes of the essays were illuminated by first person accounts. During the research for my first two books, I had interviewed more than 350 successful women. Though more than a decade had passed since the last formal interviews, I wondered if some of them, and others I had met along the way, would be willing to share their stories. I have been overwhelmed by the responses I received and the willingness of the participants presented in this book to share their full stories of their successful careers. Individually and as a group, their accomplishments are significant and impressive. Their lives exhibit creativity, risk-taking, vision, and courage. Intelligent and independent, these women stand out from the crowd. Socially conscious and personally involved from the beginning, their success has caused them to reach out. They have given back to a remarkable degree. They are also extremely interesting.

This book is organized into five chapters: (1) The New Work Landscape, with sections on Working Women, Legislation and Policies, and The Changing Workplace, (2) Organizations: Leadership and Management, with sections on the Dimensions of Management, Women in Management and Values, Ethics and Stress, (3) Work, Life and Career Strategies, which includes The Job, Women in Organizations and Organizational Career Tips, (4) On the Road to Entrepreneurship, which includes The Rise of Modern Women Entrepreneurs, Women Entrepreneurs and Success, and Patterns and the Future in a Changing World, and (5) Preparing for the Future, with sections on Getting What You Deserve, Today and Tomorrow, Technopreneurs, and the Passage of Time Through Generations. An Afterword completes the volume.

ACKNOWLEDGEMENTS

I have many people to thank. Entrepreneurs gave freely of their time to participate in this study by updating their profiles, which, in many cases, took careful introspection and thought. I appreciate their perseverance and effort and the time they took to review the finished profile for accuracy. I am especially appreciative to the Center for Women, where I have been involved as a contributor, board member, in the initial entrepreneurial woman series development program, presenter, organizer of entrepreneurial community events and, more recently, in job coaching and writing a monthly professional advancement column for the Moxie section of the Charleston *Post and Courier.* I appreciate the release by the *Post and Courier* for the rights to original columns which I have written over more than 13 years as a public service. Early on, the editorial assistance of Teresa Taylor, who started the Business major columns at the *Post and Courier,* was most helpful.

I especially acknowledge Loretta N. Poole, Associate Director, for her most generous assistance at the Berkeley Center for Entrepreneurial Studies, New York University Stern School of Business.

Special thanks go to The Citadel library and its dedicated staff for their guidance and assistance in navigating the numerous online databases.

I have found John Szilagyi, Publisher of Business and Management texts for Routledge Publishing to be the perfect editor from the first moment I talked with him at the Academy of Management meeting about the book project throughout the preparation stages. He has provided the latitude for me to work freely on developing and writing *WomenPreneurs*—this kind of autonomy has been extremely important in providing the forum for the information included in this book. I also express special appreciation to Sara Werden, Editorial Assistant, who was most helpful at every stage in providing guidelines and assistance and in answering all of my inquiries promptly and providing that special empathy so important to creativity.

This book was made possible only with the intellectual inspiration, the exchange of ideas, dedicated editorial assistance, and tireless energy and camaraderie throughout the process of completing the manuscript by my husband and lifelong champion, Jamie Wallace Moore. A Professor Emeritus of History and author of many books, journal articles and other publications, his help was invaluable in researching, framing and writing the first drafts of the entrepreneurial profiles of the successful women in this book.

My thanks also go to our wonderful German Shepherd Maxie for giving up his early mornings at the beach to help with this project.

ABOUT THE AUTHOR

Dorothy Perrin Moore, Ph.D., an international authority and speaker on women's entrepreneurship, is an Emeritus Professor of Business Administration at The Citadel School of Business, where she held the title of Distinguished Professor of Entrepreneurship. Her scholarly writings include *Women Entrepreneurs—Moving Beyond the Glass Ceiling* (co-authored), *Careerpreneurs—Lessons from Leading Women Entrepreneurs on Building a Career Without Boundaries,* which received the *ForeWord Magazine* Book-of-the-Year Gold Award in the field of Business, and was also translated into Chinese, and numerous scholarly articles, book chapters and technical reports along with practitioner writings. *Island in the Storm, Sullivan's Island and Hurricane Hugo,* co-authored with Jamie W. Moore, received the *ForeWord Magazine* Book-of-the-Year Bronze Award for Local History.

A former entrepreneur, Professor Moore received her Ph.D. in Management, Organizational Behavior and Human Resource Management from the Darla Moore School of Business, the University of South Carolina. She is a recipient of the Academy of Management, Women in Management Division's Sage Janet Chusmir Service Award and the Division's Sage Scholarship Award. She is a Justin G. Longenecker Fellow in the United States Association of Small Business and Entrepreneurship and recognized as a Small Business Administration Women in Business Advocate for South Carolina and as one of Midway College's Outstanding Alumnae.

1

THE NEW WORK LANDSCAPE

Introduction

Over the past several decades, the forces of rapid economic and technological change, an influx of women and minorities into the workforce, the rise of a global economy and an investment market emphasis on short-term profits combined to reshape organizations. There were five major components of this change—organizational restructuring, the erosion of trust, the emergence of work teams as drivers of firm performance, diversity and the accompanying presence of new styles of leadership.

The organizational restructuring that took place acquired many names: downsizing, rightsizing, flattening, streamlining, outsourcing, working smarter and others. But at the core, each described processes whereby companies took advantage of new information sharing technologies to raise productivity and simultaneously lower costs by reducing the corporate bureaucracy, trimming the number of long-term employees and reducing benefits. The impact on individual employees accelerated dramatically in the rapid economic downturn which began in mid-2008 as firms scrambled to conserve capital by reducing inventories and laying off workers.

Within organizations, the restructuring led to an ever greater reliance on teams to carry out most of the organizational work, in part because a more diverse workforce brought together people with differing backgrounds, information sets, resources, perspectives and approaches to solving problems which contributed to a collective creativity.

The new employee diversity had resulted from a wide range of demographic, economic and social pressures. Among the demographic changes, the influx of women in large numbers was the most pronounced. In the United States by 1997, women held nearly half of all managerial and executive positions (48.1 percent) and accounted for more than one-half (52.8 percent) of the employed professionals. These numbers would continue to hold.

As women were moving into work roles traditionally occupied by males, and less successfully upward toward a more balanced representation in high-status, high-profile positions, both the makeup of organizational teams and the outlook of employees were changing. In part, this was because the organizational reshaping that had made them flat, lattice style, and increasingly diverse had been accompanied by a general erosion of employee trust in management and leadership. Queried in 2009, more than half of American workers said they did not trust their organization's leaders and an even higher percentage felt their employer had violated their contractual relationship. Further complicating the problems of organizational leadership were the presence of biases inherent in workforce groupings that formerly had been homogenous.

The new organizational dilemma was this: At all levels, work team leaders had become a critical determinant in developments bearing on organizational performance and productivity. How they led increasingly diverse groups of employees not only directly affected team performance; it had become critical to organizational productivity.

Gail K. Naughton

Founder, Chairman and CEO, Histogen

The number of patients with severe burns is relatively low and it started to seem foolish to put so much into a burn product when applications in other areas could be blockbusters. I walked through the exam room with Dr. John Hansborough at UCSD Medical Center explaining why we would shift our focus away from burns when we entered a room with a motionless young boy lying naked on a gurney, infused with tubes and wires. The boy, barely 4, had been severely burned in bed when his mom fell asleep while smoking, and was heavily sedated with morphine so that the nurses could perform the extremely painful 3 x daily wound treatments on him. John simply said, "If we could tissue engineer a biological treatment for these patients it could be an amazing pain and life-saving breakthrough. By the way, Gail. How old is your son now?" He was barely 4. With Dr. Hansborough as co-inventor, our first burn product was approved in 1997.

Gail Naughton earned a B.S. from St. Francis College, Brooklyn, New York, an M.S. in Histology and a Ph.D. in Hematology from the New York University Medical Center, where she completed her postdoctoral training and served as an assistant professor of research in the Department of Dermatology, and an M.B.A. in Executive Management from the Anderson School at the University of California, Los Angeles. After embarking on a career as a medical researcher, she recognized the potential from one of her bio-technical products and co-founded a business, Advanced Tissue Sciences, and over the next 15 years, as co-inventor of its core technology, she oversaw the design and development of the world's first manufacturing facility for tissue-engineered products and established corporate development and marketing partnerships with numerous companies. From 2002 to 2011, she served as the Dean of the College of Business at San Diego State University, leaving the position in order to focus on her work as Chairman and CEO of her regenerative medicine, biotechnology company Histogen, which she founded in 2007 after discovering the potential of proteins and growth factors produced by cells grown under simulated embryonic conditions for therapeutic and biomedical applications, and developing the unique technology process to create products based on these proteins. She currently holds over 100 patents.

The recipient of numerous honors and awards, including the National Inventor of the Year award given by the Intellectual Property Owners Association (2000) and *San Diego Magazine*'s Woman of the Year (2006), Gail can answer positively the question, "Did I make a difference today in the world?" Because of her pioneering work in the field of tissue engineering, her companies have made products that help people. "While learning to engineer tissue we often heard, 'That's impossible!', so our motto became and remains 'Accomplishing the impossible ahead of schedule'," she said. "Leadership in such an environment involves finding great people who are motivated by doing something that has never been done before and giving them the tools to be successful. Such entrepreneurial risk-takers create a contagious enthusiasm for finding cures for people in need."

That enthusiasm has carried over to Histogen, where she has brought together talented people who have blazed new tissue-engineering trails with her in the past. "What is unique about this technology is that we create embryonic-like proteins by growing normal cells under conditions of low oxygen and suspension cultures," she says. "The cells are tricked into thinking that they're back in an embryonic state, and start making the chemicals that they made during fetal development, which target stem cells into dividing and generating new tissue." Histogen's first target is hair growth, but its focus is also on developing novel, non-toxic cures for cancer as well as stimulating native stem cells in muscles, bones, and nerves to generate new tissue without scarring. "We essentially mimic nature to create solutions for medical problems that have been thought to be impossible to solve," she said.

Gail has held professorships at City University of New York, Hunter College and York College. She has held positions on the boards of directors of numerous public bodies (California Health Institute, the San Diego World Trade Center and the San Diego Corporate Governance Institute), public boards (Celera, Inc. and CR Bard), private organizations (City of Hope, the Charles H. and Anna S. Stern Foundation, the Ackerman Foundation); served on the advisory boards of academic institutions (Department of Bioengineering at Johns Hopkins University and Georgia Institute of Technology) and corporate entities (Scientific Advisor at Carmell Therapeutics Corporation); and other organizations (California Health Institute, San Diego State University Corporate Governance Institute, Rotary International).

Her managerial secret? "I've learned more about being a manager from my children than anything else in the world," she says. "First, I have three, and no matter how hard I try, at any time, two of them feel neglected. It's the same thing at work. The people you work with, who you rely on, can never get everything they need. You have to balance, but also make sure they respect the time you're spending with others and know you'd give it to them if you could. But sometimes you have to deal with only the highest priorities. Dividing your time and energies and whatever else, you're never going to satisfy everybody."

Her secret to success? "If you believe in what you want to do, what others think doesn't matter," she says. "I was doing research as a postdoctorate fellow and I ended up making this serendipitous discovery. It led to a number of publications and presentations. One of the key papers I sent out for publication in a dermatology journal was rejected. The first sentence in the letter from this journal said, 'Publication of this paper would be a disservice to dermatology.' I was crushed. I lived for research. My boss said, 'It doesn't matter what he said. Your work is good, you believe in this work, it doesn't matter what the reviewer said.' I said, 'Well they're the experts.' A month later I received an acceptance from a better journal. I took the letter to my boss, I was so pleased. He said, 'Your competition obviously reviewed for the last journal. The work was good and is now accepted. You have to believe in your work and learn from each lesson.' What I learned from that single mentoring lesson has kept me in good stead all of my professional life. It doesn't matter if people put up road blocks, or tell you it's impossible; if you're doing what you believe in and think it is right, sooner or later they'll come around."

Working Women

The Movement of Women into the Workforce

Between 1970 and 2009, the last full year for which we have data, as the labor force rose from 79.7 million to 139.9 million, a 77.8 percent increase, the number of women in the labor force rose from 29.7 million to 66.2 million, an increase of 123 percent. Women represented slightly more than one-third of the employed Americans in 1970 (37.7 percent) and fewer than one-third (32.9 percent) held full-time jobs. In 2009, women made up almost half of the labor force (47.3 percent) and more than four in ten (43.2 percent) held full-time jobs. The labor force participation rate for women, 43 percent in 1970, had risen to 59.2 percent in 2009.

The numerous reasons why women sought employment include the necessity for two family incomes to maintain a standard of living and the rise in single parent families. Alison Konrad and Frank Linnehan suggest that the dramatic change in this period from the limited job market and advancement opportunities was also fueled by the impact of the Equal Employment Opportunity and Affirmative Action programs whose full effects slowly penetrated the economy in the 1970s and 1980s.

As an analysis of the mammoth data collected from the national organizations study reported in *Organizations in America, Analyzing Their Structures and Human Resource Practices* indicates, market forces were not capable of creating such a change. Theories of the efficiency of free markets and hands-off government policies are grounded in the assumption that intense competition requires firms to become more efficient. It follows that job integration would increase because firms will seek to employ the best workers available, irrespective of other factors. The same theories similarly assume that the absence of competition in government and public-policy organizations would produce job segregation. In fact, the NOS showed the reverse was true. Government and non profit organizations exhibited a considerably higher degree of gender integration.

While the advancements of women were made possible through the enactment of Title VII of the Civil Rights Act of 1964, which prohibited discrimination on the basis of race, color, religion, sex or national origin, and Executive Order 11246 on Affirmative Action signed by President Lyndon B. Johnson in 1965, which prohibited major contractors doing business with the federal government from similarly discriminating and required affirmative action to insure equal treatment of applicants, the full effects of the EEO/AA legislation were far from immediate, as Karen O'Connor and Alixandra Yanus point out. It was not until 1971 that the "U.S. Supreme Court found that the Fourteenth Amendment's equal protection clause could be read to protect women." Not until 1976 did the Court articulate "a new rule by which to invalidate state laws discriminating against women." The new standards for employment were not established until 1978, when the Equal Employment Opportunity Commission published its Uniform Guidelines. The criteria that hiring, promoting and other standards of selection must be based on the "best qualified" candidates and compliance with both the "letter and spirit of the law" arrived a year later when the EEOC published its Clarifications to the Guidelines. Twelve more years would pass before the Civil Rights Act of 1991 placed the burden of proof of nondiscriminatory practices on the employer.

Nikki Hardin

Founder and Publisher, Skirt® Magazine

YES! YES! YES! YES! I'll be first to say "I'm sorry" when I'm wrong. YES! Make it two scoops of chocolate. YES! I'll stop resisting change. YES! Let's go skinny dipping. YES! I promise to read the instructions first next time. YES! I'll up the ante. YES! Leftover

> *cold pizza for breakfast. YES! Bring on blind dates, speed dates, the online dates. YES! More vegetables, please. YES! More caresses, please. YES! I'll break up with sugar. YES! I'll risk heartbreak. YES! I'd rather be a Venus Flytrap than a shrinking violet. YES! I won't take "no" for an answer. YES! I'll take pleasure walks as well as power walks. YES! I'll find magic in the mundane. YES! I'll try not to be so well-behaved. What's on your YES! List?* (Cover essay, *Skirt!*, June, 2011)

Nikki Hardin is the founder and publisher of *Skirt! Magazine*, a monthly print publication and website for women. Two weeks out of high school, she left her rural Kentucky home on a Greyhound bus to elope with her high-school boyfriend. "If you drew a picture of my career path after I graduated," she says, "it would look like a road under construction, with plenty of detours, washouts, dead ends and exit ramps." Divorced ten years later, and with three kids to support, she entered college at age 29, and after spending the "next five years as a single mother and starting-from-scratch student," earned a B.A. from American University and later became a senior editor with a subsidiary of Prentice-Hall Publishing Company.

In 1994, Nikki says, "I was living on a tiny island off the coast of Charleston, South Carolina, broke and bored with being a freelance writer and longing to have something to read that reflected my life and the lives of the women I knew." A friend asked her what she would do if she could choose. "Start a magazine for women," she answered. It made perfect sense, she adds. "After all I had no money, no collateral unless you count a rusty used car, no business plan and no prior experience in the magazine industry. Plus I was planning to start a liberal, feminist-oriented magazine in a bright red southern state." "Nothing in my past had prepared me to start and run a business, much less one that made money," Nikki notes. "I'm what The *New York Times* once referred to in an article as an 'accidental entrepreneur.' Being undercapitalized was just one of the mistakes I made. I didn't have a business plan, I didn't own a suit. I didn't know what an editorial plan was. What I did have was this idea and a few devoted friends who believed in it or me."

When Nikki started *Skirt!* in 1994, there wasn't anything around quite like it, especially not for women. Her idea was to have a publication that spoke to all sides of a woman's personality. Fortune seemed to smile on the enterprise. A month after she moved into a new building in downtown Charleston, the building next door was torn down to reveal a sign that had been hidden for decades. It read "Skirt Factory" in big bold black letters.

The advertisements in *Skirt!* were designed to be as stylish as the editorial content, and almost immediately the publication connected with the target audience. Within a decade *Skirt!* was established and profitable, "drawing readers and contributors from around the country," but also sparking numerous imitation publications. Without funds to expand or protect her brand and trademark, Nikki had the frustrating experience of watching strangers borrow her ideas. Relief came in the fall of 2003 when "five men in suits walked up the steep stairs to our office and proposed that we do business together. They were from a media company, Morris Communications, based in Georgia." When a partnership proved too complicated to work out, they offered to buy *Skirt!* "I stalled," she says, "went back to the table, looked at the fact I was 60 and had no savings or retirement fund, named a figure and got it." Selling *Skirt!* was a benefit, Nikki explains, because it meant the business had access to resources and better benefits for the staff without giving up the independent ethos. "Before a new market launches, their staff comes to the Charleston office to train, and if we do our job right, they go back home and create their own version of a firebrand *Skirt!* Because we believe in the United Skirts of America."

Since the new agreement was reached, *Skirt!* has expanded to include eight other cities in the southeast.

As publisher of *Skirt!*, Nikki writes the cover copy for each issue. Nikki's creative and free spirit is perhaps best described in her July, 2011, short essay:

> *Have a red, white and blue spangled month.* **Be independent:** *Learn to fix your own flats and pump up your own spirits.* **Be opinionated:** *Have more to say than 140 Twitter characters.* **Be awake:** *Make a list of things you could do if the TV or computer weren't on.* **Be aware:** *Vote if you care, run if you dare.* **Be balanced:** *Live within your budget, love beyond your means.* **Be rebellious:** *Don't accept the way it's always been done.* **Be brave:** *Nurture a Ruby Slippers state of mind.* **Be strong:** *Flex your creative muscles with art, music, writing or dance classes.* **Be bold:** *Wallflowers are never in season.* **Be free:** *Let your freak flag fly forever!*

What's the next phase in Nikki's career path? Will she create yet another inspirational path that no one has thought of? Perhaps a new product line? Her reflections from her personal website at www.fridaville.com "where my imagination rents a room," focuses on looking in new directions with different lenses. "What is looking for *me*?," she asks. "Looking back, I can see that all the while the field was being prepared in the darkness, the seeds being planted. The search that I'm on, the big decisions and change that I'm aiming myself toward, seem a bit less arduous and maddening knowing that, while I have work to do on my part, something is looking for me as intensely as I am looking for it."

There are important lessons here when making career transitions. They include looking at the entire spectrum. How do I take my skills and talents and match them to the opportunities someone else is seeking?

Gender at Work

In 1999, an informative collection of scholarly studies was published in a volume edited by Gary Powell titled the *Handbook of Gender and Work.* The purpose of the book was to examine the role of gender after two decades when the workforce participation rate of women had risen dramatically. Three years later another volume of studies, edited by Ronald Burke and Debra Nelson and titled *Advancing Women's Careers,* took a close look at the reasons why managerial and professional women, as well educated and experienced as men, were not entering the ranks of senior management at comparable rates. In 2010, scholarly findings from studies in the two-volume work edited by Karen O'Connor and titled *Gender and Women's Leadership—A Research Handbook,* provided further documentation and contributed new data. Among the main findings are these:

Karen Korabik found that although research has shown that behavior at work is largely due to cultural factors and situations in which people find themselves, many people continue to believe the antiquated idea that because men and women have different biological natures, personality traits, attitudes, values and behavior preferences, job performance must be sex-based. But as Ronald Burke and Debra Nelson point out, the notion that women bring different attitudes and behaviors to the job as a product of prior socialization that teaches them to be "girls" and makes them appear less capable is completely false.

Perceptions of gender differences contribute to a more difficult organizational life for women, said Linda Carli and Alice Eagly, because hostile patterns of interaction continue to put them at a disadvantage by causing them to withdraw from mixed-sex groups and teams and thus narrowing opportunities to work on projects and exert leadership. Women try to adjust, sometimes successfully, Mark Maier said, but when organizational values reproduce masculine values and subordinate feminine values, the results give white males invisible privileges and teach women to adopt male-like behaviors. Treatment based on gender limits women's opportunities, Gary Powell reported. The small proportion of women in top management has less to do with an individual's traits, skills, attitudes and behaviors than the organizational social system and group norms such as patriarchy, discrimination and stereotypes.

Males, the majority in most organizations, define good managers and management practices in terms of masculine characteristics. But as Terri Scandura and Gayle Baugh noted, the stereotypes associated with this behavior (assertiveness, etc.) tend to be viewed favorably when displayed by men and negatively when displayed by women. This leads to a special type of disparate treatment and discrimination for women. Also at work are the long-standing organizational structures and dynamics of organizations that contain policies and practices that hinder women's progress. These include the lack of core opportunities for female employees with management potential, assumptions that women will not relocate to advance their careers and the assignment of women to staff rather than to line positions which directly contribute to profits and are thus directly related to promotion, said Viki Holton. Burke and Nelson noted there was little women could do. Hard work, behavioral skills, communication, time management, emotional intelligence, political savvy and other positive factors did not lead to advancement if they were seen as having only a supportive role in the organization and women were shunted off into "glass wall" staff assignments. Further, as Phyllis Tharenou explained, some organizations had illogical standards for measuring performance, such as rewarding employees who worked long hours over others who actually produce more. Other organizations measured performance in informal ways, which in practice meant that making the effort to accurately assess productivity was often less important to middle managers than keeping the other (mostly male) employees comfortable with the work culture. The consequence for organizations was that after doing a good job of recruiting and hiring women, most organizations had self-imposed difficulties in developing and retaining their female middle managers. So women exited the unfriendly environments and took their skills and potential out the door with them. A lack of opportunity was high on the list of reasons for leaving, sexual harassment low.

Summing up, Barbara Bird pointed to the invisible, systemic and hard to prove barriers that women (and minorities) face. They include glass ceilings, glass escalators that move men up faster, the glass cliffs of being chosen for high-risk leadership positions in times of organizational crises, and the glass walls of staff and other sidetracking assignments.

Generations

Much is being said these days about the challenge of avoiding strife and motivating people who come from diverse generations with different backgrounds, perspectives, work ethics, attitudes and expectations. But are the differences that great?

Generations in the workforce can be defined in several ways. According to a recent study at the Sloan Center on Aging and Work at Boston College, there are four of them: the Traditionalists, born before 1946; the Baby Boomers, born between 1946 and 1964 (the older set born between 1946 and 1954 and the younger ones between 1955 and 1964); Generation Xers, born between 1965 and 1980 (Older Xers born between 1965 and 1971 and Younger Xers between 1972 and 1980), and the most recent arrivals, the Yers or Millennials, born after 1980.

There are data to back up the theory of generational differences and suggested solutions. There are also contrasting studies that indicate the absence of workforce differences based on age brackets. The generational differences group includes a comprehensive study, one of the first to control for age, by Twenge and Campbell, who say Millennials rate higher in self-esteem, are more self-absorbed and anxious, get depressed and have a lower need for social approval. The authors conclude that because many of the members of this group have "unrealistic expectations, a high need for praise, and difficulty with criticism" and like to dress casually, organizations should respond with positive reinforcement (praise programs) and counter pressure (dress codes).

Clearly, the idea of separate generations with catchy names has a great deal of appeal. But is it correct? Perhaps there is something else more important and useful to leaders seeking solutions to workforce problems.

First, it takes only a few short observations to come to the conclusion that the differences among individuals within each of these "generations" are greater than any of the projected generational differences. The Twenge and Campbell study, for example, says "many" members of the Millennial group, not all of them. (The more recent findings of Twenge, Campbell, Hoffman and Lance do note changes in extrinsic and intrinsic values.)

Second, how different is a multigenerational workforce from the rest of life? A family with children in grade school is two-generational by definition. Job losses in the current recession have caused people to move back home to live with relatives. According to a recent Pew Research Center study, 16 percent of the population, nearly 50 million people, live in multigenerational households. And is making arbitrary differentiations among people based on date of birth better than looking at clearer lines of distinction among workers—veterans of military service versus non-vets, for example?

Perhaps something else is at work. If you were born between 1925 and 1942, you probably grew up in a harsh economic climate and got your entertainment and news from your radio, if you had electricity and could afford one, or your neighbor's set, if they had one, and in the city you rode a streetcar. If you grew up in the 1950s and 1960s, you saw and were influenced by, among other new things, television, lots of plastic, commonplace travel by automobile and one of its consequences, shopping centers with self-service supermarkets. This could go on, but the point is that each generational group has been partially shaped by the sharp difference in technologies and the waves that social change creates. Young people now entering the workforce, who are more comfortable with colleagues of different races and gender, did not grow up in the pre-civil rights era of strict segregation and single-income families.

Cultural differences may account for how the generations misunderstand each other. A recent Harris Interactive interview survey, conducted in coordination with the Career Advisory Board of DeVry University, examined the contrasting views of 500 Millennials aged 21 to 31 and 523 Xers and Boomers who had the responsibility of hiring them. The Millennials' priorities, listed in order, were stable employment, fulfilling or meaningful work and starting salary. Nearly six in ten (58 percent) of Millennials cited career growth and professional development as their primary goal. Two in ten would leave to take a new position at a higher salary or a better career opportunity, but at best, they said, compensation was a secondary concern; Millennials appear equally likely to leave an organization if they disliked the culture. In contrast, the Xer and Boomer hiring managers said that it was not meaningful work but salary that most concerned the Millennials. Thus, is there a generational divide in perceptions or is it just an employer (manager) employee difference?

Part of this generational misunderstanding can also be traced to new technologies, particularly the combination of iPads, cell phone checks, blog updates, Facebook, Twitter, email, and instant and text messaging that often means that people together in the same room or on the same street are talking to someone else and paying no attention to their present environment or privacy, theirs or anyone else's. It has even gotten to the point where a couple of years ago the players for a major college basketball team discovered that when they followed a suggestion from the coach and turned in their cell phones they played better because, having no one else to talk to, they got to know each other.

The effects spill over into the workplace. If you seek career advancement, it will be important to communicate openly and clearly. This begins by examining the possibility that, to a manager, acceptable office and meeting behavior does not include popping out your latest technological device to browse the internet or communicate with someone outside. And by the way, for anyone who likes to send text messages while riding a bicycle in traffic or browse the internet while writing a report in the office, the word "multitasking" is a misnomer. The verdict from the research is that doing two things simultaneously means being less efficient at both.

The best career choice is to be completely present in your actual work environment. The virtual worlds can and will wait.

The Origins of the Mommy Wars

There is a romantic and somewhat comfortable mythology of a time long ago when the norm was a "traditional" American family consisting of a husband who went off to work, a homemaker wife and children. While the majority of families could be so described prior to World War II, it is also true that there is nothing really new about large numbers of women in the American workforce.

The long-term cause of the mommy wars was the century-long reshaping of the American labor force. As recounted by Howard Hayghe, an economist in the Bureau of Labor Statistics, between 1900 and 1920, the number of women in the workforce grew from some 5 million to 8.3 million, more than 2 million of whom were married. In 1930, nearly one woman of every four (24.8 percent) had paid employment outside the home. Dual career couples constituted a relatively small 9 percent of all families. These figures changed little during the 1930s, the years of the Great Depression and record unemployment—one worker in every four without a job and one family in every five without a breadwinner in 1933—and the accompanying family disruptions and declining birth rates.

Dramatic changes in the labor force began as the Depression generation became the wartime generation. As the country mobilized, women were recruited for war work and by 1944 they accounted for more than a third of the labor force (34 percent) and more than 40 percent of workers in the aircraft industry. More than a third of them (33.7 percent) were married. They had been recruited in media campaigns that focused on the dominant role of the American male, with the subordinate females picking up the tasks he couldn't do because of more important commitments. The expectation was that after the war life would return to prewar routines. But those routines were already disrupted; the wartime effect on family life in a society consisting of (mostly) men at war and (numerous) wives at work may be gauged by two new phrases that came into the popular lexicon, "latchkey kids" and "juvenile delinquents." In the immediate postwar economy, the number of wives in the workforce declined, but only slightly and only briefly. Rosie the Riveter had come to appreciate working outside the home and by 1948 the labor force participation rate for women had regained its wartime peak of 22 percent.

More than 60 percent of all families were still traditional as the 1950s dawned, but their numbers were already declining under the severe impact of the steep rise in the marriage, birth, and divorce rates. Already, one married woman in every four was employed or seeking work. Additional shocks in the 1950s arrived in the form of the major and undeclared war in Korea in the decade's first three years, the normalization of peacetime selective service for men afterwards, and a zigzag economy that included the sharp, 61 percent increase in the unemployment rate near the end of the decade.

The economic and social cause of the mommy wars was the continuing large-scale entry of women into the workforce and the increasing proportion of dual career couples that marked the 1960s. By 1970, the number of wives entering the labor force had jumped from an average of 400,000 a year to 700,000 and the percentage of dual earning couples had risen to almost half of all families (46 percent). As Alison Konrad and Frank Linnehan have reported, the political cause of the mommy wars was related to the enactment of the Civil Rights Act of 1964, Title VII of which prohibited discrimination in employment; the promulgation by President Lyndon Johnson of Executive Orders 11246, in 1965, and 11375, in 1967, which put teeth into the enforcement of affirmative action; and the push for an Equal Rights Amendment to the Constitution, which by 1977 had been ratified by 28 states.

Cultural fireworks centered on the feminist movement, say Karen O'Connor and Alixandra Yanus, which, according to who was doing the defining, was either composed of moderates interested in pursuing legislative and judicial solutions to real issues of inequality or protesting radicals who rejected almost all contemporary social norms and values. For the grassroots activists upset with social change and shifts in power that involved gender, whose powerful backlash movement caused the ERA to fail, these were distinctions without a difference.

Changes over the last several decades have been equally influential. According to the BLS, by 2008, six of every ten women were in the labor force. Nearly three of every five married couples (57 percent) were dual earners. Fewer than one family in five (17.8 percent) was traditional in the old sense. The median percentage of wives' contribution to family income rose to 36 percent. As early as 1970, a study of women's social and economic well being reported that more than one-fourth of all children under six years of age had a mother who worked outside the home (29 percent).

In the media, the culture wars had long since turned to analysis of the pros and cons of the idea that being a mother, and a perfect one at that, is the most important thing a woman can do (not a requirement for men) plus "having it all." There were also various descriptions of what it meant to be a "good mother." Simple, said Susan Douglas and Meredith Michaels: you buy it, assemble it, install it, use it with your child, and protect your child from any defects it might contain. Women in the workforce, they more seriously continued, were being pulled between cultural riptides. Success at home required being "more doting and self sacrificing than Bambi's mother" and, at work, being "highly efficient, calculating, tough, judgmental, skeptical" and "willing to do whatever it took."

Legislation and Policies

Avoiding a Challenge of Discrimination

Every day business owners and company managers face the challenges of making personnel decisions and workforce changes in ways consistent with the policies and procedures of the Equal Employment Opportunity Commission. How did it begin and what are the basic compliance issues?

The history of affirmative action begins with a series of executive orders signed by President Franklin D. Roosevelt to reduce race discrimination in the federal government and by government contractors. Sex and age discrimination were not mentioned in the early EOs. Title VII of the Civil Rights Act of 1964 prohibited discrimination in the private sector on the basis of race, color, religion, sex, national origin or disability; required standards of employee selection based on the "best qualified" candidates; and compliance with both the "letter and spirit of the law" where the burden of proof of nondiscriminatory practices is on the employer. The Act also created the EEOC as an enforcement agency.

The EEOC enforces the statutory and case law prohibitions against employment discrimination in hiring, training and promotion decisions, reductions in the workforce, and diversity requirements for government agencies and all businesses with 15 employees or more (firms with 14 employees or fewer are exempt). Employees claiming intentional discrimination can ask for compensatory and punitive damages and the EEOC can not only ask the courts to require offending businesses to pay them but also to rule that managers and owners pay out of their own pockets additional sums that may be substantial.

What all this means is that businesses must align their in-house employment policies and procedures with those recommended by the EEOC that are in compliance with the law, train managers at all levels to assure that the guidelines are followed and consistently monitor the process. This is important in maintaining compliance to avoid uninformed or misguided management decisions. Several recent EEOC cases illustrate the kind of bad management decisions that can be costly:

- The abrupt termination of an employee who claimed race discrimination.
- Ridiculing maternity leave as a "vacation" and firing the employee seven days after a C-section.
- Terminating an employee with disabilities who parked in a handicap space even though she was satisfactorily performing her job and had a valid handicap parking placard.

- Sexual harassment that included inappropriate touching or groping of males by a male supervisor.

Do workers still feel a need for the protections provided by the employment legislation which is enforced by the EEOC? The answer is suggested by the number of cases that have been filed. In 1997, 80,680 discrimination charges were filed, in 2010 there were 99,992, an increase of 24 percent. While charges often include multiple types of discrimination, the majority of these cases were for race-based actions. Thirty-one percent of the filings were for retaliation, 29.1 percent for discrimination, 25.2 percent for disability and 23.3 percent for age, the fastest rising category.

How did employees fare? The EEOC found reasonable cause in 4.7 percent of the cases, with successful conciliations for 1.3 percent and merit resolutions for 19.2 percent. Monetary benefits, $176.7 million in 1997, increased almost threefold to $319.4 million in 2010.

Enforcement by the EEOC is not arbitrary. Discrimination and harassment of employees can be costly. It is good business to create and maintain a selection system that is not only fair to all employees but also perceived by them as just.

Americans with Disabilities

Since 1992, the Americans with Disabilities Act has prohibited discrimination against qualified people with disabilities in employment and selection and in physical accommodations in public facilities unless, in the case of private businesses, doing so would impose undue hardship or fundamentally alter the nature of the business. According to the latest statistics available from the U.S. Census Bureau, issued in December, 2008, an estimated 18.7 percent of the population, 54.4 million, had some level of disability and 12 percent, 35 million, a severe disability. Disability increases with age. According to the report, "the disability rate for each age group was higher than the rates for the younger age groups." The highest incidence of disability (71 percent) was people 80 years and older. By race, Blacks had the highest prevalence of disability (20.5 percent) and severe disability (14.4 percent); by sex, disability was more prevalent among females (20.1 percent) as was severe disability (13.4 percent) than that of males (disability 17.3 percent), severe disability (10.4 percent). In all, there are more than 28 million people 16 years and older who have disabilities.

Under the ADA Guidelines, all businesses are required to modify policies and practices to comply with accessible design standards in new construction. Those serving the public are responsible for providing auxiliary aids and services for effective communication for people with hearing, vision, or speech impairments. Since 1994, the employee selection provisions of the ADA have covered all employers with 15 or more employees. Amendments to the Act in 2008 modified definitions and applied terms in ways that enabled more people to be protected.

A 2007 study of the impact of the ADA after 15 years cites studies conducted shortly after the ADA's passage that suggested acceptance of its provisions in the business community would depend on the breadth and depth of negative stereotypical views of the disabled and, later, more hopeful studies that the Act would be helpful to the disabled, including a Harris poll indicating the internet was opening up the world of work and entertainment to people with disabilities.

Progress in gaining access to public facilities was dramatic and in the workplace direct contact with the disabled on a regular basis altered negative stereotypes. Harris Polls conducted in 1999 and 2003 found continuing massive public support for key ADA provisions. But a 1998 Harris Poll had found that some 79 percent of people with a disability were not in the labor force, compared with 29 percent with no disability, and in addition noted the life style disadvantages the disabled faced in transportation, health care and satisfaction.

In 2004, Randolph published a disability employment study which revealed that employment rates for the disabled either held steady or declined over the decade of the 1990s. Despite a period of burgeoning economy, high employment and labor shortages, some 13.3 million people (7 percent) had reported difficulties in finding a job or remaining employed due to a health-related condition. In 1999, the 15.6 million American working adults age 16 and over with disabilities had an employment rate of 34.6 percent, less than half of the 79.8 percent rate for the non-disabled. The labor force participation rate of the 5.8 million disabled at work dropped to 21 percent, less than one-third of the 69.7 percent participation rate for the non-disabled. While surveys suggested that businesses recognized the importance of hiring the disabled, few made any efforts to do so, in part because of the lack of knowledge on the part of employees, managers and owners about the ADA provisions. Only 70 percent of corporations had diversity policies or programs in place, only two out of three of these included disability as a component and only one in six (18 percent) attempted to integrate people with disabilities into the workplace. Equally serious, as Baldridge and Veiga pointed out in 2006, in work environments, even when they understand their rights, people with disabilities were often unwilling to make accommodation requests because they did not feel free to do so.

Improvements in life activities such as access to transportation, socializing, going to restaurants, attendance at religious services and political participation have been modest for people with disabilities. Despite the efforts that have been made, two Harris Polls commissioned by the Kessler Foundation and the National Organization on Disability in 2010 showed little or no gains in ten key indicators ranging from employment and income to social engagement and life satisfaction. Where polls taken a decade earlier had cited an encouraging increase in online internet access, they now showed that only 54 percent of adults with disabilities had access, compared to 85 percent of adults without disabilities. Higher levels of disability translated into lower employment status and income and a greater likelihood of living in poverty.

The progress that has been made in the 20 years since the passage of the ADA can be measured in buildings that are more accessible, automatic doors, wheelchair ramps, parking spaces, and other improvements that enable the disabled to get into and around inside public and commercial structures. These changes come as no surprise. The study published in *Work* (2007) of the attitudes of business owners toward the ADA had shown, among other things, that owners were very willing to invest in new facilities to accommodate disabled customers, less interested in investing in facilities to accommodate people with disabilities already on their payroll, and much less interested in hiring the disabled.

Another hopeful measure of progress is the slow arrival of new medical science that works to transform or at least mitigate the limitations of a disability.

Why Job Analysis?

The continuous analysis of all the jobs in an organization is at the heart of performance. But it is often overlooked because leaders and managers get bogged down with day-to-day problems and don't make time to gain a competitive edge by more efficiently designing and updating job descriptions.

When organizations begin a new initiative, they almost always carefully analyze the jobs, develop specifications and descriptions and use these to staff the positions. Unfortunately, firms seldom do this for existing jobs. In an article in the *Harvard Business Review* in 2004, Peter Drucker, the father of modern management theories, said that it is just as important to review decisions periodically as it is to make them carefully in the first place. It is for this reason that organizations should regularly update their job descriptions in order to deal with the inevitable changes that occur in a competitive and growth-oriented market.

Out-of-date job analyses may be impacting the company bottom line in several ways. An antiquated organizational frame of reference that means employee ownership of their jobs as they were originally analyzed can inhibit innovation. A "this is the way we have always done it" mentality on the part of managers suggests the organization is focusing on itself and not its customers, partners, and competitors. To avoid this organizational degeneration, position descriptions should provide for flexibility from the outset. Making it clear from the beginning that job analysis will be an ongoing process better prepares employees to endorse the future changes that are needed to stay in step with change and innovation.

Job analysis is also the first step in aligning human performance management practices for businesses with 15 employees or more to document compliance with the EEOC Guidelines and the requirements of legislation. While job analysis alone does not provide insurance against litigation, it is often the required documentation that can support human resource management decisions that have been challenged legally.

The critical element in job analysis is "validity," meaning there must be a clear and defendable (valid) relationship between the selection procedures, the job requirements and duties, and the credentials, skills, abilities, and other characteristics of people who are selected. Some work behaviors can be observed. The tasks performed by a fast food cook or an assembly line worker are examples. Analysis for jobs such as these should focus on the work behaviors and associated tasks. Other jobs require work behaviors that can't be observed. The activities of a creative chef or a research scientist come to mind. Analyses for these jobs should concentrate on the products of the work. Most jobs entail a combination of observable tasks and work products.

The system the organization uses for job analysis should provide the procedure for determining the duties and the knowledge, abilities, skills and other necessary characteristics needed to carry out the work. It should include both the critical tasks and the most important work products. It should measure the person for the job, not the person in the abstract. It must be validated for the jobs in the organization. All this requires job analysts who not only have the experience and training but the first-hand knowledge of what each job entails. Job interviews, a common method of selecting people, require a carefully structured format of tailored questions in order to match qualified candidates with the sequence of performance activities required in the position.

Without the job analysis, it is unlikely that the hiring and promotion process will meet an organization's short-term or long-range needs.

Making Performance Appraisals Effective

Long ago, the management expert W. Edward Deming, a proponent of total quality management, advocated eliminating performance appraisals. His chief argument was that in many organizations performance reviews turn into bureaucratic routines that emphasize the interests of supervisors only. The problem with Deming's solution, however, was that it placed employees in the same classification regardless of their contributions and did little to motivate employees to understand or contribute to company objectives.

Employees tend to be quick studies. While some are quite conscientious and driven to always work hard, others may quickly shift to a pace that appears to fit the system or their own needs. When organizations make it clear that extra effort does not count, some people will pull back. It is to the advantage of the organization to invest time in designing a good performance appraisal system because this places owners and managers in the position of being able to motivate people while complying with performance law.

The basic task is to establish the links between the abilities and skills that brought employees to the firm in the first place and the assessment of their productivity in order to guide goal-directed performance. This is not by any means a simple process. It first requires removing the fog of special friendships and bias. These include managers and owners who know "instinctively" who the "good performers" are. But often these so-called good performers are those who unswervingly follow the company line or reflect the ideological viewpoints of management or play up to superiors or refrain from telling hard truths. Bias can enter the review process in the form of negative stereotyping. Studies have shown that, in the workplace, men still trust a new male colleague more than a new female co-worker, consider a new male leader to have more of the requisite traits suitable to a manager, and male and female employees alike employ strong perceptions and gender stereotypes that harm evaluations of women's performance. The "halo effect" can reward someone for superior work done long ago. Leniency, a preference of the lazy or timid manager, and other projection techniques that exist only in the rater's mind, obscure reality and lead to undervaluing top quality performance.

An effective evaluation system of performance appraisal avoids measuring traits that cannot be measured. This means staying away from nebulous concepts like teamwork, compassion, cooperativeness, and collegiality. Good evaluation systems also avoid forced distribution (i.e., only the top 10 percent get the highest bonus) or a graphic rating scale that may require raters to use performance criteria (work speed, quality of work) but leaves each rater free to determine the weights for the performance elements. A good system begins with these steps:

- Employees know from the beginning of the period under review what the goals and expectations of the organization are and how their performance will be measured.
- The review tools objectively measure performance on the basis of crucial job requirements and tasks that have been carefully identified in the job analysis and to employees.
- Performance is observed over the entire review period to avoid the misleading effects of only a few direct observations, critical incidents that may contain extremes in behavior, recency effects (being influenced by the last thing the employee does), and other errors.
- The review process is professional. Comments by the rater relate to the performance objectives and are impersonal. "Jack, the quarterly report you turned in makes no sense" is

a personal attack. "Jack, let's see how you can structure your next report so we get the information we need" is directed at the work product.

- The review notes positive contributions. It is not the occasion where 100 good things are forgotten so the rater can spend time on the two not-so-good things and the one bad thing.
- The review process is open. The rater really listens to the comments of the employee rather than pushing past them to get to the next thing on the list.
- The review is objective oriented. For an employee whose performance is unsatisfactory but correctable, an action plan will be introduced to help improve future performance. In cases where an employee who has performed satisfactorily but circumstances prevent the deserved promotion or a salary increase, there is a plan to keep the employee motivated and on track for success in the next review period. For the satisfactory promotable employee, there is a plan for career development.
- The review process protects the organization. If an employee is not doing satisfactory work, what he or she needs to do to correct the problem is clearly spelled out and the unsatisfactory work documented.
- There is an appeal process for employees who feel they have not been fairly evaluated without the fear of retaliation.

Employees need feedback on what they have done. They also need to be guided by positive strategies in areas where improvements are needed. A well-thought-out and -conducted appraisal may not leave everybody feeling happy, but it will convey to most employees the feeling that their performance has been appraised fairly and equitably. This enables improved performance as individual and company goal alignment makes it possible for the organization to remain competitive, proactive and successful. Finally, it is important to remember that once performance appraisals are tied directly to monetary or promotional awards, a bridge to litigation has been created if the process does not incorporate job-related criteria and a valid system for appraisal.

There is no better ambassador for an organization than an employee who feels treated fairly. It is the least expensive advertising campaign one will ever do as a manager or an entrepreneur.

The Gender Problem of Performance versus Potential

In today's uncertain business climate, it would seem like the smartest firms would be finding ways to bring all of their best minds to the table and put resources behind them. So why don't they? A survey conducted for the *Wall Street Journal* by Vikram Malhotra, chairman of the Americas for McKinsey & Company, concluded a key reason is that middle-management women get promoted on performance while middle-management men are promoted on potential. From the outset, the playing field is not level.

Organizations that want women to succeed must work at it, says Viki Holton, and this means breaking down the barriers that often isolate women. One cure is "signposting," meaning creating opportunities for women to gain the same access that men do through their networks and mentors. In organizations where men are the majority and women lack mentors, women need help from above.

Organizations that want to retain women would do well to understand that gender role stereotypes and work role expectations are congruent for male and conflicting for women executives. Men are expected to be decisive, rational, unemotional, blunt, direct and even argumentative. These are stereotypically "boss" behaviors. Women are stereotypically seen as indecisive, emotional, and conventional—just the opposite. It's a no-win situation in an organization whose culture is ruled by stereotypes. A woman who manages in-role is seen as ineffective, a woman managing in the male model is out of place.

As Mary Mattis points out, with women making up roughly half the middle managers in organizations and the costs of replacing senior managers and high-tech professionals substantial, the retention of women professionals and managers is emerging as a key concern of firms. Quoting J. Michael Cook, the former CEO of Deloitte and Touche LLP, the practice of firms, his included, of hiring increasing numbers of women and then watching them leave at an equally high rate can be called the "stupid curve."

The solution to the problem requires a series of steps. First, the organization must identify, understand and adopt equitable practices and then apply them irrespective of sex. The benchmarking begins with understanding and developing the business case for gender diversity and tying the diversity strategies to the firm's strategic plans. Actions to be taken range from identifying and recruiting the best and brightest talent to eliminating barriers to success to enhancing opportunities for all. Once the higher-ups are for it, a company "best practices" plan to retain and encourage the development of talented women can be written. This is the easy part.

A harder part is to put in place the necessary programs and systems to measure the plan's effectiveness. The really hard part is for the CEO to reach down and change the organizational culture in order to shift the outlook of the (mostly male) middle managers who with their autonomy are capable of ignoring any plan or rendering it ineffective by giving only lukewarm support.

All it takes to create an environment unfriendly to women is an immediate superior who neglects to follow the organization's published policies, even EEO requirements, because he sees them as getting in the way of his job or who views himself as superior. What it takes to create an equitable environment, as Eleanor Tabi Haller-Jorden reported at the 2009 Brussels Jump Forum, is passionately engaged leadership that believes the advancement of women also advances the company, an internal culture amenable to women's contributions and policies of recruitment, retention and advancement. There is more to it than just checking off the boxes.

The Changing Workplace

How Women Have Changed the Business Landscape

> *I am five feet tall and female and people do not take me seriously right off the bat. You need to be bigger and more masculine to intimidate people; they pay attention to you. It's like an elephant. An elephant gets more attention than a mouse. But if the mouse is the president of the company and it needs to be run effectively, then the mouse needs to learn how to manage the elephant. And that is what we do. We manage at least one elephant every single day.* (Linda Horn, L. R. Horn Concepts Inc., Women's Business Advocate of the Year, 2009. The quotation is from Moore, D.P. *Careerpreneurs,* p. 89.)

According to *Key Facts about Women Owned Businesses 2008–2009 Update,* published by the Center for Women's Business Research, there were 10.1 million privately held businesses that were at least 50 percent woman-owned; of these, 7.2 million were 51 percent woman-owned. The 50 percent woman-owned financially stable and growing firms generated nearly $2 trillion in revenues and provided some 13 million jobs. Businesses operated by women of color made up slightly more than one-fourth (26 percent) of this total. Firms with at least 51 percent woman-ownership generated $1.1 trillion in revenues and provided 7.3 million jobs. The number of women-owned firms continued to increase at twice the rate of male-owned businesses. Women who own 50 percent or more of their businesses now accounted for 40 percent of all privately held firms. One in five firms with revenues of $1 million or more are woman-owned.

For some time, women have been founding firms at rates higher than men. The most successful generally establish their businesses in sectors or industries similar to their previous work environment or deal in familiar products and services. Most also start firms in fields where there is a medium level of female participation but recently many have been branching out into such traditionally male industry areas as communications, transportation, wholesale trade, manufacturing, and construction. At three times the rate for all start-ups, women of color constitute the fastest growing group of female entrepreneurs.

Corporate experience explains much of the growth. By 2007, women accounted for more than one-half (51 percent) of all workers in the high paying management, professional and related occupations. While the desire to be in charge, to be one's own boss, is a strong reason for founding a business, people already in the workforce are three to four times more likely to start one. The success of women entrepreneurs in particular can often be traced back to the financial, marketing, management, technical and networking skills and confidence gained while working in organizations owned by others.

As Moore and Buttner found, female entrepreneurs with previous corporate experience, most commonly for 10 to 12 years, tend to fall into one of two groups. The "Intentionals" understood the advantages of practical experience and gained it prior to fulfilling lifelong ambitions of creating businesses of their own. The "Corporate Climbers," by contrast, started out pursuing the American dream of advancing within an organization. A growing sense of their own personal ability to run things along with corporate restructuring, downsizing, rightsizing, and systemic attitudinal and perhaps organizational barriers to career advancement led many to consider entrepreneurship.

While few women entrepreneurs started businesses because they had faced systematic discrimination, many launched in reaction to the negative impact of hitting a corporate roadblock or a desire to live in a better work climate. For the overwhelming majority who exited corporations, the motivations were the pull of an entrepreneurial idea, the joy of seizing a marketplace opportunity, and the challenge of controlling one's destiny.

Whatever their reasons for leaving an organization, nearly all understood that amid rapid technological changes and culture shifts the days of counting on a traditional pattern of career progression were over. The new business landscape required an aptitude to evaluate risks, find opportunities both within and outside corporate life and, as Mainiero and Sullivan say in *The Opt-Out Revolt,* to find balance. Entrepreneurs are more likely to survive if they ultimately leave their previous organization to establish a business in the same type of firm or industry. But most felt out the terrain before becoming a full-time, dedicated entrepreneur. Consequently, nearly two-thirds (65 percent) of all new women business owners were employed elsewhere at the time of their business start-ups. They were also more likely than men to layer full-time and part-time work and delay making a complete break from the organization to concentrate on their venture.

Owning a business is a big job. As an enlightened woman leader and entrepreneur, the business owner is the vision-setter, information resource, motivator and analyzer. As the firm manager, she is the ambassador, taskmaster, auditor and servant. As the owner, the buck stops with her.

Denise L. Devine

Founder, CEO and President, Nutripharm, Inc. and Froose® Brands, LLC

I found myself in the somewhat unique position of being an executive with a major food company by day and a frustrated consumer by night (actually, let's face it: by day too!). I was consistently concerned by the lack of nutritious food products for young children in the marketplace. A major culprit of bad nutrition in my household was fruit juice. My son wanted to drink it all day long, filling him with empty calories and leaving him not wanting to eat at mealtime.

Denise L. Devine graduated first in her class at Villanova University with a B.S. in Accounting, earned an M.S. in Taxation from Villanova Law School and began her career as a licensed Certified Public Accountant with Arthur Andersen & Company, where she rose to become a member of the firm's national, closely held business team. After moving to the Campbell Soup Company, she was responsible for negotiating, pricing and executing financings, mergers, acquisitions and divestitures. After a promotion as Campbell's senior manager of finance and investment strategy, the company underwrote her subsequent study at the Wharton School where she earned an M.B.A.

Long before clinical studies proved the link between health problems, obesity and too much juice consumption, she says, "My motherly instincts told me that too much juice for young children was not good." Painstaking research led her to conclude that the excessive consumption of fruit juice posed immediate and long-term risks to children's health. With two children (she has three now) and her husband starting his own financial valuation firm, she chose to leave corporate life and in 1997 founded her own company, Nutripharm (and its subsidiary Devine Foods), in Media, Pennsylvania, "to develop a nutritious alternative to juice that would incorporate the whole food—complex carbohydrates, vitamins, minerals and fiber—that young children need to grow." Over time, she developed and marketed patented whole food products and beverages for children and adults and acquired a one-third stake in a bottling plant in Western Pennsylvania. Her company now holds 17 national and international patents on various formulations of a portfolio of products that includes kids' drinkable snacks, a drinkable nutrition product, frozen confections, ingredient bases, a natural fiber blend, and dietary supplements.

In developing her products, Denise has received strong backing from the Ben Franklin Technology Partnership, the U.S. Department of Agriculture and scientists at the International Food Network in Ithaca, New York, who use the facilities of Cornell University. Because it is exceedingly difficult to get new products into supermarkets where shelf space is at a premium, Denise began by marketing in natural food stores and creating inroads into college and university cafeterias to gain acceptance and eventual product placement by the national chains.

Denise's early work on a non-dairy frozen confection caught the attention of research chemists at the Agricultural Research Service of the U.S. Department of Agriculture and led to a decision to combine technologies to develop a non-fat milkshake that is low in sugar and high in fiber. Her continuing dedication to children's nutrition and serious commitment to providing solutions to prevent childhood obesity and positively impact lifelong health resulted in Froose Brands, with several products now in the market. The flagship product is Froose®, a drinkable snack that tastes like juice but contains fiber, vitamins, complex carbohydrates and grain/fruit nutrients that juice doesn't have. The "Froose team," as Denise calls it, is "a group of like-minded parents and parents-to-be who converge on the same passionate commitment to better nutrition for young children." As a company, she says, "We take the lead in improving what's there or creating what's not."

It wasn't easy to abandon a successful career for an uncertain new enterprise, but her "dream just wouldn't let her be." "I couldn't give up," she says. "I had to make it work one way or the other." Denise Devine's numerous honors and awards include the Best 50 Business Women in Pennsylvania (1999), the Villanova Alumni Gold Medal, the highest honor bestowed on a graduate of the university (2000), a gubernatorial appointment to the Pennsylvania Blue Ribbon Business Tax Reform Commission (2004), Entrepreneur in Residence at The Wharton School (2003 and 2004), and the Girl Scouts of America "Take the Lead" Award (2007).

With regard to today's world of work, in answering the question of whether or not the playing field is level or stacked in favor of or against professional women, she says, "It largely depends on the industry you are in and the particular people you have to do business with. However, when it comes to raising large amounts of financing, women are still, by and large, 'capital access' challenged."

Glass Floors, Ceilings, Walls, Elevators and Cliffs

Women's careers are not affected by barriers related to gender differences but they are affected by the differences that gender makes.

Each year, in March, Catalyst, a New York City research organization, presents awards to Fortune 500 companies to honor innovative cultural initiatives in women's recruitment, development, and advancement that incorporate diversity and inclusion. In 2011, Kaiser Permanente was recognized for increasing the number of women holding senior executive positions (47 percent to 50 percent in 2009), the mix of racially/ethnically diverse women (rising from 12 percent to 18 percent), the percentage of women board directors (from 21 percent to 36 percent over an eight-year period) and tripling the number of racially/ethnically diverse women on its board. McDonald's Corporation, another award winner, was recognized for writing an inclusion strategy into its business plan and corporate values statement, the presence of women in management positions (Europe, 52 percent, the US, 64 percent), and raising the percentage of women on the board of directors from 14 percent in 2006 to 23 percent in 2009.

That's the good news. The bad news is that in the overwhelming number of organizations women find the glass ceilings still exist and the glass floors are slippery. The "think manager—think male" mindset is persistent, durable and global.

Recalls a California former public sector professional, now head of a retail firm, "The chain was absolutely vertical. During the entire 12 to 13 years, I was never consulted nor did I have the authority to hire or fire a secretary who worked for me." Reports a San Francisco entrepreneur, "I had an overwhelming feeling of not fitting in. At first I had the feeling that this meant something was wrong with me instead of with the situation." The abundance of evidence continues to tell us that at each stage of advancement men move up at least twice as fast as women. A 1998 Catalyst study reported that for most women the corporate ladder is not tall enough to reach the top.

The most recent Catalyst (2010) statistical report tells us the picture has not changed that much. The glass elevator continues to speed men upward while women are trying to climb the too-short corporate ladder.

Surveys continue to show women exiting organizations at high rates. Up to 22 percent of female entrepreneurs who have been in business less than 10 years left their corporate careers because they hit the glass ceiling. As a female marketing, consulting and seminar provider once summarized, "The only way through the glass ceiling is to go out on your own." "The guys still run the major corporations in America today."

Women who make it to upper management often confront the additional barrier of a second level of discrimination. One said she awakened only when she reached the top echelons. "My view of the corporate world was that you continually go up. It was when I got to the most senior levels of the corporation, I was one of the ten highest ranking women in a 15,000 person corporation, that's when I found the glass ceiling." Another, who left after a long career, looked back and concluded, "I had gone as far as I could go. I was just tired of solving their problems." Some women in senior management found themselves confined by the glass walls of being slotted to positions dealing with staff with little access to power or the opportunity to make an impact. As a Pulitzer Prize winning columnist put it in his recently published, bestselling novel, "That was what [the organization] did with smart women . . . made them managers and pushed them up the promotion ladder. It was a kind of repressive tolerance. Pretty soon they weren't fit for real operations any more, and they weren't given an opportunity. They fell uphill."

The number of women at the top has declined recently. Fewer than 3 percent of the Fortune 1000 companies have female CEOs. Women hold only 14.4 percent of the executive positions in the Fortune 500 companies and occupy only 16 percent of the seats on their boards. Perhaps the glass cliffs are the reason. The term has two applications. The first is that when firms downsize or close, women senior leaders are three times as likely to lose their jobs. When the economic crisis hit hard in 2008 and company fortunes headed down, female CEOs were disproportionally blamed and not the economy. The other is that when the bad times hit, there was a recognition in some male dominated firms that their "think manager, think male" mindset wasn't working and therefore there was a willingness to take a new look at women's suitability for senior positions. However, the "think crisis, think female" syndrome meant that women were offered the often impossible opportunities to turn things around quickly under conditions where success was problematic at best and in positions where men had failed already.

The glass cliff may also help explain why in the US male CEOs last an average of 8.2 years in the job compared to 4.8 years for female CEOs.

Eleanor Tabi Haller-Jorden

General Manager, Catalyst Europe AG

Positive experiences with mentoring have made me even more committed to mentoring others. The benefits of a few minutes of well-timed mentoring have legs; these benefits are long-lasting and far-reaching. In the final analysis, what makes a mentoring relationship so compelling is that it introduces the idea of personal sponsorship into an inherently impersonal system. As a result, the act of mentoring can be as rich and varied as the individuals involved.

Eleanor Tabi Haller-Jorden attended Princeton University as an advanced standing scholar and graduated magna cum laude from Bryn Mawr, where she received the Helen Taft Manning Prize in History. She holds a Master of Science degree in Industrial Relations from the London School of Economics and Political Science and is a Sage Fellow at Cornell University. Between 1987 and 1990, Tabi served as a Director and then as Vice President of Advisory Services, Catalyst, New York. She also founded and directed the Public Policy Center in Philadelphia. From 1991 to 2005, she worked in cross-cultural talent management and strategic planning as the Founder and Managing Director of the Paradigm Group. Here, she focused on international human resources research, corporate change initiatives, performance management, business coaching and cross-cultural diversity with projects from planning to consulting at J. P. Morgan. In 2005, Tabi became a Strategic Advisor for Catalyst Europe and in 2006 the General Manager of Catalyst Europe AG, a Switzerland-based organization established to work with corporate and academic members in Europe to encourage solutions to organizational inclusion and innovation in a region of great cultural diversity. She is particularly interested in addressing the lack of mentoring, which Catalyst research consistently finds at the heart of the factors that inhibit the advancement of women.

Tabi's understanding of the importance of mentoring began with her first mentor, her mother. "I was raised in a household of mavericks," she says, "individuals who chronically challenged conventional wisdom. My mother was a beacon in that regard. A world-renowned Japanese linguist, she showed me firsthand the strength that comes from displaying professional commitments alongside personal convictions. On numerous occasions, when our school calendars permitted, she demanded that her children be allowed to accompany her on business trips so that her absences did not come at too high a personal cost." Tabi's first professional mentor was her manager at Morgan Guaranty Trust Company. "He was a risk-taker and stretched my comfort zone with almost maddening frequency," she says, "I recall his request that I make a presentation to the chairman at the ripe young age of 23. Surely, I asserted, I wasn't experienced enough to venture into the hallowed board room of Morgan Guaranty Trust Company. Yet my mentor primed me for success with his vast professional experience, good humor, and uncompromising faith in my ability to deliver. In short, he helped me get out of my own way."

Tabi's response to the challenge women face in finding an influential mentor is for organizations to go beyond the idea that mentor means a single individual and work to create corporate networks that place the traditional employer–employee interactions in settings that also consider the broader cultural issues surrounding women in the workplace. Her particular concern is one of the double bind difficulties women encounter as they advance. While they may begin with supportive networks, she has found that, in order to advance, women must adopt traditional male behaviors to gain respect. In the process, their original network support disappears. Organizations benefit from creating a more complete and flexible employer/employee relationship in corporate social networks, as Tabi calls them, because they become "employers of choice" for women and retain skilled, increasingly productive workers. Their women employees benefit because the existence of the corporate social networks enables them to advance their careers as they progress through various stages of life.

As an international expert on women in leadership positions, the impact of organizational change, and mechanisms and devices that increase organizational effectiveness and global diversity, Tabi is the author of several publications, a frequent lecturer and presenter at institutions such as the International Institute for Management Development (IMD) in Lausanne, the London School of Economics and Political Science, the Yale School of Organization and Management and Columbia University Business School. She has been designated a European Thought Leader on behalf of IBM's Global Innovation Outlook initiative and appears in the *Profiles in Diversity Journal 6th Annual Women Worth Watching*™ issue, which showcases leading business women. Tabi is also a single mother of two boys, an avid windsurfer, a poet who creates poetry onstage and has performed in Zurich, Oslo, and London and is the owner of the Living Gallery, a virtual art space and gallery in Switzerland.

Women on Board—The Business Case

A rapidly growing body of research is showing that increasing the number of women on corporate boards immediately improves firm performance.

The initiatives began in Norway, the world's third leading exporter of oil (behind Saudi Arabia and Russia), named in the

2001 United Nations Human Development Report as the best country in which to live (the United States ranked sixth), where 40 percent of all elected officials are women and, in 2010, 52.6 percent of ministers were women.

In 2002, Norway mandated that public companies fill at least 40 percent of the seats on the boards of directors of public companies with women (and similarly at least 40 percent of the seats with men). State-owned enterprises had until 2006 to comply, public companies until 2008. In times of ongoing change and crisis, thinking went, to make sense of global complexities and act in broad and imaginative ways to develop and grow, firms needed all minds at the table. In practical terms, this meant women in sufficient numbers to contribute to firm innovation and elevate strategic planning.

Finland, with a present-day board representation of 23.4 percent, followed with a requirement that women constitute at least 40 percent of board members in companies wholly owned by the state, an objective achieved in the spring of 2006, and, in 2010, a corporate governance code saying that public companies need representation from both genders on the board of directors or have a very good reason to explain why not. Sweden (23.9 percent women on corporate boards) enacted a corporate governance code in 2008 for public companies requiring them to strive for equal gender distribution on boards.

The ripple effects continue. An equality law introduced in Spain in 2007 required public companies with more than 250 employees to "develop gender equality plans with clear implications for female appointments to the board" and insure, by 2015, that at least 40 percent of board members are female. Joining Iceland, Finland, Denmark, Ireland and probably the Netherlands in mandating quotas, the French parliament gave final approval to a law requiring large companies to have at least 40 percent female board members within six years. In Italy, where women have only a 6.8 percent representation, the Italian lower house approved a 30 percent quota for corporate boards and the Senate recently passed an amended version of the law. Rejecting quotas, but clearly making gender equality a priority, the British government endorsed the conclusions of a report it had commissioned that stated that by 2015 women should make up at least 25 percent of the boards of the largest British firms. Most recently, the Australian government has mandated that by 2013 all companies with 100 or more employees must report their gender statistics to the Equal Opportunity for Women in the Workplace Agency.

Are there implications for American companies? I recently had the opportunity as a visiting professor at the Norwegian School of Management BI, Oslo, to participate in a day-long international conference "Women on Board: Lessons from Norway." Here is what I took away: Given the differences in the society and culture (the Norwegian population is relatively homogenous, ours is diverse), legal structures and the political and economic systems—large sectors of the Norwegian economy, especially energy, are wholly or partially state-owned, for example—there is little likelihood that the United States could or would mandate a gender diversity quota. According to some statistics, women currently make up 15.7 percent of the corporate board membership of publicly traded U.S. companies large and small.

According to the most recent research, adding highly qualified and motivated women to corporate boards in sufficient numbers to be effective yields positive results. With a 39.5 percent representation on Norway's corporate boards, women have proved valuable "for their ability to exert a positive impact on tasks of a qualitative nature," "contribute to a diversity of thought," "broaden discussions on strategic issues" and generate "higher quality decision making related to organizational strategies and practices." A study of French firms during the 2007–2008 financial crisis linked high performance with the number of women on boards.

According to S&P GovernanceMetrics, U.S. companies with a board membership of at least 22 percent women show the highest board performance, companies with 13 percent, the lowest. Catalyst has reported that companies with three or more women on their boards increase their return on equity 112 percent. To be innovative and competitive, American firms will need to work to bring women into more corporate board rooms and in greater numbers. This was one of the reasons the Securities and Exchange Commission adopted, in February, 2010, a regulation that public companies and mutual funds must disclose whether or not diversity is considered when directors are named and, if so, how the policy will be implemented and its effectiveness evaluated.

This is only a starting point. In selecting directors, companies need to be increasingly mindful of the fact that to ignore half of the population is bad business. Not only are many women qualified to be directors, they are more likely to recognize the potential from the firm's female customers who control over 80 percent of personal and family expenditures and suggest how the business might profit from focusing on that group.

References

Introduction

The analysis of leadership styles is discussed in Whitaker, L. D. (2010). Overview: History of women's public leadership. In K. O'Connor (Ed.), *Gender and women's leadership: A reference handbook* (Vol. 1, pp. 61–69). Thousand Oaks, CA, London, & Singapore: Sage Publications.

For other sources, see the article from which this discussion is extracted: Moore, D. P., Moore J. L., & Moore, J. W. (2011). How women entrepreneurs lead and why they manage that way. *Gender in Management: An International Journal, 26*(3), 220–233.

Profile: Gail K. Naughton

Final approved profile developed from interview data, materials furnished by entrepreneur, and review of on line websites. See also http://www.cit.cmu.edu/about_cit/events/2010/04_12_innovation_invention_naughton.html; http://people.forbes.com/profile/gail-k-naughton/76336 and http://www.prnewswire.com/news-releases/gail-k-naughton-phd-named-national-inventor-of-the-year-for-her-innovations-in-tissue-engineering-73734807.html

Working Women

The Movement of Women into the Workforce

Department of Labor, Bureau of Labor Statistics, Current Population Survey. Civilian labor force participation rate 16 yrs or over in April, 2011. Retrieved from http://www.bls.gov/cps/

Kalleberg, A. L., Kooke, D., Marsden, P. V., & Spaeth, J. L. (1996). *Organizations in America, Analyzing their structures and human resource practices.* Thousand Oaks, CA: Sage Publications (based on the national organizations study). See review by Moore, D. P. (2000). *Journal of Organizational Behavior, 21*(1), 113–115. doi: 10.1002/(SICI)1099-1379(200002)21:1<113::AID-JOB6>3.0.CO;2-F

Konrad, A., & Linnehan, F. (1999). Affirmative action: History, effects, and attitudes. In G. Powell (Ed.), *Handbook of gender and work* (pp. 429–452). Thousand Oaks, CA, London, & New Delhi: Sage Publications.

O'Connor, K., & Yanus, A. B. (2010). Overview: History of women's public leadership. In K. O'Connor (Ed.), *Gender and women's leadership: A reference handbook* (pp. xii–xv). Thousand Oaks, CA, London, & Singapore: Sage Publications.

U.S. Department of Education, National Center for Education Statistics. (2010). *Condition of Education 2010,* Table A-23-2.

Profile: Nikki Hardin

Final approved profile developed from entrepreneur's featured panel presentations, website materials, and additional material furnished by the entrepreneur. Quotations cited to original *Skirt!* and *Fridaville* references used in text.

Gender at Work

Powell, G. (Ed.) (1999). *Handbook of gender and work.* Thousand Oaks, CA, London, & New Delhi: Sage Publications. Authors referenced from this work include:

Carli, L., & Eagly, A. Gender effects on social influence and emergent leadership (pp. 203–223).

Konrad, A., & Linnehan, F. Affirmative action: History, effects, and attitudes (pp. 429–452).

Korabik, K. Sex and gender in the new millennium (pp. 3–16).

Maier, M. On the gendered substructure of organizations: Dimensions and dilemmas of corporate masculinity (pp. 69–94).

Powell, G. Introduction: Examining the intersection of gender and work (pp. ix–xx).

Roos, P., & Gatta, M. The gender gap in earnings: Trends, explanations, and prospects (pp. 95–124).

Burke, R. J., & Nelson, D. L. (Eds.) (2002). *Advancing women's careers.* Oxford & Malden: Blackwell Publishers. Authors referenced in this work:

Burke, R. J., & Nelson, D. L. Advancing women in management: Progress and prospects (pp. 3–14).

Holton, V. Training and development: Creating the right environment to help women succeed in corporate management (pp. 119–138).

Scandura, T., & Baugh, G. Mentoring and developmental relationships (pp. 161–173).

Tharenou, P. Gender differences in explanations for relocating or changing organizations for advancement (pp. 97–116).

O'Connor, K. (Ed.) (2010). *Gender and women's leadership: A reference handbook* (Vols. 1–2). Thousand Oaks, CA, London, & Singapore: Sage Publications. Authors referenced:

Bird, B. Overview: Women leaders in the business and profit sector (pp. 419–426).

O'Connor, K., & Yanus, A. B. Overview: History of women's public leadership (pp. xiii–xv).

Generations

Aparna, N. (2010). Getting to the foundation of talent management. *T+D, 64*(2), 20. (This article addresses the employer readiness for aging-related businesses and is based on Boston College's Sloan Center for Aging and Work Research.)

Career Advisory Board (Jan. 28, 2011). *Executive summary—The future of millennials' careers.* DeVry University and Conducted by Harris Interactive. (Poll of 500 U.S. Adults aged 21–31 and 523 Hiring Managers Dec. 29 to Jan. 10, 2011.) Retrieved from http//www.harrisinteractive.com

Pew Research Center Publications (March 18, 2010). The return of the multi-generational family household. Retrieved from http://pewresearch.org/pubs/1

Pitt-Catsouphes, M., Matz-Costa, C., & Besen, E. (2009). Age & generations: understanding experiences at the workplace (Research Highlight 6). Sloan Center on Aging & Work at Boston College. Retrieved from http//www.bc.edu/research/agingandwork/projects/generations.html

Twenge, J. M., & Campbell, S. M. (2008). Generational differences in psychological traits and their impact on the workplace. *Journal of Managerial Psychology, 23*(8), 862–877.

Twenge, J. M., Campbell, S. M., Hoffman, B. J., & Lance, C. E. (2010). Generational differences in work values: Leisure and extrinsic values increasing, social and intrinsic values decreasing. *Journal of Management, 36*(5), 1117–1142.

The Origins of the Mommy Wars

Douglas, S. J., & Michaels, M. W. (2004). *The idealization of motherhood and how it has undermined women—The mommy myth.* New York, NY: Free Press.

Hayghe, H. V. (March, 1990). Family members in the work force. *Monthly Labor Review,* 14–19.

Konrad, A., & Linnehan, F. (1999) (full reference above).

O'Connor, K., & Yanus, A. B. (2010) (full reference above).

U.S. Department of Commerce, Economics and Statistics Administration and the Executive Office of the President Office of Management and

Budget for the White House Council on Women and Girls (March, 2011). *Women in America—Indicators of social and economic well-being*, Washington, DC: U.S. Government Printing Office. Retrieved from http://www.whitehouse.gov/sites/

U.S. Department of Labor, Bureau of Labor Statistics (BLS) (accessed 2011). *Annual social and economic supplements (ASEC) 1968–2009*, Current population survey (CPS), Tables 23 and 25. Retrieved from http://www.census.gov/hhes/www/cpstables/032009/pov/new46_10012501.htm (Dataset 10035).

Legislation and Policies

Avoiding a Challenge of Discrimination

EEOC clarifies the definition of who is an "applicant" in the context of internet recruiting and hiring (2004). *Fair Employment Practices Guidelines* (587), 1–4. Retrieved from EBSCO*host*.

Executive Order 11246 on Affirmative Action.

Konrad, A., & Linnehan, F. (pp. 429–452) (full reference above).

Legislation: Title VII of the Civil Rights Act of 1964; Age Discrimination in Employment Act of 1967; Americans with Disabilities Act (ADA) of 1990; The Civil Rights Act of 1991; ADA Amendments Act of 2008. See also http://www.eeoc.gov/laws/guidance/index.cfm. On enforcement see http://www.shrm.org/LegalIssues/FederalResources/FederalStatutesRegulationsandGuidance/Pages/Uniformguidelinesonselectionprocedures.aspx and http://www.eeoc.gov/eeoc/statistics/enforcement/charges.cfm. In fiscal year 2008, the EEOC received 24,582 charges containing ADEA allegations (an increase from the 19,103 ADEA charges received in fiscal year 2007). In fiscal year 2009, the EEOC received 22,778 ADEA charges.

Smith, A. (2008). Definition of "applicant" will not change. *HRMagazine*, *53*(5), 23. Retrieved from EBSCOhost.

Uniform Guidelines on Employee Selection Procedures Part 1607 (1978). See series of PDF files showing the relationship between selection procedures applying to all employment decisions and discrimination. Specifically applies to ADA, Job Analysis, and Performance decisions in sections addressed below. Retrieved from www.access.gpo.gov/nara/cfr/waisidx_00/29cfr1607_00.html (Clarifications, 1979).

Americans with Disabilities

ADA Guidelines. Retrieved from http://www.ada.gov/business.htm. Surveys can be found at www.2010DisabilitySurveys.org

Department of Commerce, Economics and Statistics Administration, U.S. Census Bureau (Issued Dec., 2008). Brault, M. W. Americans with disabilities: 2005. Retrieved from http://www.census.gov/prod/2008pubs/p70-117.pdf

Baldridge, D. C., & Veiga, J. F. (2006). The impact of anticipated social consequences on recurring disability accommodation requests. *Journal of Management, 32*(1), 158–179.

Brault, M. W. (Statistics: Issued Dec., 2008). Americans with disabilities: 2005. U.S. Department of Commerce, Economics and Statistics Administration, U.S. Census Bureau. Washington, DC: U.S. Government Printing Office.

Moore, D. P., Moore, J. W., & Moore, J. L. (2007). After fifteen years: The response of small businesses to the Americans with disabilities act. *Work, 29(*2), 113–126.

Randolph, D. S. (2004). Predicting the effect of disability on employment status and income. *Work, 23*(3) 257–266.

See Polls and Surveys of Those with Disabilities:

Harris Poll #41 (July 26, 2003). Support for key principles of ADA still overwhelming but awareness of ADA and support for principles declines somewhat. Harris Interactive. Retrieved from http://www.harrisinteractive.com/Insights/HarrisVault.aspx

Harris Poll #59 (Oct. 7, 2000). Conflicting trends in employment of people with disabilities 1986–2000. Harris Interactive. Retrieved from http://www.harrisinteractive.com/Insights/HarrisVault.aspx

Harris Poll #30 (June 7, 2000). How the internet is improving the lives of Americans with disabilities. Harris Interactive. Retrieved from http://www.harrisinteractive.com/Insights/HarrisVault.aspx

Harris Poll #30 (May 12, 1999). Overwhelming majority of Americans continue to support the Americans with disabilities act. Criticisms and attacks on the ADA have had no impact on massive public support for the key provisions of the 1990 law. Retrieved from http://www.harrisinteractive.com/Insights/HarrisVault.aspx

Harris Poll #56 (Oct. 14, 1998). Americans with disabilities still pervasively disadvantaged on a broad range of key indicators: Huge differences between those with and without disabilities, in employment, income, transportation, health care and life satisfaction. Harris Interactive. Retrieved from http://www.harrisinteractive.com/Insights/Harris Vault.aspx

Kessler Foundation/National Organization on Disability (Oct. 5, 2010). Survey of employment of Americans with disabilities. Retrieved from http://www.2010disabilitysurveys.org/

Kessler Foundation/National Organization on Disability (July 26, 2010). Survey of Americans with disabilities. Retrieved from http://www.2010disabilitysurveys.org/

Why Job Analysis?

Drucker, P. (2004). What makes an effective executive? *Harvard Business Review, 82*(6), 58–63. See Also Response to article in HBS by: Beloshapka, V. (2004), *82*(10), 152–153.

Other Valuable Resources Include:

Cascio, W., & Boudreau, J. (2010). *Investing in people—Financial impact of human resource initiatives* (2nd ed.). Upper Saddle River, NJ: Pearson Education. (Unique aspect of book: HR measurements aligning HR investments with organizational goals.)

Hersey, P., & Goldsmith, M. (1980). The changing role of performance management. *Training & Development Journal, 34*(10), 18. Retrieved from EBSCO*host.* (Discusses role for Uniform guidelines in selection procedures.)

HR Guide to the Internet: Job Analysis; Law/Legal Issues; Federal Guidelines. Impact of the Uniform Guidelines on Employee Selection Procedures. See specifically Sections 60-3.9-Section B.; 60-3.14-Section A; and 60-3.14-Section C.2. Retrieved from www.job-analysis.net/G002.htm

Mathis, R. L., & Jackson, J. H. (2011). *Human resource management: Essential perspectives.* Mason, OH: South-Western Cengage Learning. See specifically: C3, Equal employment and diversity management (pp. 39–60) for more in-depth coverage of major equal employment laws, types of discrimination, compliance, diversity management and affirmative action; C4, Staffing: the nature of job analysis, job description and specifications, recruiting, selection and placement (pp. 60–82). C7, Compensation strategies and practices (pp. 126–149). (A good way to evaluate an HRM text is by carefully reviewing the Appendices to determine whether references are provided for case law and the Uniform Guidelines and unlawful practices as in Appendix B to this work (pp. 211–213). Also examine scholarly background of authors and level of recent research.)

Making Performance Appraisals Effective

Some HR Recommended References for Developing Effective Systems:

Caleo, S., & Heilman, M. E. (2009). Differential reactions to men and women's interpersonal unfairness. Academy of Management Proceedings Abstract, Chicago.

Cascio, W., & Boudreau, J. (2010). (Full reference above).

Daniel, C. (2001). Separating law and professional practice from politics. *Review of Public Personnel Administration, 21*(3), 175. Retrieved from EBSCOhost.

Performance Appraisal and Standards (2011). In Encyclopedia of Business (2nd ed.). Guide and overview retrieved from http://www.referenceforbusiness.com/encyclopedia/Per-Pro/Performance-Appraisal-and-Standards.html

Scholtes, P. R. (1998). Performance without appraisal: What to do instead of performance appraisals. Copyright © Scholtes Seminars and Consulting 1996–2006. Retrieved from http://www.pscholtes.com/pscholtes/performance/and referencing Dr. W. Edwards Deming, often referred to as the father of the Quality movement, named annual appraisals, merit ratings and similar practices as one of the

"Seven Diseases" that stand in the way of building healthy companies. See also Scholtes, P. S. (1998). *The leader's handbook: Making things happen, getting things done.* New York, NY: McGraw-Hill. (In chapter 9 Scholtes provides detailed explanations on why performance appraisals are so harmful and why they don't make sense, and also references Deming.)

Spector, M. D., & Jones, G. E. (2004). Trust in the workplace: Factors affecting trust formation between team members. *Journal of Social Psychology, 144*, 311–321.

The Gender Problem of Performance versus Potential

Haller-Jorden, E. T. (April 23, 2009). Brussels jump forum for advancing women in the workplace—Can women rescue the economy? Retrieved from http://www.forumjump.eu/files/report_2009.pdf

Holton, V. (2002). (Full reference listed under Burke & Nelson above.)

Malhotra, V. (April 12, 2011). Where are all the senior-level women? *Wall Street Journal.* Retrieved from http://online.wsj.com/article/SB10001424052748704013604576246774042116558.html

Mattis, M. C. (2002). Best practices for retaining and advancing women professionals and managers. In R. J. Burke, & D. L. Nelson (Eds.), *Advancing women's careers: Research and practice* (309–332; Statistics and reference to material, pp. 310–311). Malden, MA: Blackwell Publishers. Mattis, the former head of the Awards evaluation process at Catalyst for eight years, notes that the best practices in her chapter are excerpted from Catalyst (2000). *Cracking the glass ceiling: Catalyst's research on women in corporate management, 1995–2000.* New York, NY: Catalyst.

The Changing Workplace

How Women Have Changed the Business Landscape

Bureau of Labor Statistics (2010). Women in the labor force, 1970–2009. Data from current population survey (CPS). See also Women in the Labor Force: A Databook (2010 ed.), BLS Report 1026 (Dec., 2010). See also Table 10. Employed persons by major occupation and sex, 2008 and 2009 annual averages (pp. 26, 27). Current Population Survey, U.S. DOL, U.S. Bureau of Labor Statistics, Washington, D.C.

Center for Women's Business Research (2010). *Key facts about women owned businesses, 2008–2009 update.* Retrieved from http://www.womensbusinessresearchcenter.org/

Mainiero, L. A., & Sullivan, S. E. (2006). *The opt-out revolt: Why people are leaving companies to create kaleidoscope careers.* Mountain View, CA: Davies-Black Publishing.

Mattis, M. C. (2004). Women entrepreneurs: Out from under the glass ceiling. *Women in Management Review, 19*(3), 154–163.

Moore, D. P. (2010). Women as entrepreneurs and business owners. In K. O'Connor (Ed.), *Gender and women's leadership, a reference handbook* (pp. 443–451). Los Angeles, CA: Sage Publications.

Moore, D. P. (2000). *Careerpreneurs—Lessons from leading women entrepreneurs on building a career without boundaries.* Palo Alto, CA: Davies-Black Publishing. (See Intentional Entrepreneurs at p. 5; Corporate Climbers at p. 89. See also Linda Horn quotation at p. 89.)

Moore. D. P. (1999). Women entrepreneurs: Approaching a new millennium. In G. Powell (Ed.), *Handbook of Gender in Organizations* (pp. 371–389).

Moore D. P., & Buttner, E. H. (1997). *Women entrepreneurs—Moving beyond the glass ceiling.* Thousand Oaks, CA, London, & New Delhi: Sage Publications. (Quote at p. 30.)

Profile: Denise L. Devine

Final approved profile developed from interview data and additional material furnished by the entrepreneur. Quotation by Denise on financing for women first appeared in "Pennsylvania's Best 50 Women in Business," in the *Philadelphia Business Journal.* See News about Devine Foods. Retrieved from: http://www.devinefoods.com/pages/news_pa_50.html

Glass Floors, Ceilings, Walls, Elevators and Cliffs

Carter, N. M., & Silva, C. (2009). Opportunity or setback? High potential women and men during economic crisis. Retrieved from http://catalyst.org/etc/hipo/ (Statistics on women senior executives).

Catalyst (2011). Catalyst award winners. Retrieved from http://www.catalyst.org/page/69/catalyst-award-winners. See detailed reports on each winner for 2011: Kaiser Permanente, McDonald's Corporation and Time Warner Inc.

Catalyst (Aug., 2011). U.S. Women in Business. Pyramids, citing Catalyst, 2010 Catalyst Census; Fortune 500 Women Board Directors (2010); Catalyst, 2010 Catalyst Census Fortune 500 Women Executive Officers and Top Earners (2010). http://www.catalyst.org/publication/132/us-women-in-business

Catalyst and the National Foundation for Women Business Owners with support of The Committee 200 Foundation (1998). Women Entrepreneurs: Why companies lose female talent and what they can do about it. References for leaving organizations are cited on p. 13. In the private sector these are: flexibility, 51 percent; glass ceiling, 29 percent; unhappy with work environment, 28 percent; unchallenged, 22 percent. See p. 22 for change in percentage of women starting businesses with an entrepreneurial idea: 20+ years = 51 percent; 10 to 19 years = 48 percent; and less than 10 years = 35 percent.

Ignatius, D. (2011). *Blood money: A novel of espionage.* New York & London: W. W. Norton & Company (quote at p. 17).

Ryan, M. K., & Haslam, S. A. (2007). The glass cliff: Exploring the dynamics surrounding the appointment of women to precarious leadership positions. *Academy of Management Review, 32*(2), 549–572. (Extensive discussion of the glass cliff and other related concepts.)

Profile: Eleanor Tabi Haller-Jorden

Final approved profile developed from entrepreneur's featured presentations, website materials, and additional material furnished by the entrepreneur. *The Profiles in Diversity Journal 6th Annual Women Worth Watching*™ issue, which showcases leading businesswomen, designated Ms. Haller-Jorden as one of its Women Worth Watching.

Women on Board—The Business Case

Catalyst C-News (Aug., 2011). Changing work places, changing lives, *3*(7).

Catalyst (2011). U.S. Women in Business. Pyramids, citing Catalyst, 2010 Catalyst Census; Fortune 500 Women Board Directors (2010); Catalyst, 2010 Catalyst Census Fortune 500 Women Executive Officers and Top Earners (2010). Retrieved from http://www.catalyst.org/publication/132/us-women-in-business

For statistics see the following: United Nations Report (2001); Governance Metrics (March 8, 2011).

Catalyst (1998). Catalyst, the National Foundation for Women Business Owners (NFWBO), with support of The Committee 200 Foundation. (Full citation above.)

Globewomen Issue 80 (Dec. 17, 2010). Retrieved from http:globewomen.org.

Nanivadekar, M. (2010). Overview: Women's leadership in the global context. In K. O'Connor (Ed.), *Gender and women's leadership: A reference handbook* (pp. 293–303).

Soares, R., Combopiano, J., Regis, A., Shur, Y., & Wong, R. (2010). Women on boards. See also 2010 Catalyst Census: Fortune 500 Women Board Directors (Catalyst, 2010), pp. 1–16. Retrieved from http://www.catalyst.org/publication/433/women-on-boards

Other Valuable Resources:

Hillman, A. J., & Cannella Jr. A. A. (2007). Organizational predictors of women on corporate boards. *Academy of Management Journal, 50*(4), 941–952.

Konrad, A. M., Kramer, V., & Erkut, S. (April–June, 2008). Critical mass: The impact of three or more women on corporate boards. *Organizational Dynamics, 37*, 145–164.

Terjesen, S., Sealy, R., & Singh, V. (2009). Women directors on corporate boards: A review and research agenda. *Corporate Governance: An International Review, 17*(3), 320–337.

Torchia, M., Calabrŏ, A., & Huse, M. (2010). Critical mass theory, board strategic tasks and firm innovation: How do women directors contribute? Academy of Management Paper. Montreal, Canada.

2

ORGANIZATIONS: LEADERSHIP AND MANAGEMENT

Introduction

Leadership expert Bernard Bass tells us that while there is an overlap in management and leadership they involve quite different qualities. Managers perform functions associated with planning, investigating, organizing, and control. Leaders deal with interpersonal aspects and are involved in setting the company strategic vision and plans for reaching goals. Both are required for success. Unless the leader has a clear vision and the managerial skills to turn the vision into action, there can be no successful implementation. Leadership and management must go hand in hand. At each phase of the decision-making process, as one Georgia entrepreneur explained, "Basically the buck stops here. I have to deal with the problem effectively, or somebody is disgruntled." There is no one sure-fire management style, no quick-fix solution—to add water and stir. The secret is that you get to decide.

There are, however, several important general theories that offer management guidance, and it is useful to know what they are and something about their evolution.

The first management theories came into being when large business organizations arose as a consequence of the 19th century industrial revolution. As David Nadler and Michael Tushman, *Competing by Design—The Power of Organizational Architecture,* have suggested, the combination of building new materials (structural steel), new company needs (centralizing workers in production units, controlling numerous business units over vast differences) and the appearance of collateral technology (factory and office machines, the telegraph and telephone) meant it became possible to both physically build massive factories and modern skyscrapers and create the large firms necessary to manage far-flung operations.

What we today call traditional or classical management, organizing work in the image of the machine so operations were structured, orderly and impersonal, involved a couple of basic ideas and gave rise to a number of management concepts.

Frederick Winslow Taylor's approach, scientific management, focused on the individual worker and the best ways to select, train, and motivate employees. Organizational management sought efficiency by dividing management by function and level of authority and instructing managers through comprehensive rules. Power was concentrated at the top; the firm was seen as a pyramid-shaped hierarchy. When it soon became apparent that the idea of a fixed and permanent organization structure did not fit when times changed, a new, human relations approach appeared. It contended that organizations changed internally as they responded to unpredictable environments and aimed at understanding how psychological and social processes interacted with work to influence performance.

New approaches emerging after World War II described organizations as complex evolving systems. Organizational behaviorists such as Douglas McGregor described contrasting ways of managing employees. His Theory X identified managers who assume that most people are not ambitious, don't want responsibility, dislike work and try to avoid it. These managers give detailed and complete instructions and maintain control. McGregor's Theory Y describes managers who assume that employees are internally motivated and capable of self-direction and self-control in working toward organizational goals.

Quantitative theories of management appeared when computers allowed us to process huge amounts of information. Management scientists used mathematical models of the decision-making process to compare alternative courses of action as precisely as possible. Systems analysts viewed complex organizations as a collection of related subsystems rather than individual parts, as was the focus in the classical period of management.

Consider a restaurant. The diverse items going into the system (capital, land, equipment, materials, customers, and information) are called inputs. What comes out of the system (product, service, and information) are called outputs. The system itself is called the transformational process. Open subsystems (waiters serving customers) interact with the external environment. Relatively closed subsystems (the kitchen staff) infrequently interact with the external environment. Decisions made independently at the subsystem level (the cook decides to buy the cheapest ingredients available rather than the best, the front end manager schedules too few waiters to serve customers) can impact the organization negatively. The systems perspective thus assumes that the whole is greater than the sum of its parts, that any change in a subsystem can affect other parts of the organization and therefore the organization must be managed as a coordinated entity.

Contingency theory offered a way to pull everything together. It assumed that the effectiveness of a particular management style varied according to the situation and the people involved because everything is impacted by a variety of external and internal factors.

Any of the above management perspectives can be used alone or in combination depending on the situation. But at the heart of the approach is the recognition that change is inevitable and good managers are those who can adapt.

Current leadership theories call for using different techniques to fit different conditions. In a construction firm, for example, once the project had been settled on and the goals agreed to, the entrepreneur might manage architects using Theory Y because they are creative professionals and disinclined to do their best work if forced to conform too closely. She might employ scientific management principles to decide the best way to perform component tasks (whether to pour concrete walls at the site or use preset slabs). Elements of the classical management style with strict rules and bureaucratic regulations might guide workers on a job site (start time, hardhats must be worn, etc.). Janet Marie Smith, Architect and Urban Planner, described in an interview with *Working Woman* how, as the team's project supervisor for the Baltimore's Oriole Park at Camden Yards, she moved between facilitating and hierarchical management styles as circumstances dictated.

Rebecca Smith

Founder and President, A. D. Morgan Corporation

> *The low-key but serious leadership style is very effective for me. I am a positive leader. I place such great emphasis on rewarding excellence and celebrating good work that a slight departure from that norm sends a clear message of dissatisfaction. I am generally upbeat and emotionally steady, moving around the office chatting and laughing while encouraging and promoting my team's renegade spirits and innovations. My continuing message is that we have an agreement to each do our part of the job, which together makes a successful team.*

From the beginning, Rebecca Smith knew she wanted to own her own building company. As her profile in the *Suncoast Builder/Architect* describes, she began at an early age by "helping her father on home projects and watching him prepare engineering drawings." In the ninth grade "she opted to take wood shop in lieu of home economics" and hers was one of the three architectural designs selected from those submitted from the school's five shop classes and entered in a final competition among junior high schools. "The only girl in the competition," she took first place. After earning her B.A. in Architecture and an M.S. in Building Construction from the University of Florida, Rebecca worked for a construction firm for five years to learn the practical side of the business. An outsider in the male dominated world of construction, in the early days as an employee she took great care to "blend in." "There were issues of sensitivity. Soon I had earned their respect as part of *their* team. Later, I overheard comments from the existing crew to the new arrivals like 'That's no girl, that's Rebecca'."

Rebecca had set a goal of owning her own business by the age of 30 and, in fact, beat that by one year. At age 29, in the middle of an economic slump (1989), she negotiated a loan from her father and started the A. D. Morgan Corporation. The company was named after her golden retrievers, Addie and Morgan. She had one employee and an $8,000 renovation contract in hand when she opened for business. "I wanted to be a contractor," she said, "the fact that everybody else was going out of business didn't matter. I truly believed that if there was only one contract to compete for, we were going to get it." In the early years she dealt with the problems of being a woman in an overwhelmingly male dominated industry by focusing on construction projects and what her company could deliver rather than gender issues. Many of the early employees had worked with her before so they knew she understood the business of construction and was an effective manager and leader. But there were others in the company who were working with a woman in construction for the first time, let alone having one as their boss. The challenge she faced with her previous co-workers was more related to the transition from being a peer to becoming their leader. "In this field, I find myself leading and managing men 99 percent of the time," she notes. "They differ in both age and levels of management. We have the superintendents in the field who supervise the subcontractors and laborer force, as well as project managers, and some very sophisticated clients. This is not a group of men who will react to the same style of management."

Developing a client oriented level of services that included both design and construction phase services (cost estimating, site development, scheduling, management, wireless communications, life cycle cost analysis and monthly status reports), along with a focus on superb quality and cost savings, Rebecca's company grew at a rate of approximately 100 percent per year during a time when many other companies had difficulty surviving. In 1998, A. D. Morgan was named a Small Business of the Year by the Tampa Chamber of Commerce. Rebecca was further honored by the University of Florida as their distinguished Alumna for the School of Building Construction for 1998–1999. Another very distinguished honor was awarded to Rebecca as the Ernst and Young, State of Florida Entrepreneur of the Year for the Industry of Construction and Real Estate. In 2000, the A. D. Morgan Corporation, now the fourth largest woman-owned business in the Tampa Bay area, received the internationally recognized LEEDs certification (Leadership in Energy and Environmental Design), then a relatively new program endorsed by the state of Florida to incorporate higher attention to environmentally sensitive construction projects. The same year, Rebecca was honored with a Distinguished Women in Business Award.

The challenge came immediately after the September 11, 2001 attack on the twin towers when $16 million in contracts were canceled, a significant part of A. D. Morgan's revenue. By the end of 2003, the company had worked through its backlog and reached a critical point. The turn came at the end of the year, when Rebecca learned her company had been awarded renovation projects for three elementary schools that totaled over $10 million. In 2007, A. D. Morgan marked its 18th anniversary with total revenues exceeding the $400 million mark and at its high point employing 50 people with annual revenues of approximately $80 million.

The fact that Rebecca operated a diversified company allowed her to focus on renovation projects when the 2008 economic downturn triggered three straight years of decline in the state of Florida construction industry. As a Class "A" certified general contractor, Rebecca's company has offices throughout the state in Tampa, Bradenton, Sebring, Cocoa and Ocala. The current list of A. D. Morgan's projects and developments includes some

48 K-12 and 25 higher educational institutions, 18 health care and research facilities and 15 correctional institutions, in addition to office buildings, parking garages, public and retail structures and broadcasting facilities. In 2009, Rebecca was recognized as one of Tampa Bay's 100 most influential business leaders.

Rebecca's style of management begins with knowing everything about the job—"I don't ask them to do anything that I wouldn't or couldn't do myself," she says. But the real key to her success is her ability to bring out the best in her employees. In developing an outline for a large project analysis report, a creative task, she asked the team to assume they were the client and asked how they would like to see the report formatted. "I took notes, offered suggestions, and at the end of the meeting handed them an outline plan to deliver the report. The outline was influenced by my experience as a project manager but included my perspective as a president, one who reviewed many reports." The process gave the project team the opportunity to participate while getting immediate feedback on their ideas. "It was a learning process for them and an opportunity for me to gauge their abilities." The resulting outline met Rebecca's goal to obtain information while the process allowed for team growth and learning. As an added benefit, the project team gained greater insight as to what, how and why the report was necessary and left the meeting more energized to undertake the task with enthusiasm.

Dimensions of Management

Approaches to Management

There are any number of books that explain the basics of good management. But few managers have the time to read widely and certainly not everything. One solution to the problem of staying up to date is to get a revised textbook and keep it in the office as a reference.

Management principles and concepts are considered so important that nearly every school of business administration offers required courses at both the undergraduate and graduate levels. The requirement exists because there is an agreed-upon body of knowledge that is set down and formally passed on from one generation of managers to the next—irrespective of changes in technology, environments and organizational designs and structures.

Ten years ago, after more than 20 years as a professor of management, I set out to examine the differences in the approaches across leading textbooks in the field. Revisiting the analysis in 2011, I discovered that the authors have not strayed far from the basics Peter F. Drucker set out long ago in *The Practice of Management*, which consists of setting goals, organizing activities, motivating and communicating, measuring performance and developing people.

The texts vary in their approaches. Most common and dominating in the field until recently was the traditional approach to teaching management that emphasizes organizational goals and processes. As Thomas S. Bateman and Scott A. Snell, *Management: Leading & Collaborating in a Competitive World* (8th edition), say, delivering strategic value requires planning (analyzing the present and anticipating the future), building a dynamic organization (assembling and coordinating the human, financial, physical, informational, and other resources), flexibility (through attracting and retaining the very best people), leading (stimulating, motivating, and communicating with employees), and controlling (continued organizational learning that leads to changing things when necessary). Theirs is a modernized, results oriented, functional approach focused on delivering value and achieving goals as efficiently as possible. Stating at the outset that "effective management is the result of hard work and careful planning," authors Don Hellriegel, Susan E. Jackson and John W. Slocum Jr., *Management: A Competency-Based Approach* (11th edition), take a similar approach in discussing the development of six core managerial competencies (self-management, strategic action, planning and administration, global awareness, teamwork, and communication). In addition, each chapter includes a discussion of ethical challenges.

By contrast, Richard L. Daft, *Management* (10th edition), holds that today's demands go well beyond what is traditionally taught in management courses. Written with the assistance of Patricia G. Lane, the volume describes the challenges in confronting the array of ethical dilemmas, crises, rapidly changing technologies, globalization, outsourcing, government regulation, social media, global supply chains, and the Wall Street meltdown. Dealing with change in its forms is at the heart of the book. Also calling attention to the rapidly changing environment, Gary Dessler, *Leading People and Organizations in the 21st Century,* suggests that managing today is increasingly based on technologies that both allow and require "managing at the speed of thought." In his discussion of the complexities of the ever-changing workplace, economy and environment, John Schermerhorn, *Management, 11e* (2010), includes a discussion of the problems a manager faces in trying to achieve lifelong career success. Those seeking a valuable assessment tool will benefit from Schermerhorn's *Personal Management Workbook,* developed with Robert L. Holbrook, Jr., that provides 30 self-assessments that explore the important dimensions of management strategies.

Why the different emphases? Managers operate at organizational levels and do different things in a multitude of environments, each of which is unique in some respect. One management size philosophy does not fit all. What you do as a manager depends, in part, on who you are in the organization. It also depends on what you actually manage—what decisions you get to make.

What works best? There is no one simple answer, but considerable research points in the direction where answers may lie. Tom Peters and Robert Waterman, authors of *In Search of Excellence,* found that America's best-run companies responded to conditions quickly, had a relatively simple structure with few hierarchical levels, and stayed close to their customers. Research also suggests that the various employee empowerment programs have a few common ingredients for success: Management has to gain the trust of employees by behaving with honesty, openness and integrity, employees must be able to make decisions without fear for their jobs, and everyone, from management to the newest worker, should feel responsible for the company's welfare. The value of this advice as an effective management strategy has not changed.

The most difficult part of the process? For employees to have power, someone in management has to give it up.

Leadership, Management and the Information Revolution

New styles of management appeared as managers increasingly dealt with rapid change, unpredictable external environments, a rising flood of information and evolving technologies.

Organizational efficiency in the age of the information revolution, said David Nadler and Michael Tushman in *Competing by Design: The Power of Organizational Architecture*, requires organizational creativity, and that means managing teams of people to use their collective abilities. In essence, as an overview of the book states, "All the reengineering, restructuring, and downsizing in the world will merely destabilize a company if the change doesn't address the fundamental patterns of performance—and if the change doesn't recognize the unique core competencies of that company."

Attention has turned to finding leadership styles that did not leave people feeling they were controlled, managed or manipulated. One of the most comprehensive that came to the fore described the transformational leader, a leader who articulates an organizational vision that can be shared, gives subordinates power and encouragement, guides by motivating and serves as a role model. According to Bernard Bass, rather than formalized and rigid procedures and visible demonstrations of power that marked the authoritarian leadership style, the transformational style emphasized flexibility, the encouragement of employee innovation and the integration of people and ideas. John Kotter, in his book *Force for Change: How Leadership Differs from Management,* takes a similar approach to that of Bass and also points out that most organizations are usually lacking in either leadership or management competencies and in most cases it is in leadership competency. "Over time, the most passionate leaders move on ... while layers of management build up ... gradually transition to a complacent mentality, where management reigns supreme and leadership is in short supply." This, he says, ultimately kills organizations as managers may not have the foresight to inspire change rather than imposing or simply reacting to it.

Managers who want to learn more about transformational leadership may want to start with award winning authors James M. Kouzes and Barry Z. Posner, Professors of Leadership at Santa Clara University's Leavey School of Business, authors of *The Leadership Challenge* (over 1.8 million copies in print and named one of the Top 100 Business Books of All Time), for a more detailed discussion of these concepts and practical applications.

Information is also available from some of the best known leadership institutes. These include the Wharton Center for Leadership & Change Management, the Ohio State University Leadership Center, the Center for Creative Leadership, in Greensboro, NC, and the John F. Kennedy School of Government at Harvard University, which offers Leadership Strategies for Senior Executives and a special leadership program for women.

Nearly all the major research universities and most colleges have developed creative leadership programs for managers. Many also have made information available to the public. For a motivational pick-me-up you can access the Ohio State online Leadership Moments at www.ag.ohio-state.edu. Each week a featured column addressing a leadership moment appears online. These are also archived.

To catch up on a broad base of literature, you might want to turn to the Wharton Suggested Reading List for the M.B.A. class of 2011. The current listing of 40 books introduces you to classics across the field of management, leadership, ethics, finance and all the disciplines in the business major. In addition, you may find it valuable to check out sources such as the Chief

Executive Leadership Institute, Danish International Continuing Education, Federal Executive Institute, General Electric Company, ImprovEdge, International Leadership Association and the Center for Advanced Study of Leadership, University of Maryland or the Peter Drucker Foundation, among others.

A final note: Much of what you will read on the websites is derived from the basic principles underlying the concepts of transformational leadership.

Closing the Gap—Moving Beyond Buzzwords

Owners and executives searching for ways to create the most productive work environment are always interested in the newest ideas on leadership and management, the best approach to motivating people, methods to cut costs and raise productivity and more. The problem is sorting through the mountain of available information. In the first five months of 2011 alone, publications on these topics included no fewer than 11 bestsellers, some 64 new books that made somebody's "must read" list, and reminders of the 22 classics that continue to be popular and relevant. (For the listing, see LeadershipNow.com.) Supplementing all this is the avalanche of "how-to" popular books and a proliferation of audio and videotapes, books that you can download, and short fix-it approaches, all explaining how to become a more effective leader.

Aside from checking out the latest volume on the bestseller list and then waiting for the next one or taking a refresher course in Management 101, finding one's way through the endless advice can be daunting.

Warren Bennis is one of the world's foremost experts on leadership, with more than 30 books and numerous articles on leadership, change, and creative collaboration. You might want to start with one of his books. The *Financial Times* named his *Leaders* one of the Top 50 Business Books of All Time. His other works include *An Invented Life, Geeks & Geezers,* co-authored with Bob Thomas, for which he received a Pulitzer Prize nomination, *Leading for a Lifetime,* and *On Becoming a Leader,* named among the 100 Best Business Books of All Time. Bennis' *Still Surprised: A Memoir of a Life in Leadership* was selected as the Editor's Choice on LeadershipNow.com. No time to read? The audio cassette for his *Managing People is Like Herding Cats* suggests how you can learn to accomplish this feat on your way to work.

Among Bennis' observations:

- Managers are the people who do things right, while leaders are people who do the right thing.
- The most successful organizations in the 21st century won't be managed but led.
- Leaders will recognize that "the only capital that really counts is human capital."

There are also some common sense nuggets mixed in with the numerous approaches to becoming a great leader. For example, Sam Deep and Lyle Sussman, the authors of *Smart Moves*, published in *Working Woman*, list seven basic management principles. Each draws on situations that everyone has experienced or observed:

- Parkinson's Law (activity expands to fill the time allotted to it).
- The Law of Effect (behaviors immediately rewarded increase in frequency, behaviors punished decrease).
- GIGO (garbage in, garbage out).
- The Peter Principle (people tend to be promoted beyond their competencies).
- Pareto's Law or the 80–20 rule (the significant people in any meeting usually constitute only a small part of the group).
- The Pygmalion Effect (what we expect from others determines how we behave toward them).
- Murphy's Law (if anything can go wrong, it will).

Lists like this vividly highlight what can be causing problems. Acquiring the management skills to deal with them is a bit more difficult, particularly the most basic one: making the leap from your individual identity as a performer to that of a manager. It requires you to move from a specialist role in performing specific tasks, thereby accomplishing objectives through your own efforts, often working independently, into becoming a generalist who coordinates diverse tasks, relying on others to get things done, building networks and working in a highly interdependent world.

The next leap after that is to a more diverse environment and broader span of control and responsibility.

Women in Management

Women, Power and Leadership

Considerable confusion still arises from the idea that there is a style of management particular to women, a concept that became popular with the publication of "Ways Women Lead," a 1990 article in the *Harvard Business Review* by Judy Rosener, then a Professor of Management at the University of California at Irvine, who argued that women often did not have the same access to formal power and, therefore, had to rely on personal power, influence, and teamwork. It was an "interactive" style of leadership to get work accomplished, said Rosener, a style distinguished by the fact it encouraged participation by others, involved sharing power and information rather than hoarding it, and emphasized positive leadership skills which enhanced the value of others and got people excited about their work by allowing them to participate in real decision making.

Rosener's article was immediately followed by fierce debates. One was between women celebrating the superiority of a feminine style of management and others wary because the idea of a special style suggested that women are not inherently tough enough to hack it in corporate life. Some dismissed Rosener's revelations as little more than good evidence that women do not have to follow male management models to be successful. Still others, like business writer and consultant Nancy K. Austin, for example, pointed to the dangers from emphasizing feminine styles. Said Austin, about half the "leadership seminars" for women she investigated were designed around the gender stereotype that, before they can become leaders and managers, women somehow needed to correct a batch of career derailing defects.

As Moore reported in *Careerpreneurs*, "It can be useful to remember that, to date, not a single research study has uncovered any gender-based differences between men and women in the desire for power, the drive to acquire it, management style, or the anxiety that comes from being in charge. Several streams of research do suggest there are culturally based differences between women and men in views about holding and exercising power." As Moore and Buttner said in *Women Entrepreneurs*, "this is where we get the stereotypes such as the now discredited ideas that women managers have difficulty in the workplace because many men and women are raised to expect male authority and female compliance or that from childhood boys supposedly place value on autonomy and self-sufficiency while girls tend to be more relationship and group oriented."

In 2011, Moore's coauthored work showed that the number of studies isolating any effects of gender on productivity is slight, though there is at least one strong suggestion of a positive linear relationship between gender diversity and productivity. The value of including women members in teams has been supported in studies of IPO firms, small firm performance, and military settings. Findings suggest that when the number of women on a team increases, collaboration, solidarity and conflict resolution, reciprocity and self-sustaining action all rise.

Current research suggests that, while evidence for sex differences in leadership is mixed and leadership styles depend upon context, in general, women tend to employ a transformational approach, are more likely than men to do so and specifically employ a relational approach. The body of research further suggests that more than men, women behave democratically in leadership situations, use interactive skills, place emphasis on maintaining effective working relationships and value cooperation and being responsible to others while working to achieve outcomes that address the concerns of all parties involved.

In evaluating situations, it can be helpful to remember that, while broad cultural stereotypes abound, there is no reason to adopt them or feel constrained to act within them. Successful management techniques run the gamut from the fiercely hierarchical to the widely participatory. What works in any given situation depends on a number of complex factors.

Including you.

Maria L. Maccecchini, Ph.D.

President and CEO, QR Pharma, Inc.

I think that if we can tell women—or minorities—that if they like something, if they have a dream, they should just go for it. Martin Luther King did not say, "I have a budget," he said, "I have a dream." And so if you just follow your dream you are going to get there sooner or later, but the reality is that it is not linear. It absolutely is not linear.

Maria L. Maccecchini began her studies in Switzerland, came to the United States because it had "much better science," earned her Ph.D. in biochemistry from Rockefeller University and then spent two years at the California Institute of Technology as a postdoctorate fellow in molecular biology. Liking academics but wanting to develop a product, "to have a drug," she took her first job in industry as an entry-level research scientist and after six years was in charge of a group of 35 people as manager of molecular biology. But frustrated with the pace of product development amidst the slowness of the corporate bureaucracy, and also with her prospects for advancement—"I think we were talking about the glass ceiling"—she moved to Bachem Bioscience, a U.S. subsidiary of a Swiss company, as general manager. Under her leadership, the company grew from one to 20 employees and increased U.S. sales twentyfold in five years.

Following that success, in 1993 Maria started her own biotech company (Annovis after mergers, acquisitions and a name change) that developed, manufactured, and marketed a variety of nucleic acid-based products and services for businesses in the life sciences sector. She had also found the new problems of raising money and credibility; specifically, "You have the big boy's organizations and you don't quite belong." "But in order to succeed you have to go and work the old boy networks." The combination of her track record and networking led to success. "I went to a financial meeting," she recalls, "and somebody says, 'This lady saved two companies.' If I were to say the same thing nobody would believe me. But when he says it they all listen." By 2001, Annovis was profitable, growing between 30 percent and 100 percent per year, and employed over 120 people worldwide. In May, 2008, the company was acquired by the publicly traded Transgenomic.

Taking a break, as she put it, "to run around the world," Maria climbed Mount Everest and then went on to dog sledding in Alaska. Needing "to get my brain moving again," she joined a local angel investment network, "a great parking lot for people who want to keep mentally stimulated but do not want to commit to the 24/7 whirlwind that encircles any start-up."

Excited by a new idea, in May, 2008, Maria founded a new company, QR Pharma, to test and bring to market compounds to treat Alzheimer's. Again she ran into the start-up challenge of access to funding, this time to finance the expensive clinical trials required to develop new drugs. "If you have results in one mouse," she says, "investors want to see them in two mice. If you have them in two mice, they want to see them in a rat, then in a dog. By asking for progressively more data they reduce their risk, but also you have run out of money. When you are a large pharma company with 50,000 employees, that's not a problem. When you're QR Pharma with three employees and 13 consultants, it's a little trickier."

Currently, Maria is President and CEO of QR Pharma and also the director of two angel funds in which she not only invests in early-stage companies but also mentors them in start-up, strategy, management and finance. She holds over 40 patents, has authored numerous technical as well as business articles and frequently participates in scientific and business conferences as speaker or panelist.

Regarding leadership, "I know my management style: I don't want to control. I want to be a leader by vision and I respect other people's visions. If you tell me about your vision, I will let you pursue it. I am a very good boss for people who don't like bosses; however, I am a terrible boss for those who need direction. I absolutely can't stand to tell somebody that they have to put their name in the upper left-hand corner. If somebody who needs a lot of help works for me, I will try to have them report to somebody else. It took me a while to figure out what my leadership style was. Those who have vision, I promote and foster, for the others, I have to find a boss."

Up to a point. "As long as we reach our goals," she continues, "it is easy for me to give up control. But when I feel things are not going well, I shake things up, pull them apart, see how they fall and change direction. So I do eventually take over if things don't work out."

"I am a strong believer in people pursuing their dreams and I encourage everybody to do so," she continues. "I have two examples of people that followed what their gut told them contrary to what everybody else said. One liked microorganisms (bugs). He did not want to develop cures against them, he did not want to use them for production, food, consumer goods or pharma purposes, but instead he wanted to characterize them. Well what do you do with a bunch of newly discovered bugs? You become professor of microbiology at a university and the world expert on rare bacteria and fungi. The other loved high altitude orchids—these are tiny little flowers that grow in inclement weather in cracks with very little soil. Supposedly they are beautiful, but you can see their beauty only under a microscope, because they are so small. He wrote several books on high altitude flowers with beautiful pictures of these minusculous orchids. And again there is a happy ending. I am further a strong believer in reinventing oneself. Getting a Ph.D. may sound crazy, but is perfectly normal if you consider that you will live into your late eighties or nineties. You will be able to use that Ph.D. for 30 years."

Picking a Management Style

Begin with the obvious. Avoid being a bad manager. This may not be as easy as it sounds. Organizational value systems become embedded in formal and informal rules for getting things done. They continue even when times change, irrespective of whether the process leads to economically, ethically, and socially sustainable objectives. The fallout from outdated systems of leadership and management has been a matter of record in the recent economic downturn.

In the modern age, access to timely, relevant information is crucial in operating a successful business. Organizations need to become transparent and cultivate a culture of candor, say Bennis, Goldman, and O'Toole, and create the conditions for "the free flow of information within an organization and between the organization and its many stakeholders, including the public. Like a central nervous system, "an organization's capacity to compete, solve problems, innovate, meet challenges and achieve goals—its intelligence, if you will—varies to the degree that information flow remains healthy. That is particularly true when the information in question consists of crucial but hard-to-take facts, the information that leaders may bristle at hearing—and that subordinates too often, and understandably, play down, disguise, or ignore. For information to flow freely within an institution, followers must feel free to speak openly, and leaders must welcome such openness."

Bad work climates generate any number of negative organizational fallouts. To cope with perceived organizational injustice, employees withdraw or adopt behaviors that are counterproductive. The most common triggers, according to Sidle, include "unjust compensation/reward systems, social pressures to conform, negative/untrusting attitudes, ambiguity, performance standards which are unrealistic, unfair rules, and violating employee trust." When this goes on long enough, it can lead to the opt-out revolts, especially when there are alternatives.

The lesson in all this is simple. If management at the lower level is not good, the reaction of subordinates to the whole organization can become negative quickly. Higher management and boards of directors can make no better investment than to insure that managers at all levels are operating in ways that insure all employees are being treated equitably and fairly.

Is there a "best" style of management? Much depends on the size of the organization and your place in it.

As a top level manager, you may be charged with the organization's overall performance. Your focus will be on the vision and long-term objectives for survival, growth, and overall effectiveness. In entrepreneurial firms, small or large, the business owner must attend to all levels of management in addition to having knowledge of all of the business functions whether strategic, tactical, or operational. The smaller the firm, the greater the span of owner knowledge required.

You might be a middle level manager, falling somewhere between the top managers noted above and the frontline managers. The military term for this position, where management scholars borrowed it, is "tactical manager." In this role, you are responsible for bridging the gap in day-to-day operations, customer relations and frontline managers and employees to assure smooth completion of operational objectives.

Frontline managers are the operational managers, often called supervisors or sales managers depending on the nature of the company. In modern organizations, frontline managers are no longer directed and controlled from the top but called upon to be innovative and entrepreneurial in carrying out the company mission.

The eminent management scholar Peter Drucker, in an interview in 2004, provided some important tips on what it takes to be successful. While he applied his list to successful executives, there are a number of items that can easily be adapted to the decision-making strategy of successful managers at all levels.

- Ask "What needs to be done" rather than "What do I want to do."
- Write a priority list based on what you are best at doing. Then be sure the necessities get done, but not by you.
- Take on only one or two major projects on your list at a time. When finished, scrap the list and start with a new one rather than returning to priority number three.
- Take responsibility for your decisions.
- Focus on opportunities. Recognize when you need to abandon projects.
- Create a clear line of communication with all parties you are dealing with by clarifying your projects and explaining how they fit with the organizational goals.

All employee empowerment programs have a few common ingredients for success: Management must gain the trust of employees by behaving with honesty, openness and integrity. Employees have to be able to make decisions without fear of the consequences. Everyone, from management to the newest worker, should feel responsible for the company's welfare. Why is such a simple thing so difficult in practice? Because it means sharing knowledge and power and building trust. Everyone needs to feel responsible for the organization's welfare. This happens only when employees have a sense of ownership.

The critical element involves power. For employees to have power, management must share it.

Understanding Diversity and Why It Should be Cultivated

Taking care of business in a rapidly changing nation of more than 300 million people increasingly requires understanding the demographic shifts that are making our workforce more diverse. Americans now speak more than 300 different languages, live in a country with a falling native birth rate and an aging population, and are experiencing a tidal wave of new immigration. These changes are just the beginning.

In today's world, organizational success is determined by how well one manages people. This means understanding that dealing with diversity is not the same as affirmative action, and not just a human resource management issue to be contained within a single office, department or division but an integral part of a company's operation. The management, client and customer relations in a diverse society require the firm to recognize when change is needed, what kind, and the wisdom to act on this knowledge. Successful leadership includes the knowledge that treating people as if they are all alike may be counterproductive. Recognition of differences and the true contributions that each employee can bring to the table in pursuit of the organization's goals brings people into the process and aids in the formulation of a stronger organizational culture.

In most organizations, there are at least two groups of people, and often more. Most commonly, the majority and dominant group is composed of those who hold power, occupy the decision-making positions, allocate the resources and control the flow of information and rewards. The organizational minorities are diverse and varied, but their primary and common characteristic is that they operate on the margins. Whether defined in terms of age, gender, abilities, ethnicity, race or sexual orientation, or any of the secondary interactive components such as the level of education, work background, income, marital status, parental status, military experience, religious beliefs or geographic locations, minorities enjoy fewer granted rights and have lower status.

The numbers of people operating on the margins are expected to increase dramatically. Presently, the United States has more than 28 million people 16 years and older who have disabilities, and the population is aging. Women and people of color represent 70 percent of the yearly new entrants in the workplace. Not quite half of all U.S. children (44 percent) live in immigrant communities.

More dramatic changes lie ahead. Consider some projections for the year 2020, when only 68 percent of our workforce will be white non-Hispanic (a decrease of almost 10 percent since 1995), 14 percent Hispanic, 11 percent African American and six percent Asian. There will be as many women in the workforce as men. Twenty percent of the population will be 65 or older. Population migration will increase dramatically in the areas of manual labor, professional and high technology because replacement immigration will rise rapidly to offset native population declines and the effects of the aging workforce.

What does this mean if you are the chief executive officer, small-business owner, or manager today? To begin with, some in this new population will be customers for your goods and services. Others will work for you. Here are some questions for owners and managers at all levels:

- Is your organization one of those companies on the bottom rung of the ladder that denies that diversity exists or, if it does, that seldom acknowledges that it is important or should affect operations?
- Is the business at the next rung, the minimal stage, happy to sell to anyone and inserting "compliance with EEOC and Affirmative Action" in the position advertisements, but when filling positions anxious to hire only "people like us."
- Has the company moved beyond the lip service second tier to cultivating an inclusive and supportive climate that values individual identity and rights and recognizes that there are differences in talents and what each person brings to the table?
- Or, best of all, has the organization advanced to the top rung, exhibiting the supportive organizational climate that seeks out the best from everyone?

There are some simple indicators. Can employees talk to managers and leaders candidly about problems and expect positive changes? Does the company's leadership try to "straighten out" or target employees who raise difficult questions or don't seem to "fit in?" If so, the company is in danger of turning away customers or losing talent because people do not feel valued, included or heard.

Shabnam Rezaei

President, Big Bad Boo

We believed strongly in the social value of what we wanted to create. We felt that major stations were not representing minorities on television. While you have a show like Maya and Miguel *or* Dora, *they're not really representing an ethnicity. As an example, we pitched* Mixed Nutz *to a very large corporation to raise money. And this was an entertainment company. They said, "Well, we really like the idea. But why don't we take Jae, and instead of Jae being Korean, we'll make him Asian, you know, because that will hit a larger demographic." And we thought, "Well, that's exactly what's wrong with what's on television right now, trying to think of it as demographics as opposed to "Well, maybe the Korean holiday of Thanksgiving is really interesting. So why don't we explore that? Americans would be interested in that."*

Ten-year-old Shabnam Rezaei left Iran with her family during the Iran–Iraq war and with her brother was enrolled in the American International School in Vienna. Along with her studies, she learned to speak English, German, French and bits of Croatian, in addition to her native Farsi. "It was really eye-opening to see what one language can do in terms of endearing you to someone who doesn't speak any other languages," she says. "It opens up a whole other world." After graduating from the University of Pennsylvania with a B.S. in Computer Science and a B.A. in German Language and Literature, she went to work for the financial services consulting firm Exis Consulting, where she rose to become a global sales manager, while simultaneously earning her M.B.A. from New York University. "My father is an engineer; my mother is a doctor. As a good Iranian girl, I was meant to do something that was going to pay the bills.

My goal was to get a good job with a good company and become a productive member of society," she says.

Shabnam spent the next 10 years at financial consulting firms in London and New York but longed to do something more meaningful. Following the attack on the twin towers and sensitive to shifting attitudes toward Middle Eastern immigrants, she began her entrepreneurial career by working nights and weekends while hanging on to her day job as head of professional services for the treasury and capital markets division at financial software solutions provider MISYS. "After 9/11, the world was not a good place, and I wondered if there was anything I could do to change that," she remembers.

By 2004, she had created the website PersianMirror.com, a website for showcasing Iranian culture to a Western audience. Invited by a viewer who was a television writer who wanted to create a short, animated feature for Iranian-American children—"sort of like *A Charlie Brown Christmas*," she says, "but celebrating the Iranian New Year," she agreed to help promote the project.

"There are 5,000 years of Persian history; I wanted to show the positive side, the fun side, that Iran was not just what you see on TV, and also to connect to the immigrant community. Here was something that could really change the lives of children. Instead of being embarrassed by the food they eat or speaking Farsi to their parents in front of their friends," she continues, "we could make those things fun, and something to be proud of." In 2005, Shabnam and her husband and business partner took their plan to the NYU Stern Business Plan Competition, which they won. "Everybody got what we were trying to do, right away," Shabnam says, "even if they weren't Iranian—and actually, nobody was Iranian. I was the only Iranian. Even the guy who got in touch through the site and started this whole thing was only half Iranian. That didn't matter. Everybody understood the need for this."

Encouraged by the competition's judges to think beyond the niche of a single special to a larger enterprise with a greater cultural reach, in 2006 Shabnam and her husband co-founded a production company to produce with their own money the direct to DVD, dual language (Farsi and English) animation *Babak and Friends—A First Norooz.* After encountering and overcoming numerous financial, production and particularly distribution difficulties, and using famous voice-over artists, they succeeded in bringing the story of an 8-year-old boy stuck between the two cultures of his Iranian life and his American life to museums, Apple stores and the DVD audience. Asked later whether it was her artistic side that prompted her to leave a successful career to start an animation studio, she answered: "I couldn't draw a stick figure if my life depended on it."

From this success she learned about a big gap in the market for culturally rich content for immigrant families. In 2007, Shabnam and her husband co-founded Big Bad Boo Studios and, lured by strong financial incentives in the form of 40 percent tax credits on production, shifted their production facilities to Vancouver, Canada, though retaining offices in New York. Shabnam left her job with MISYS to become her firm's managing director. In 2009, her company was selected by a panel of judges to participate in the Ernst & Young Entrepreneurial Winning Women program. Ernst & Young had developed this program to apply their system of networks and resources "to jump-start the growth and success of women-founded companies."

In 2010, the animated children's television series produced by Big Bad Boo for the 5–8 age category, *Mixed Nutz,* made its debut on 27 public broadcasting stations. The series episodes feature Babak (Iranian) and his friends Damairs (Cuban), Sanjay (Indian), and Jae (Korean), who all go to school in the fictional Western town of Dyver City (pronounced "Diversity") and learn about each other's cultures. The endless interaction opportunities include the visit of Jae's Korean grandfather, which adds generational barriers to the mix. The company's new property, *1001 Nights,* features for the first time animated stories of the Arabian Nights, a universal set of stories that are over 1,000 years old, as told by Persian Princess Shahrzad. The series will launch on Disney, Teletoon, CBC Radio Canada, Al Jazeera

Children's and other channels. Most recently, Shabnam and her husband have launched Oznoz.com, a platform for teaching language and culture through cartoons, books and games. Oznoz offers content in Arabic, Chinese, Indian, Korean, Persian and Spanish among others and is the exclusive distributor for *Sesame Street* in multiple languages. "By incorporating a second language into a child's life, through full immersion, cartoons, books and every day activities, we can ensure they learn that language like a native," says Shabnam, who learned German in Vienna primarily by watching TV.

For her work, Shabnam has been recognized by major media outlets such as NPR, CNN, Entrepreneur and Forbes, as Iranian-American Woman of the Year (2009) by *Persianesque Magazine*, as one of *Business in Vancouver*'s "40 Under 40," and a Stevie Award for Women in Business in New York.

Shabnam, a creative modern woman entrepreneur, represents that unique capacity to bring to the term "copreneur" an accurate interpretation—the importance in engaging at every level in a joint venture where all minds are at the table. "If you are going to be an entrepreneur," Shabnam says, "having a good partner is really important." Her diversity initiative is at the forefront of 21st century global challenges to open new levels of cultural understanding at the ground and basic roots level in the USA and around the world.

Avoiding Skilled Incompetence

Organizations don't learn, the people in them do. And when they do it right, the result is a learning organization, one that adapts to shifts in technology, public demands, customer preferences, competitors and all the other environmental forces.

Surprisingly, learning organizations are not the norm. Many of the largest and most powerful public and private sector organizations of 50 years ago, or even 30, have been upstaged or replaced by newcomers.

What these dying organizations have in common is the failure of their leaders to pay attention to those who are raising questions the company needs to address. There are many reasons why. Some are people reasons. Among the most prominent are CEOs who assume the future will be the same as the past (think buggy whip manufacturer at the dawn of the automobile age), managers who insist things be done the same way (because that's the way we've always done it) and bosses who prefer (and pay and promote) people who tell them what they want to hear instead of what they need to know.

There are also systemic reasons for organizational malperformance, chief among them the fact that what is best for the organizational member is not always best for the organization. Examples include CEOs and directors under pressure from stockholders to maximize profits in the short run over making a needed organizational investment or the regional vice president who offers overly generous discounts to customers to pump up the numbers in order to get a bonus.

According to the experts, the key ingredient in determining organizational success or failure is how people in organizations approach problems and learn from them. The type of business doesn't matter, the field of business doesn't matter, and neither does the geographic region and local culture.

Chris Argyris, the father of organizational learning research, said there are two types of organizational learning. An example of the first type is people who take the feedback from various sources about how to improve the product, deliver it better, and the like. It is learning focused on improving what the organization is already doing (Can we make an animal-friendly buggy whip?). Argyris called this single loop learning. The second type of organizational learning involves more fundamental issues and facing questions that require rethinking basic assumptions (Can we put a motor in this buggy?). It is the type of organizational learning that reshapes organizations so they can adjust to new conditions. It is learning of the most critical kind. Argyris termed it "double loop learning." (If we add a motor, is it still a buggy?) Organizations that did not learn in this way, he said, suffered because "skilled incompetence" was at work.

There are many examples of skilled incompetence. We have all met people who respond defensively when anyone questions their pet project and are clever enough or powerful enough to keep it going. Many of us have observed or even participated in meetings where the groupthink of the participants overruled the facts at hand. The more sophisticated examples of skilled incompetence include the bright people who are capable of recognizing an error or potential problem (our new product has important defects) but bypass the threat (we should go ahead and release it on schedule) by acting as if they are not engaged in wishful thinking (we have so much invested in development and manufacture that we cannot delay market entry).

Double loop learning takes place when the realization dawns that instead of applying the usual model to the problem at hand the organization should consider another. This sounds simple, and it is. But in real life the execution is anything but easy. Recognizing that there are other approaches to solving problems, including ones not yet tried, requires a frank discussion.

In some environments, supervisors, managers, and leaders are wary because they are supposed to be on top of things, or at least want to appear to be. Confusing criticism of their decisions with disrespect for their authority, they find open discussions uncomfortable and avoid them. Managers can be uncomfortable admitting, "I simply do not have the answer to this problem right now."

One of the fascinating things that Argyris found was that women were more open to discussion and thinking creatively than men.

Organizational learning has considerable relevance to career development. Finding out whether or not you are in a learning organization is important. Consider just one change. In the past, top decision makers exercised organizational control in part because they were privy to and had near exclusive control of critical information. Nothing in this system allowed for (nor did anyone at the top particularly wish for) suggestions and criticisms from people lower down. Top management could continue to do this when the early computers arrived because, large, heavy and expensive, they were located at headquarters and anyone wanting to access the information in them had to go through management. It is still possible for an organization to operate in the old fashion mode, and many do. But operations today are likely to be accompanied by a blizzard of electronic messages zipping freely through the formal and informal organizational networks connecting to all sorts of electronic computing devices.

Good ideas may lie within. In the learning organization, they will get a hearing. How are things in your company?

Judith V. Moore

Founder and CEO, Charleston Cookie Company, LLC

There's a Charleston tradition to give an unexpected gift called a surcee. While no one quite knows the origin, there is a Scots word, "sussy," meaning to care.

My secrets to success? Hard work, luck, good people skills and I've learned to live sleep-deprived.

Judith V. Moore (no relation), founder and CEO of the Charleston Cookie Company, brought to her business start-up a varied background of experience in sales and finance from her tenure at American Express and Dun & Bradstreet and educational credentials that include a B.S. in Psychology from Temple University, an M.S. in Marriage and Family Therapy from the University of Maryland and a B.A. from Corcoran School of Art in Washington, DC.

During the Christmas holiday of 2001, Judith went on a quest for the perfect chocolate chip cookie. When she started looking for that perfect recipe, Judith couldn't find the irresistible formula or even one she liked enough to really get excited about, so she turned to creating her own. It had to look good, she said, and have a complex flavor. She succeeded when she found and added her secret ingredient. That Christmas, when she went to visit her daughter and son-in-law, they mentioned to her that a local cookie company had revenues the previous year of $9 million—a number that caught her attention and imagination. Returning to Charleston, she found that there was no Charleston Cookie Company, so she locked up the name because the South Carolina port city was such a popular tourist destination.

Family and friends were her first test market. Encouraged by the response to her creations, she speculated that she might be able to bake cookies (which she loved doing), sell them and turn the process into a lucrative business. During the 2002 Christmas season she personally baked, packed and delivered in 14 days 200 dozen cookies as a test project. Over the next year she researched the business side, sought out and took advice from the non-profit business counselors at SCORE, and worked and reworked through cash flow projections until she had a break-even business model. In October, 2003, she launched the business.

In the early days, Judith did not have the advantage of being able to purchase flour, sugar, chocolates, eggs, vanilla and other ingredients at prices equivalent with those paid by the mass volume supermarket chains or cookie companies like Pepperidge Farms or Deborah Fields. No one asked the giants, each time, "Are you sure you will have enough money to pay for these supplies?" Rather than trying to personally bake every single gourmet cookie, set of brownies (and the famous Charleston Rainbow Row Gingerbread Houses for the Christmas holiday season), she hired an extremely talented and experienced (former) Executive Pastry Chef, Judy Papadimitriou. Together they worked on new cookie recipes, allowing her to develop her target market in creative ways. Her marketing strategy was to offer cookies to people she met and provide samples for business and other events at The Citadel, the Medical University, the College of Charleston and numerous special programs throughout the Charleston region. Not inexpensive and also time consuming, but very effective. Money that others would spend on print advertising, she spent on feeding people cookies, allowing them to sample her products first hand. Over time, Judith created a reputation for quality based on special ingredients such as the "heavenly eggs" laid by the hens at nearby Mepkin Abbey and then delivered straight from the hen house.

Critical to her success was that, as soon as her Charleston Cookie Company began to prosper, Judith began to explore alternatives. "I had learned that I was not in the cookie business," she says. "I was in the gift business." Experiments led to her development of saleable frozen unbaked "cookie pucks," as she describes them. It was this product line that gave the Charleston Cookie Company the versatility to deal successfully with the decline in discretionary spending in the economic downturn that began in 2008 by quickly shifting to selling frozen unbaked products to wholesalers and private label companies.

As President and CEO, Judith is responsible for product development, marketing, product packaging, image and placement. In addition to the items described above, her product lines include gift baskets, corporate gifts and recipes. The Charleston Cookie Company has been on the Food Network show *Road Tasted*, and featured in an episode of "Your Business" on MSNBC. Judith is a recipient of the United States Chamber of Commerce Blue Ribbon Small Business of the Year Award (2008), been recognized as an Entrepreneur of the Year by Enterprising Women (2011) and the U.S. Chamber of Commerce Dream Big Small Business of the Year (2011) and participated in a special panel for the United States Association for Small Business and Entrepreneurship.

Judith's success is not just a good story. It is a lesson in the economics of business development and job creation. She had a very difficult time finding capital to buy the equipment she needed and, in fact, had to buy her first piece of equipment with cash because she couldn't obtain an equipment loan from a bank. When seeking initial capital to start Charleston Cookie Company and after going to many different banks, she found a banker willing to give her a $150,000 home equity line. With that loan, which she repaid, Judith established a business that created 27 jobs. That works out to $5,556 per job. Three years ago, the state of South Carolina lured the Boeing Company with a pack of incentives totaling more than $900 million, according to published sources, to set up an assembly plant in the Lowcountry. The initiative, declared the proud politicians, would create between 4,000 and 5,000 jobs. At best, that works out to $180,000 of taxpayer money per job. Think of the possibilities if the many other women like Judith who have an idea could get the support they need to establish or grow their businesses.

Values, Ethics and Stress

When Companies are Unethical, Everybody Loses

The issues raised by Sherron S. Watkins, Enron's Vice President for Corporate Development, in her unsigned whistleblowing letter to Enron Chairman Kenneth L. Lay, is an example of a crisis in ethics. Responding to his invitation to place concerns in a comment box, Watkins tried to bring what she called an "elaborate accounting hoax" to Lay's attention. When her comment went unaddressed, she sought a face to face meeting. Instead of seeing her, at a meeting a month later Lay, announced to company employees that "our financial liquidity has never been stronger" while behind the scenes he was exercising $1.5 billion in stock options just ahead of Enron's announcement of a $618 million quarterly loss. As Sharon Watkins later described in an address at the Academy of Management, when congressional investigators uncovered her letter buried in boxes of documents, they brought her before the United States Senate to testify.

The bold outlines of the story were widely reported. Enron borrowed heavily to create a number of limited partnerships to purchase Enron assets that were in trouble, the board of directors suspended the company ethics code so Enron executives, for lucrative compensation, could run some of these limited partnerships, and when the assets in the partnerships declined in value Enron pledged its stock to cover the bank loans. The financial manipulations kept debt and losing ventures off

Enron's books and resulted in inflated or nonexistent earnings. Enron concealed these activities by limiting public disclosures.

When Enron stock began to lose value in the general market decline, the whole business was revealed as a financial house of cards and Enron collapsed. In the troubled period before the full extent of Enron's problems were known, Chairman Lay was cheerleading employees to believe in a bright future and to hold on to their company stock. Many would soon lose jobs, pensions and their investments.

Fortunately, unethical companies are not the norm. But can employees spot potential trouble? There are no sure answers. The best advice is to retain your independence and stay alert. Organizations work very hard to encourage a loyal and dedicated workforce. The importance of teamwork or "being on the team" is voiced constantly. There is nothing inherently wrong with this, but carried too far the team culture can merge into groupthink. And groupthink tends to redefine ethics and appropriate behavior in terms of follow-the-leader norms and organizational loyalty, creating the conditions in which misdeeds can occur. When leaders begin to refer to everybody in it as a "family" and everyone seems to sign on, it can be an early warning sign. Companies are not families. (Families don't retrench in difficult times by laying off children and telling them to find another place to eat and sleep.) Pay attention to your organization's statements of principle. Companies may call these documents a mission, a values or a vision statement (or all three) but the language always speaks to high standards of performance and ethics. Compare what your organization is actually doing with what it is publicly professing, and also to your own standards.

If ethics and company actions begin to diverge widely, you may face the problem down the road of whether or not to draw the line in complying with what you are asked to do. No one likes to discover bad news. But knowing is better than not knowing. It is in your interest to know as early as possible if your organization is heading down a dangerous path.

The Whistleblowers

When illegal, immoral, illegitimate or, at the very least, inappropriate practices take place in an organization over a period of time, a small number of employees may conclude they have a responsibility to reveal what is going on in a way that ensures corrective action will be taken. Who are these whistleblowers and what pushes them to action?

Examining a sample of over 3,000 military and civilian air force employees, authors Marcia Miceli, James van Scotter, Janet Near and Michael Rehg found that several important personality traits appear to suggest who is likely to blow the whistle. One set of candidates consists of people who are upbeat and positive. Active, alert and outgoing, with high levels of self-esteem and optimistic about their chances of success in initiating organizational change, they are less constrained than others when faced with conduct they perceive as wrongdoing. Two other groups of potential whistleblowers come from opposing ends of the employee spectrum. The first is made up of people who strongly identify with the organization. Believing the company will always treat them fairly, these organizational loyalists assume they will be supported and report wrongdoing so the higher-ups can correct it. In direct contrast are the employees who care little about the organization. Among these near-outsiders are people who experience more anxiety, anger, fear, guilt and stress than the average person. Because they interpret neutral or ambiguous situations negatively, they can be more likely than others to spot organizational wrongdoing early on and react by blowing the whistle on the conduct.

A recent study published in the *Journal of Finance* that examined more than 216 cases of alleged corporate fraud describes the complexity of whistleblowing. Sixty-four of the cases studied were caught by the board of directors. Analysts, rating agencies and bankers detected 42 more. News reporters uncovered 20 cases. Auditors caught another 16 and the Securities and Exchange Commission, an additional 10. Attorneys searching for class action lawsuits found only five cases. One problem, the study found, was that people with the incentive to expose fraud lacked the necessary information while many who had the information often lacked the incentive; and sometimes, as in the case of stock analysts and auditors, blowing the whistle threatened to end their own careers. "Employees have it worst," the authors found. "Of those who went public, 82 percent were fired or reassigned, or quit under pressure."

Whatever the motivation, few whistleblowers take their concerns outside the organization and then only as a last resort. Nearly all first attempt to get the problems corrected internally.

But it's not just about the whistleblowers. Most employees who observe the misdeeds or inappropriate activity do nothing about it. But they are severely affected, and as knowledge of wrongdoing in the firm spreads, which it will, it communicates something demoralizing. Uncorrected wrongdoing causes employees to lose confidence. People begin to distance themselves from management. Commitment to the job declines. Everyone has read of the unfavorable publicity and lawsuits reaped by organizations whose misdeeds became public knowledge. Corporate misdeeds also carry high costs in the form of negative employee attitudes that affect work performance.

What can companies do to encourage whistleblowing? A recent study published in *Decision Sciences* suggests employees should be specifically assigned the responsibility of reporting any problem they uncover to a supervisor. To insure employees are comfortable, management must create an organizational climate of trust that includes a management history of responsiveness.

The first step to take if you encounter what appears to be unethical behavior in your work environment is suggested in an article published by Leibowitz and Reinstein in the *Journal of Accountancy*. Though you may not be a Certified Public Accountant, you can employ a variation of the CPA analysis of the situation in terms of three possible conclusions:

- This is acceptable because a reasonable and informed third party would conclude that no one has compromised the rules.

- This is a threat because the evidence suggests the rules have been violated.
- This may be a threat. We need to do something to reduce the risk.

Ethics and Dealing with Corrupt Companies

Maintaining a high standard of ethics is always the best course to follow. Economist and social critic Robert Frank explores work in economics, psychology, and biology to argue that honest individuals often succeed, even in highly competitive environments, because their commitment to principle makes them more attractive. Dale Meyer counsels that because the balance between money and business decisions is at the core of many ethical dilemmas, issues of telling the truth versus lying "must be examined through an ethics lens." For a series of easy to read cases based on sound research, see Archie Carroll's *Business Ethics: Brief Readings on Vital Topics* and his co-authored book, *Business & Society: Ethics, Sustainability and Stakeholder Management.*

But what can you do if you discover that you are working in a company that is acting illegally and especially in a recessionary job market where your family is counting on you? Could you be a manager waiting to see if your company is going to be investigated and your possible involvement revealed?

How might this happen? Consider this scenario. You are well regarded by both colleagues and senior management. You have advanced fairly quickly, now earn a good salary, have substantial benefits and have been told that you have a real future with the company. You and your spouse, who holds a full-time job at another firm, enjoy life in the community. Your youngest child has a serious medical condition. Fortunately, the doctors expect improvement in time. For now, you are grateful for your company's comprehensive health care coverage which pays nearly all of the medical expenses. It is also reassuring to know that you work for a company that publicly embraces the highest standards. The written guidelines contain numerous statements of business ethics, including this one: "Compliance with the law and ethical standards are conditions of employment, and violations will result in disciplinary action, which may include termination. Employees are asked to sign a statement indicating that they have read, understand and will comply with this statement and employees are periodically asked to reaffirm their commitment to these principles."

Things seemed to be going well three months ago when you were assigned to head a new project that is both important to the company and a test of your leadership. Recently, however, after becoming increasingly concerned about your company's business practices, exotic accounting methods and financial reporting, you have come to realize that what your company is doing may be illegal. The expert outside advice you quietly sought confirms this.

After gathering the facts, you approached first your boss and then the chief financial officer. The message they sent is clear. We have been doing things this way for years and the practices are blessed by the firm's lawyers. The policies will remain as they are and your full cooperation is expected.

What can you do? You have roughly four choices.

The first is to go along. Convince yourself the bosses and attorneys are right, that all businesses do these kinds of things and that you should be a great team player. Downside: You are right about the illegality, and by going along you will be participating in a criminal conspiracy.

You can resign. Leaving the firm removes you from any legal risks, and your reputation stays intact. Downside: Finding a new position in this economy will be difficult. Resignation may require relocation with both you and your spouse job hunting while having to pay high medical bills.

Blow the whistle. Stay on the job, inform federal and state regulatory authorities of what is going on and cooperate in building a case against your company. Downside: While some whistleblowers have been compensated, even written bestselling books, many did not accomplish anything aside from putting their families through extreme misery. The company will suffer from what the bosses have done, but many will blame you with names such as "outsider," "traitor," "difficult" and "not a team player." Any mitigating effects of the whistleblower protections in the recently enacted financial regulatory legislation are as yet unknown.

The last choice seems attractive, at least on the surface: ***To live two lives.*** You cooperate in carrying out the company policies but guard your future by regularly warning against inappropriate actions and keeping copies of emails, memos and other records. If there is no investigation, your life sails along. If there is an investigation, you assume that you will be protected because you have kept records. Downside: You could not be more wrong. If your company is investigated, you will either voluntarily or be forced to turn your records over to the authorities. Your own written record shows that you knew criminal activity was taking place but continued to work at the company and thus participated in the scheme. As these records are among the strongest possible evidence of criminal intent on your part, prosecutors will have no problem indicting and convicting you.

The sketch above is hypothetical but based on actual events. The description of personal life is taken from a compilation of the experiences of the employees at WorldCom. The ethics language is quoted directly from Enron's statement of ethics.

So what can you do if you uncover indisputable evidence that your company is acting illegally?

According to the experts, there is only one choice: to leave the organization even if the immediate consequences to your life will be terrible.

It sounds unfair, and it is. But as a career choice, when the company is corrupt, nothing is attractive. Only quitting immediately keeps you out of harm's way and preserves the personal brand of ethical behavior that you have worked so hard to create.

Work Environments and Stress

Excess stress is a common health risk. With corporate costs of worker disabilities running as high as $340 billion annually, employers have found it good business to invest in work site wellness.

Stress comes from perceptions of opportunities or threats that appear important and the fears we can't deal with them. The major stressors, according to the Rose Medical Center in Denver, Colorado, involve life-changing events: the death of a spouse or a close family member, marital separation or divorce, personal injury or illness, getting married, retiring from work, experiencing a major natural disaster and the like. Lower on the scale, but still important, are common life events like buying a home, moving or even entertaining guests.

Nearly everyone experiences work-related stressors. Some people face uncomfortable working conditions, have assignments and responsibilities that are unclear, or are given a work overload (an underload is equally bad). Demanding assignments and promotions are stressful, as are the conflicts, disagreements and misunderstandings that arise with superiors, subordinates, or co-workers. Research by Lilia M. Cortina and Vicki J. Magley shows that workplace incivility can cause stress, distraction, and low job satisfaction. When workplace bullying emerges in these uncivil environments, stress increases. Then there are the stresses that arise out of work–life links. Conflicts between job requirements and family responsibilities are not unusual. Less common, but perhaps more difficult, is the stress that comes when work requests violate personal values.

The ability to handle stress varies from individual to individual. Coping with stress involves two strategies. The first is problem-focused, the steps one can take to deal directly with the sources of the stress. The second is emotion-focused, and includes rest, exercise, and getting support from others. Making a conscious effort to re-evaluate the situation is often useful. To cite a textbook example: Thinking "I'll never get this project done on time" is a stress builder. Thinking "If I stay focused and take it one step at a time I'll make steady progress" is a stress breaker.

Both Steven Sauter, Coordinator of the National Institute of Occupational Safety and Health's Work Organization Stress-

Related Disorders Program and Paul J. Rosch, M.D., President of the American Institute of Stress, believe that stress results from the job itself, not the worker. According to Lyle H. Miller, who has been studying stress for 30 years and who directs the Bio Behavioral Institute, a non-profit research organization focused on stress and behavioral health, some of the early warning signs of stress are anger, headaches, intestinal issues, shortness of breath, hair loss, changes in appetite, fatigue and panic attacks.

Entrepreneurs and middle managers are particularly susceptible to stress because the problems of subordinates are often pushed upward and the pressures from above are continuous. It is a common misperception that those at the top of the organization feel the impact of stress the most. In reality, it is those who are squeezed in between, those with less control, who feel the greatest impact.

What can be done to improve the work environment and especially when changes in the economy place even greater stressors on employees? First, as a manager or entrepreneur, it is important to remember that there are benefits to be gained in improved productivity by applying standards which can be interpreted clearly by all employees.

Employees cannot do well if they are confused. They need clear explanations from the outset. It is much more difficult to patch things up later after the operation has been botched.

When changes are made, particularly job changes, make sure that those to be involved in the change participate in the process. Consider everyone and how the change affects them. Make sure that those who will be affected participate in the process.

Imprecise road signs make navigation difficult. Map changes clearly. Avoid conflicting demands on employees. Telling clerks, for example, that customer satisfaction comes first and then raising the number of customers you expect them to deal with each hour sends a contradictory message.

Expect employees to bring personal baggage to work and understand that this impacts their attitudes and productivity. Sometimes the best of us struggle to cope with work/life stressors.

I learned this from the research for my book (co-authored with my husband) *Island in the Storm: Sullivan's Island and Hurricane Hugo* and from our life in the months after the center of the Category 4 hurricane crossed over the island. As one woman put it, "It was much easier to get over the death of my spouse than to get over Hugo."

It may be important to adjust the work at least temporarily to enable the employee to continue to function more effectively on the job. Or it may be just as simple as showing "I care." Many large organizations are taking positive steps to retain valued employees by enhancing facilities, work flows, flexible work schedules, granting personal days, and courier services, and providing day care centers for children and aging parents, and exercise facilities. They all say "the company cares."

Reduce work environment stressors by making it ergonomically sound. Nobody is happy when their feet hurt, their back hurts, or their hands and arms go numb. Insure that safety precautions are followed and that workers are not exposed to unnecessary danger or toxins.

If drastic steps are necessary, run a class act. Give advance notice of termination and provide fair severance pay and counseling services to reduce the negative effects of layoffs or other threats to workers' economic well-being. It is better to have exiting employees who are ambassadors for your business.

Keep a sense of humor. Try to find something to laugh about every single day, and share the laughter. Lowering stress can be contagious. This is not a cliché. It is good business.

Work–Life Balance

By the year 2000, two out of every three married couples was a dual career couple. More than four in ten married women with children (41 percent) worked full time. More than one-half of all mothers employed when they gave birth returned to work within three months and nearly two-thirds (63 percent) were back at work by the time their child reached the first birthday. Finances dictated many of the choices. The cost of raising a child, up to \$145,000 for a middle income family in 1960, rose to \$165,000 in

1999, a 13 percent increase. The scramble to afford a house in a "good" school district meant taking on a mortgage in a market of rising home prices and stagnating middle income wages.

Balancing work and family had become exceedingly difficult, according to data compiled by the organization Mothers and More in 2001. Nearly two-thirds of working fathers and mothers (64 percent) said the time pressures on working families were getting worse. Seventy percent felt they didn't have enough time with their children. One working woman in every four said they had to cut back on their work schedule at least one day out of every seven to meet caregiving obligations. The most severe pressures were felt in families where the mother had a part-time job. Of a possible 236 industries, more than half of part-time working mothers were concentrated in 10 of them where the hourly wage averaged $8.27.

As Mainiero and Sullivan show in their book *The Opt-Out Revolt*, the need for balance makes it worth seeking, but the dream that another path will magically lead to balance is not reality. Reality is that women with full-time jobs still shouldered the burden of work at home. Averages from the Bureau of Labor Statistics Annual Time Use Survey for the five-year period 2005–2009 show that, for married couples with children, women spent more time doing housework, preparing meals and cleaning up, shopping, caring for and helping children, and hauling them around. Men spent more time on lawn care and leisure activities, principally watching television. This was true irrespective of the ages of children, whether both parents were employed full time or the father worked full time and the mother part time or only the father worked outside the home. The main difference was that mothers who worked part time did more household chores than mothers who worked full time and mothers not in the workforce did more than both the other groups. Compared to mothers who worked full time, mothers at home more than doubled the hours devoted to household activities and child care. (The place was kept cleaner and as a bonus the homemaker wives averaged 45 minutes more sleep a day.)

As for men, on an average day, nearly two-thirds of married fathers (65 percent) who were employed full time engaged in some household activities and nearly seven out of ten (68 percent) helped in caring for children. In other words, it wasn't that fathers working full time weren't doing something at home, it was just that they weren't doing as much of it as the mothers. On any given day in 2009, for example, more than half the mothers (51 percent) and 20 percent of fathers did housework and more than two-thirds of mothers (68 percent) and 40 percent of fathers prepared meals or cleaned up afterward.

It helped a great deal if one was employed by a company that supported a work–personal life balance. According to one study, where these organizational values were present, managerial women and men alike reported greater job and career satisfaction, less stress at work, a more positive outlook and greater family satisfaction. The unexpected finding from the study was that the organizational support benefited men more than women, possibly because of the woman's greater "second shift" duties.

The new work/family dynamics gave rise to four theories about the work careers of mothers. Powell and Mainiero's River of Time Model focused on the two major concerns of career and personal achievement on the one hand and family and personal relationships on the other. Brush's Integrative Perspective looked at the power of two distinct sets of relationships: one in professional life and the other in personal life. The Projection Theory of Cohen, Swerdlik and Phillips examined how women arranged circumstances within their power to do so to make them consistent with their own needs, fears, desires, impulses and conflicts. My Careerpreneuring Model looked at how over time women created different environments and established different cultures in order to seek balance and minimize conflicts at different stages in their business careers and family conditions. Common elements in all the approaches help explain why women business owners, more than men, tend to provide work environments consistent with their own values and establish organizational cultures that minimize conflicts among employees.

The models have in common the recognition that, for most working mothers, work is a vehicle for fulfillment and satisfaction and not just a paycheck; that it is impossible to be superwoman, and therefore expectations must be kept realistic; that whether a parent works is not important, but how that work impacts the home in terms of parental stress, mood and energy level is important; that having a working mother does not predict how children will assess their mother's parenting skills; and that both families and careers change over time.

For insight into need for balance and the dream that another path will magically lead to balance, see Mainiero and Sullivan's *The Opt-Out Revolt.*

References

Introduction

Bass, B. M. (1990). *Bass & Stogdill's handbook of leadership: Theory, research, and managerial applications* (3rd ed.). New York, NY: Free Press (4th ed. published with R. Bass, 2008; quote at p. 383).

Nadler, D., Tushman, M., & Nadler, M. B. (1997). *Competing by design—The power of organizational architecture.* New York, NY: Oxford University Press.

Taylor, F. W. (1911). *The principles of scientific management.* New York, NY: Harper & Brothers.

Profile: Rebecca Smith

The draft profile corrected and approved by the entrepreneur incorporated materials from Watkins, P.J. (Jan., 2008). The A. D. Morgan Corporation. *Suncoast builder/architect* (pp. 27–28). Retrieved from a press release link at the entrepreneur's website. http://www.admorgan.com/press_area/content_details.asp?id=57. See also Kauffman Foundation—The Entrepreneurship Resource Center. Constructing a Money Tree at http://www.entrepreneurship.org.

Dimensions of Management

Approaches to Management

Bateman, T. S., & Snell, S. (2008). *Management: Leading & collaborating in a competitive world* (8th ed.). New York, NY: McGraw-Hill.

Daft, R. L. (2011). *Management* (10th ed.). Mason, OH: South-Western and Cengage Learning.

Dessler, G. (2000). *Leading people and organizations in the 21st century* (2nd ed.). Upper Saddle River, NJ: Prentice Hall.

Drucker, P. F. (1954, 1986). *The practice of management.* New York, NY: HarperCollins.

Hellriegel, D., Jackson, S. E., & Slocum, J. W. (2007). *Management: A competency-based approach* (11th ed.). Mason, OH: Thomson Higher Education.

Peters, T., & Waterman, R. (1982). *In search of excellence.* New York, NY: Harper & Row.

Schermerhorn, J. (2010). *Management, 11e* (1st ed.). Hoboken, NJ: John Wiley & Sons, Inc.

Leadership, Management and the Information Revolution

Bass, B. M. (1990). *The Bass & Stogdill's handbook of leadership: Theory research, and managerial applications* (3rd ed.). New York, NY: Free Press (4th ed. published with R. Bass, 2008; quote at p. 383).

Kotter, J. P. (1990). *A force for change: How leadership differs from management.* New York, NY: Free Press. See cited material and Steps of change: http://www.kotterinternational.com/kotterprinciples/ChangeSteps.aspx

Kouzes, J. M., & Posner, B. Z. (2002). *The leadership challenge.* San Francisco, CA: Jossey-Bass (original, 1997). Also see the *Leadership practices inventory* (LPI) by Kouzes & Posner (2nd ed.).

Nadler, D., Tushman, M., & Nadler, M.B. (1997). *Competing by design: The power of organizational architecture.* For quoted material see description of book at http://market.android.com/details?id=book-qSAZcL02usMC

Closing the Gap—Moving Beyond Buzzwords

Bennis, W. (2011). *Leaders.* Editor's choice of 50 top ranked leadership books. Retrieved from http://www.LeadershipNow.com

Deep, S., & Sussman, L. (June, 1991). Eight management principles you can't work without. *Working Woman,* 61–63.

Women in Management

Women, Power and Leadership

Austin, N. K. is best known for co-writing the bestsellers *A passion for excellence* (1985) and *The assertive woman* (1975). Between the two books more than a million copies have been published in seven languages. She also co-founded the Peters Group.

Moore, D. P. (2000). *Careerpreneurs.* (Quote at pp. 104–106.)

Moore, D. P., & Buttner, E. H. (1999). *Women entrepreneurs.* (Quote at p. 30.)

Moore, D. P., Moore, J. W., & Moore, J. L. (2011). How women entrepreneurs lead. *Gender in Management,* 220–233. (Quote at p. 222.)

Rosener, J. (1990). Ways women lead. *Harvard Business Review, 68*(8), 119–25). See also: Rosener (1997). *America's competitive secret: Women managers.* New York, NY: Oxford University Press.

Other sources on women's leadership styles:

Hill, L. A. (2003). *Becoming a manager: How new managers master the challenges of leadership* (2nd ed.). Boston, MA: Harvard Business School Press. (See Transformation of Identity, Exhibit I.I., p. 6.)

Roberson, L., & Kulik, C. T. (2007). Stereotype threat at work, *Academy of Management Perspectives, 21*(2), 24–40.

Profile: Maria L. Maccecchini

Final approved profile developed from interviews with entrepreneur, featured presentations, website materials, and additional information furnished by the entrepreneur. The Alliance of Women Entrepreneurs (AWE) has designated Maria as the recipient of the 2011 Iris Newman Award for "connecting, educating and inspiring women entrepreneurs." Retrieved from: http://www.phillyawe.org/mc/Page Id=129618.

Picking a Management Style

Bennis, W., Goldman, D., & O'Toole, J. (2008). *Transparency: How leaders create a culture of candor.* San Francisco, CA: Jossey-Bass. (Quote at pp. 3–4; see also pp. 20–27.) See also O'Toole, J., & Bennis, W. (2009). What's needed next: A culture of candor. *Harvard Business Review, 87*(6), 54–61.

Karlgaard, R. (Nov. 19, 2004). Peter Drucker on leadership. Retrieved from http://www.forbes.com/2004/11/19/cz_rk_1119drucker.html

Sidle, S. D. (2010). Counterproductive work behavior: Can it sometimes be good to be bad? *Academy of Management Perspectives, 24*(3), 101–103. doi: 10.5465/AMP.2010.52842956. (Cite at p. 102.) Research brief of findings from Krischer, M. M., Penney, L. M., & Hunter, E. M. (2010). Can counterproductive work behaviors be productive? CWB as emotion-focused coping. *Journal of Occupational Health Psychology, 15*(2), 154–166.

Understanding Diversity and Why It Should be Cultivated

BLS for Workforce. (For statistics see the citations to the U.S. Department of Labor BLS in Chapter 1.)

Diller, J. V. (2011). *Cultural diversity: A primer for the human services* (4th ed.). Belmont, CA: Brooks/Cole Cengage Learning.

Intuit (Oct., 2011). The Intuit 2020 Report—Twenty trends that will shape the next decade. Retrieved from //http.intuit.com/http.intuit/CMO/intuit/futureofsmallbusiness/.pdf

Wikipedia (2011). Marginalization is defined in the U.S. as "the social process of becoming or being made marginal or relegated to the fringe of society." The encyclopedia covers the individual, community, professional, public policy, social practice aspects. Retrieved from http://en.wikipedia.org/wiki/Marginalization

Profile: Shabnam Rezaei

The draft profile corrected and approved by Shabnam incorporates the opening quotation and other materials from Brennan, M. (2009). Transcript: Teaching traditions. Retrieved from http://www.forbes.com/2009/12/17/shabnam-rezaei-thought-leaders-mixed-nutz.html. Other sources consulted include: Cheers for Big Bad Boo http://www.upenn.edu/gazette/0310/pro03.html; ExpatWomen.com; http://expatnetrepreneur.com/shabnam-rezaei-expat-success-story/and http://www.persianesquemagazine.com/2010/01/08/iranian american-woman-of-the-year-shabnam-rezaei/

Avoiding Skilled Incompetence

Argyris, C. (2002). Double-loop learning, teaching and research. *Academy of Management Learning & Education, 1*(2), 206–218.

Argyris, C. (2000). *Flawed advice and the management trap.* New York, NY: Academic Press.

Argyris, C., & Schon, D. A. (1996). *Organizational learning II.* Reading, MA: Addison-Wesley.

Argyris, C., & Schon, D. A. (1978). *Organizational learning. A theory of action perspective.* Reading, MA: Addison-Wesley.

Profile: Judith V. Moore

Final approved profile developed from interviews with entrepreneur, featured USASBE Plenary panel presentation in 2011, website materials, and additional information furnished by the entrepreneur. Reference for Boeing citation: Investigative reporting by the *Charleston Post and Courier* in early 2010 estimated the total package of incentives for Boeing to locate in South Carolina to be worth $900 million or more. By Nov., 2011, Boeing had created 5,000 direct jobs. See Stech, K. & Slade, D. (Jan. 17, 2010). Boeing's whopping incentives: Analysis: Package at least double first estimates. Retrieved from http://archives.postandcourier.com/archive/arch10?0110/arc0117920489.shtml Nov. 1, 2011 and Wise, W. L. (Nov. 18, 2011). Aviation a $7B area dynamo. *The Post and Courier,* 6B.

Values, Ethics and Stress

When Companies are Unethical, Everybody Loses

Pearce, J. L. (2003). Presidential introductory remarks of Sherron S. Watkins Academy of Management Address. *Academy of Management Executive, 17*(4). (Address at p. 119.)

Watkins, S. (2003). Former Enron vice president Sherron Watkins on the Enron collapse, Academy of Management Address. *Academy of Management Executive, 17*(4), 119–125. doi: 10.5465/AME.2003.11851888

See also: Beenen, G., & Pinto, J. (2009). Resisting organizational-level corruption: An interview with Sherron Watkins. *Academy of Management Learning & Education, 8*(2), 275–289. doi: 10.5465/AMLE.2009.41788851

The Whistleblowers

Leibowitz, M. A., & Reinstein, A. (2009). Help for solving CPAs' ethical dilemmas. *Journal of Accountancy, 207*(4), 30–34. Retrieved from EBSCO*host*. (Cited list at p. 31.)

Martin, J. A., & Combs J. G. (2011). Does it take a village to raise a whistleblower? *Academy of Management Perspectives, 25*(2), 83–85. doi: 10.5465/AMP.2011.61020808. (Cites at pp. 84, 85.) Research brief of the findings in Dyck, A., Morse, A., & Zingales, L. (2010). Who blows the whistle on corporate fraud? *Journal of Finance, 65*, 2213–2253.

Miceli, M. P., Van Scotter, J. R., Near, J. P., & Rehg, M. T. (2001). Individual differences and whistle-blowing. *Academy of Management Proceedings & Membership Directory*, 2001, C1–C6. doi:10.5465/APBPP.2001.6133834

Near, J. P., Rehg, M. T., Van Scotter, J. R., & Miceli, M. P. (2004). Does type of wrongdoing affect the whistle-blowing process? *Business Ethics Quarterly, 14*(2), 219–242. Retrieved from EBSCO*host*.

Waples, C. J., & Culbertson, S. S. (2011). Best-laid plans: Can whistleblowing on project problems be encouraged? *The Academy of Management Perspectives, 25*(2), 80–82. Research brief of findings in Keil, M., Tiwana, A., Sainsbury R., & Sneha. S. (2010). Toward a theory of whistle-blowing intentions: A benefit-to-cost differential. *Decision Sciences, 41*(4), 785–812.

Ethics and Dealing with Corrupt Companies

Carroll, A. B. (2009). *Business ethics: Brief readings on vital topics.* New York, NY and London, UK: Routledge Taylor & Francis Group.

Carroll, A. B., & Buchholtz, A. K. (2011). *Business & society: Ethics, sustainability and stakeholder management* (8th ed.). Mason, OH: South-Western, Division of Thompson Learning.

Enron Ethics Statement. Enron's 64-page Code of Ethics. Retrieved from http://www.thesmokinggun.com/archive/0130061enron1.html (see excerpt: To: All employees; From: Ken Lay Department: Office of the chairman. Subject: Code of Ethics; Date: July 1, 2000).

Frank, R. H. (2004). *What price the moral high ground: Ethical dilemmas in competitive environments*? Princeton, NJ: Princeton University Press. (As cited by G. D. Meyer at http://www.gdalemeyer.com.)

Meyer, G. D. (2011). Selected books for examining ethical practices in business and societal relationships. Retrieved from http://www.gdalemeyer.com/Suggested_ percent20Reading.htm

Thomas, T., Schermerhorn Jr., J. R., & Dienhart, J. W. (2004). Strategic leadership of ethical behavior in business. *Academy of Management Executive, 18*(2), 56–66. doi: 10.5465/AME.2004.13837425

Work Environments and Stress

Avey, J. B., Luthans, F., & Jensen, S. M. (2009). Psychological capital: A positive resource for combating employee stress and turnover. *Human Resource Management, 48*(5), 677–693.

Claussen, L. (Ed.). (2011). Stress in the workplace—Keeping stress in check could create a healthier and safer workforce. Reprinted from Safety+Health, *183*(3), National Safety Council (see p. 45). Retrieved from http://www.accuform.com/files/pdfs/sh0311Stress.pdf

For a debate on how some of the figures are derived, see: Nguyen, S. (Jan. 9, 2011). The true financial cost of job stress. Retrieved from http://workplacepsychology.net/

Moore, J. W., & Moore. D. P. (2006). *Island in the storm: Sullivan's Island and Hurricane Hugo.* Charleston, SC, & London, UK: History Press. (Referenced areas, pp. 123–141, cite at p. 123.)

NIOSH Working Group. *Stress at Work,* DHHS Publication No. 99-101. (Cite at p. 4.) Retrieved from http://www.cdc.gov/niosh

Sidle, S. D. (2009). Workplace incivility: How should employees and managers respond? *Academy of Management Perspectives, 23*(4), 88–89. doi: 10.5465/AMP.2009.45590142 Research Brief of: Cortina, L. M., & Magley, V. J. (2009). Patterns and profiles of responses to incivility in the workplace. *Journal of Occupational Health Psychology, 14*(3), 272–288.

Work–Life Balance

BLS, Annual Time Use Survey Table (2009). Source provides: Time spent in detailed primary activities and percent of the civilian population engaging in each detailed primary activity category, averages per day by sex, 2009 annual averages (Table A-1); Averages per day by sex on weekdays and weekends, 2009 annual averages (Table A-3); Percent of the population engaging in activities by time of day, 2005–2009 (Table A-7); Time in primary activities by married mothers and fathers with own household and children under 18; By employment status of self and spouse and age of youngest child; average for the combined years 2005–2009 (Table A-6).

Brush, C. G. (1992). Research on women business owners: Past trends, a new perspective and future directions. *Entrepreneurship Theory and Practice, 16*(4), 5–30.

Burke, R. J. (2002). Organizational values, job experiences and satisfactions among managerial and professional women and men: Advantage men? *Women in Management Review, 17*(5), 228–236.

Buttner, E. H. (2001). Examining female entrepreneurs' management style: An application of a relational frame. *Journal of Business Ethics, 29*(3), 253–269.

Buttner, E. H., & Moore, D. P. (1997). Women's organizational exodus to entrepreneurship: Self-reported motivations and correlates with success. *Journal of Small Business Management, 35*(1), 34–46.

Cohen, R. J., Swerdlik, M. E., & Phillips, S. M. (1996). *Psychological testing and assessment: An introduction to tests and measurement.* Mountainview, CA: Mayfield. (Reference at p. 424.)

Grady, G., & McCarthy, A. M. (2008). Work–life integration: experiences of mid-career professional working mothers. *Journal of Managerial Psychology*, 23(5), 599–622. doi: 10.1108/02683940810884559

Heraty, N., Morley, M. J., & Cleveland, J. N. (2008). The work-family dyad: Multi-level perspectives. *Journal of Managerial Psychology*, 23(5), 477–483. doi: 10.1108/02683940810884496

Mainiero, L. A., & Sullivan, S. E. (2006). *The opt-out revolt: Why people are leaving companies to create kaleidoscope careers.* Palo Alto, CA: Davies-Black.

Moore, D. P. (2007). Careerpreneurs: The 21st century strategic women-preneurs. In A. D. Bührmann, K. Hansen, M. Schmeink, & A. Schöttelndreier (Eds.), *Entrepreneurial diversity—Unternehmerinnen zwischen Business-plan und Bricolage* (pp. 190–209). Münster: LIT Verlag.

Moore, D. P. (2005). Career paths of women business owners. In S. I. Fielden & M. J. Davidson (Eds.), *International handbook of women and small business entrepreneurship* (pp. 42–51). Cheltenham, UK: Edward Elgar Publications Ltd. See also: Moore, D. P. (2004). The entrepreneurial woman's career model: current research and a typological framework. Special edition: Advancing women's careers. *Equal Opportunities International, 23*(7/8), 78–98.

Mothers and More (July, 2001). Work/life balance statistics. Retrieved from http://www.mothersandmore.org/press_room/statistics.shtm#work_lifebalance

Powell, G. N., & Mainiero, L. A. (1992). Cross currents in the river of time: Conceptualizing the complexities of women's careers. *Journal of Management, 18*(2), 215–237.

3

WORK, LIFE AND CAREER STRATEGIES

Introduction

Until recently, people tended to think of the world of work in separate categories. People either worked in someone else's business or in their own. The distinction between being an employee and being an entrepreneur was clear. The rapid changes in the economy in the past three decades have blurred the lines. What counts now are portable skills and knowledge, meaningful work, on-the-job learning, and the right contacts at the right time. In today's world, people must be ready to move from position to position, into entrepreneurship and back again, from one alliance to another. The terms "occupations," "jobs", and "careers" have taken on very new meanings.

For women, business ownership can be a progressive step, a strategic window of opportunity or a programmed stage in an evolving career. In my research, I identified eight distinct paths. Seven of these involve work outside the home: corporatepreneurs, intrapreneurs, entrepreneurs, boundarypreneurs (women who move back and forth from entrepreneurship to corporate life), globalpreneurs, technopreneurs (women involved predominantly in fields of technical expertise), and gazellepreneurs (fast-growth, high-volume, capital-intense, multifaceted business owners). The eighth group consists of women who own home-based businesses and when used in conjunction with motherhood are often referenced as mompreneurs.

While the stories of successful women entrepreneurs are very much individual, the origins of nearly all of their firms have an important plot line in common. At a critical time in the entrepreneur's career, someone with whom she had connected offered encouragement, pointed out an opportunity, provided financial backing or in some other important way lent a hand. It happened because these entrepreneurs had continually constructed networks with extensive links connecting to many people and thereby multiplied the possibilities of getting assistance at just the right moment.

What does this networking entail? Is it a chance meeting, a blind phone call, an informal introduction, the passage of a business card, perhaps a referral or a personal introduction? In a Kentucky state-wide, women's business leadership conference, the three keynote speakers introduced some strategies that had proved successful. The theme running through all their presentations was the essential role of alliances. Said one, "If we make a blind phone call, we can measure the effectiveness of that in the 1 percent category. An informal introduction may lead to an increase in the effectiveness of our contacts by 15 percent. If someone gives us a referral, we might count on 50 percent effectiveness in closing or joining a business relationship. However, if someone takes time to give us a personal introduction and makes the links in the alliance between the two parties clear, this will lead to a 90 percent chance of a sealed business relationship with long term ramifications."

The choice of employment or self-employment is deeply embedded in not only relationships but also individual characteristics and valued outcomes. One's course will be based on a collected set of skills, abilities, experiences and opportunities. While we cannot control the future, the key to maximizing opportunities seems to be the ability to maintain a high level of personal self-esteem, self-knowledge, and a sense of control.

Ruth Ann Menutis

Founder, The Grove and Branded Works

We were the first to go into airports and open our little nut stands. And then along came the big boy Host Marriott and they started exactly what we were doing in a whole slew of airports. I could have thrown my arms up and said, "Well, I can't compete with them. They're too big." But the idea that I was the moving target, that they were going to get my business, I wasn't going to let them do that. I had to develop a strategy that would be more successful than theirs. I knew that this meant we had to personalize everything we did. We had to give extremely good customer service. We put all this extra training into developing this plan. It had taken me ten years to open ten airport nut shops. Marriott opened in ten airports in one year. Our drive for quality and service made it necessary for them to close all ten within five years. You are a moving target. Measuring success is a continuous process. You measure by saying, "What did they do wrong and what did I do right? What do I have to keep doing to continue growing this business?"

Ruth Ann's Menutis has built a succession of successful companies. Small wonder she has served as Louisiana Chairperson to the National White House Conference on Small Business, and as president of the French Market Corporation. She is a recipient of the Chamber of Commerce Person of the Year award and State of Louisiana Small Businessperson of the Year award.

How did it all begin? Ruth Ann's introduction to the business world was performing promotional spots on a local television program. After graduating from high school, she married a Houstonian and at the age of 20 started her first entrepreneurial venture, a clothing boutique. Building a reputation as a talented designer, she moved to New Orleans and grew the firm to a chain of 16 clothing shops in New Orleans, Houston and New York. She sold the stores after the manufacturer changed its business focus and traveled while planning her next move. In Denver, she spotted the then novel concept of selling natural food snacks at the airport. She returned to New Orleans, consulted her attorney and friend, Paul Valteau, who telephoned Jerry Glazer, Chairman of the Board of the New Orleans Airport at that time, to explain her idea. Offered a three months lease, the partners launched the Grove Natural Snack company in 1980 with a risky investment of $20,000 for a short-term trial. The gamble succeeded and the next year they bought the Denver-based company.

Growth did not come easily. "We now owned a company with the ability to expand, but no place to expand to! We had contacted most airports and always heard the same song and dance: 'Your company is too small to come into our airport.'" "We had opened at Lakeside Mall, but the store was only marginally profitable, so we knew the concept was not for shopping malls."

Then an opportunity opened up through networking. "One day Paul and I were purchasing key man insurance for the business," Ruth says. "The salesman was Danny Abramowitz. He was a New Orleans Saint but selling insurance on the side. We told Danny how we had tried to get into the Dallas Fort Worth Airport but with no success. Danny says, 'Oh, I know the Director, I'll introduce you.' He makes the call, sets up the appointment and we travel to Dallas and walk into the Director's office. He was an obvious football lover who worshipped Danny. As we walked in and Danny introduced Paul and me, we got a nod and then it was football talk for one solid hour. I sat there thinking, what am I doing here! Then the big question came. It was addressed to Danny, ignoring Paul and me. 'Well, Danny, what is it you want in my airport?' Danny replied, 'Oh my friends want to put in a 42 square foot nut stand.' His answer, 'Got any pictures?' I pulled out a picture, handed it to Danny, who laid it on his desk. The Director looked at it for two seconds and said, 'Sure Danny, move it in anytime.' That was airport number two and the rest is history. Once in DFW, airports all over the U.S. were calling us to set up." In time, the Grove would grow to 100 locations at 19 major airports across the country and expand into theaters and Texaco service stations, and operate a bottled water division and maintain a 24,000-square-foot processing facility in Arlington, Texas.

In 2004, Ruth Ann and her partner sold the Grove to concentrate on their other company, Branded Works, which they had formed in 1994 and partnered with the airport-based Hudson Group, a wholly owned subsidiary of international duty-free travel retailer Dufry AG of Basel, Switzerland, to operate news, books, stationery and jewelry stores and specialty shops and cafes in airports. For 16 years now Ruth Ann has been a partner with Hudson News in the airport news stands, where she holds an interest in six of their 100 or more airports. She frequently visits and works in each of these locations, which include Boston, New Jersey, New York, Washington, Charleston and Cincinnati/Northern Kentucky.

Ruth Ann also moved into real estate, beginning with the transformation of New Orleans French Quarter properties into profitable office buildings and from there spread to investments elsewhere. After Hurricane Katrina destroyed most of her New Orleans investment properties, together with her son Dimitri, she turned her attention to the development of a 33,000 square foot building in Lafayette, Louisiana, which had remained vacant after two major oil companies moved out. One year later, after extensive renovation, including an up-to-date media center, Travis Technology Center is fully occupied. The occupants, mostly in the field of technology, include a Women's Business Center.

Recently, Ruth Ann and her son acquired the rights to Raising Cane's Chicken Finger. This is a quick serve restaurant offering Chicken Tenders that are prepared fresh rather than after having been frozen. The first location opened in the San Antonio Airport in 2009, with more to follow. In 2011, Ruth Ann and her son, through a public bid process, acquired the rights to Pinkberry Yogurt for airports. The first location is due to open in the Dallas Fort Worth Airport in 2012. She has, she brags, "airport fever," her favorite place for business.

Ruth Ann today continues her real estate development with her son Dimitri and daughter Jamie. Her latest venture is the development of 24 two-bedroom town houses. The modern, all metal Warehouse District Lofts feature green elements.

Throughout her career, Ruth Ann considers her greatest accomplishment to be enabling and helping other entrepreneurs realize their dreams. During idle time she coaches other men and women who are seeking information on how to start new businesses. She is also preparing to write a book, *Making My Dream a Reality*, in response to the demand of many of those she has mentored and nurtured who wanted to make a special tribute on how she has contributed to their success.

The Job

Job Hunting

You have not been looking for the perfect new position, just one to enable you to keep your home, pay your bills and take care of the needs of your family. But everywhere you look there are no openings for someone with your qualifications. How can you make it better?

Perhaps you fear it is your job history. You may be getting ready to graduate and you have held only part-time jobs, been an intern or a volunteer, and worry that you are at a competitive disadvantage. You may have a so-called "impractical" degree or one that is dated, lapses in your work resume due to time out for family, illness or additional education and training, or a series of low-paying or temporary jobs. Your experience may be in the hardest hit sectors of the economy or with companies that suddenly ceased to exist. You may have even gone back to school to update your resume by boning up on computer high-tech skills, accounting, marketing and management practices or in a host of other areas that experts advise. But still you see no connections between your background, education, job history and the advertisements you read in the paper.

Maybe the problem is not you. Your job search strategy might be bogged down. Most likely, you have become accustomed to thinking of the job market and your credentials in a specific and defined way. This is why it is so important to get a fresh perspective on the job market and on your credentials.

First step, check out the good advice that is readily available. CNNMoney.com introduces you to some of its trusted career coaches. Ford Myers, President of Career Potential and the author of *Get the Job You Want, Even When No One's Hiring*, recommends that you first become crystal clear about what you can offer and then develop the ability to show prospective employers how you can provide solutions to their problems. John O'Connor, president and CEO of Career Pro Inc., similarly says, "You must study each lead and customize each application very carefully; lots of jobs are available but apply right." Barbara Safani, President of Career Solvers, advises to make your job search a full-time job. Daniel King, Principal of Career Planning and Management Inc., flatly points out that it is not the most qualified person who gets the job; it's the one who best knows how to market their qualifications. And Gerry Crispin, co-owner of CareerXroads, strongly suggests "Never, EVER, apply for a job again without first getting an employee in that firm you've targeted to 'refer' you." Kathy Robinson, founder of TurningPoint, says network effectively. "Instead of saying, 'I'm so great in XYZ career and you should hire me,' good networkers say, 'I have been really interested in XYZ career, and have been setting up conversations with people to learn more about what's new in the field."' Cheryl Palmer, a certified executive career coach at Call to Career, says always be prepared. "You should be constantly updating your skills and keeping your network viable. Too many people get too comfortable in their jobs and don't think about what may come next. These are the people who tend to be totally devastated when they are laid off."

Second step, get help from a career coach and or job counselor. Each expert you consult will offer a different perspective based on his or her own frame of reference and level of knowledge. Job coaches are not equally knowledgeable, but the good ones are helpful because of their experience and understanding of what works. Find it scary to go and ask someone for a fresh perspective on what you have to offer and what the best new approach might be for you? Refocus. Think of how someone could offer you the insight you need. And don't forget the value of consulting a career coach in the location where you want to land your next job—just think of the inside alliances they have within the local market.

One more thing. Develop a "job trailer." It will be to your job search what a movie trailer is to a film: a well-planned 30-second piece with highlights that draw in the prospective employer. Begin crafting your job trailer by candidly answering these questions (10 seconds each):

- What makes me the unique choice for this job?
- Here are my capabilities and the problems I can solve.
- Here is how I can help your company meet your objectives.

Retooling

A new beginning requires re-examining one's skill set. To assist you in this, educational institutions of all kinds have skill building, certification and other offerings that address the needs of workers in transition. The objective, perhaps best stated by the Massachusetts Institute of Technology, is to enable people to "reconnect, renew, refuel, relaunch, reenter, retool, reinvent, rekindle, reinvigorate, redefine, recreate, rethink, reestablish and reequip."

What does this mean to anyone in transition who has no definite job prospect?

First, make an inventory of your talents. This will enable you to examine the full spectrum of job and career options, not just look for an opening like the last job you had. Then do some research on the kinds of businesses that employ people with your competencies. It will take time, but it is worth doing because then you can use this knowledge to construct a flexible search for a new career.

Second, package your knowledge, talents, experience and skills to fit what's out there. Developing a new profile and self-image can lead to creating a job niche because the position you are seeking may only exist after you show a prospective employer how hiring you can contribute to the firm's bottom line. For example, assume an applicant is a recent journalism graduate or laid off reporter. Jobs in the newspaper business are tight for a variety of reasons: fewer readers, especially among the young; competition from the electronic media; fewer pages due to the reduction in subscriptions and advertising and higher print costs.

How does this person take her set of writing skills, which the majority of people in the labor market do not have, and turn it into a creative position? If she presents herself as a reporter primarily, she has not renewed, refueled or relaunched. She is presenting an image that narrows job opportunities. She is showing a limited group of employers her skill set in a closed box.

The real skill she has is the ability to write, to articulate, to communicate, to market, to state things clearly, to improve the numerous essential documents all firms generate. She can do the things that are at the top of the list of employer complaints about what they can't find in the labor market—people who can write clearly. That is what should be marketed.

Suppose the applicant's background is in fabric design. But due to the large number of textile companies that have left the country, there appears to be no way for her to get a foot in the doors that remain. How can she use her creativity to launch the job search in new directions? Looking at the field more broadly is one beginning. She should closely examine the spectrum of jobs that are currently being advertised and project where additional openings might occur. Then she should determine what business skills might best fill a resume for these potential openings. As a designer of fabrics, she might want to add some courses in marketing and advertising from a local college or technical school to expand her job search opportunities and also to develop new networks, friends or associates who may recommend her to an employer.

Some general suggestions. If the job seeker is still in school, she is probably already aware of the vast array of services offered by the institution's career service center. Graduates, and sometimes those unable to complete a degree, may not be aware that these services are also available to them. In many cases, schools waive fees for the services in the interest of building goodwill (and possibly attaining future donations from grateful alumnae). Many institutions extend these services to members of the community as well.

If you elect retooling by taking a new program of study, it will be important to determine as nearly as possible what your future set of skills will be and how they will relate to the job market. And be careful. Before enrolling, check to see what percentage of enrollees complete the program, how long they take, and their subsequent employment records. Be especially wary of for-profit and internet-based institutions that boast about the high percentage of graduates who obtain high-paying jobs whose enrollment offices say they will assist in getting loans for you. The costs of some of these programs can be substantial and you will be on the hook for repayment. Before investing in education or training, focus on the return on investment for your time, effort and dollars.

Finally, remember effort and perseverance count. Stay socially healthy; strive to make at least three new contacts every day; and avoid hibernation. Stay physically healthy; get started; and keep up an exercise and fitness program.

Answering Key Questions

I am a recent newcomer and I feel like you can't get a job (not a good job) in this market unless you have the right connections. How can I get a foot in the door and be taken seriously?

Preparation is essential. Start with a self-analysis. Identify your strengths and the best way to highlight these in an attractive way to the market you want to enter. Once you know what your strengths are, identify strategies that will enable you to not only showcase your skill set but enlighten a company as to how you can apply these skills to best serve their needs. The approach "Here I am, here is what I have done" will not interest many recruiters. Anyone with a job opening is interested in what you can do for them. And they are not interested in the rambling, nonspecific version. Are you the best person to assess your strengths? Possibly not. This is why it is important to take advantage of the job coaching sessions that are usually available at non-profits for a minimal fee and at university and college career centers. You can only gain from having a fresh set of eyes look at your resume of accomplishments and make some recommendations.

Market your skill set. Your education, background and employment record will be important, but sending the same resume and cover letter to 50 different potential employers and following the same personal script at any resulting interviews leaves you as one of the crowd.

Target the job. Make the position you apply for your sole focus. Do the research to find out what the company is likely to want. Tailor your resume and cover letter to their position description. If you gain an interview, explain how hiring you will advance their interests.

Create networks. Who you know and who knows you is important. As a newcomer, attend professional meetings and events related to your skills or the job you want. Start with your alumni network if you have one. Get involved in community and social organizations and your church. Circulate. Engage, which means listening as well as talking to people. Volunteer. Keep busy and always be professional. Why do this? Because your application will go to the top of the list if someone inside an organization can say, "I know her, and she's good."

Be proactive. Let's suppose you have special training in hospitality management and are a specialist in event planning where the economic downturn has had a strong negative effect. The old "Here I am, never mind the problem" approach will not land you the job, no matter how many people you know, how long you have been here or how intricate your network is, because there aren't that many jobs. Instead, start thinking, "What can I offer from my experience that no one else has thought of to increase somebody's profit and how do I get this information to a prospective employer who needs it?"

Do the research. Searching for a job as a newcomer doesn't just involve checking the want ads but completing the in-depth research on the financials, marketing strategies, to better understand what you can bring to the table. It also means being fully engaged, going to events where professionals in your field are and being prepared for each potential job with a business card, an effective resume, cover letter and a careful follow-up. Don't forget the value of sound communication skills—this means providing accurate information in an easy-to-read form without grammatical errors. Find out the right way to write the letter, to format the resume, and the proper way to address the person who will be reading it. Find out the right titles to use prior to your meetings. For example, addressing one of your male professors as Dr. and your female professors as Mrs. or Ms. when both have the same Ph.D. is an expression of poor etiquette. Forget the out-of-date regionalisms such as, in the South, calling a woman Miss Jane or a man Mr. Thomas.

What about dress? *How do I know what is considered the right attire for the job I am applying for? I keep reading that the way I dress and carry my body makes a difference. What does that mean?*

Appearances count. Most people make up their minds about someone in the first 10 seconds. A friend of mine, a specialist in interviews, once told me: "When she came for the interview, I knew she was wearing the most appropriate clothes she thought she had." The last thing you want the interviewer to focus on is whether your clothes are appropriate or not.

Proper attire and the projection will affect not only every job interview but also every potential business and social encounter. It starts not with what everyone else is wearing on a daily basis but *what they are wearing in the place you want to be.*

Classic always works. This means well-tailored slacks that come to the appropriate ankle length, or a skirt that comes below the knees and is not tight, a blouse with sleeves below the elbow or at the wrist, that is not see through, tight or showing cleavage. Accessories should be on the light side; avoid long hanging earrings or big loops, jangling bracelets, long finger-nails, and take time to professionally groom your hair to avoid bangs that block your vision. Sandals and flip-flops are out—you want shoes that enclose the toes and avoid high heels that can get caught in a grate, sidewalk, or carpet. Walk with the best of posture, shake hands firmly. Leave people feeling that you would make a great representative. Practice the best etiquette, because the next to last interview could be a lunch and knowing how to handle your silverware is a must. Turn down the wine if offered.

Here is some good advice from Rebecca Smith, an extremely successful business owner. "I know some very capable women who have undermined their own careers because they confused their role as a businessperson with their presence as a woman. The issues of being a woman versus being non-sexual are more subtle than issues of appearance. If a woman approaches me with questions about being successful, the first thing I do is look at her appearance, what she is wearing, her posture, makeup, and jewelry. If she has the basics of a good, strong presence and seems to be articulate with reasonably good command, then I might comment on a few simple things like clothes, jewelry, etc. If she doesn't have the basics, I don't bother commenting on the details. There are some characteristics which are absolutely essential to success in a non-traditional field. The same skills a man must possess to be a leader must be exhibited by a woman, with even more refinement."

Remember the importance of the first 10 seconds. Practice pitching your voice low and speaking slowly and clearly. Shake hands firmly. A shrill, piercing voice, nervous laughter and a handshake like a bear or a fish will make a strong negative impact.

Upset that anyone says projecting a professional appearance in your job search excludes piercings, tattoos, strangely colored cosmetics, miniskirts, high spikes and the sexy clothes you see on TV? OK, go ahead and make a strong statement of your personal right to express yourself. Just understand that you will probably need an independent income for the very long duration of your job search.

Career Networking

Two different kinds of networks exist in the world of work. Men have traditionally been able to make and take advantage of informal organizational contacts both in and outside the workplace. Women have had the more difficult task of learning to network in order to be able to tap into the informal organization. The higher up the organizational ladder, the more restrictive the networks, making them a difficult barrier for senior women to penetrate. While corporate networks for women have existed for more than 25 years, only recently have they been seen as a pipeline for the senior development of women in management. For this reason, women are now moving away from individual networking to collectively working to enhance their status.

The positive impact networks have on finding jobs and advancing careers and on business start-ups is well established. For one thing, as Tabi Haller-Jorden notes, according to many employees, “the very experience of participating in a network builds skills. It’s your opportunity to position a point, make an argument, or give a presentation that is so beneficial.” Further, “corporate networks can, among other things, provide a kind of social mentoring that may not entirely replace but can certainly supplement the traditional one-to-one relationship. Call it ‘distributed mentoring’; the network is the mentor.”

Constructing networks is therefore a vital part of career planning. The basic network consists of support people who are close: family, old friends, shared experiences. More distant personal and professional associations come next. As for the social media, be wary. It may intuitively seem to be a good avenue, but no study has yet established the effectiveness of internet contacts.

For the professional woman, successful network-building strategies involve five types of networks. Each works at a different level.

Personal networks, developed on the basis of interpersonal bonds and relationships, are valuable for their emotional and coping support.

Professional networks are necessary for keeping up to date. Their effectiveness varies based on their exclusiveness and accessibility. Warning: in-group networks that share valuable information only among a few may confer short-term advantages, but over time can stifle growth because the network excludes the diversity it needs to keep fresh.

Formal organizational networks consist of the more open ways of getting and receiving information. Their only limits are one's field, interests, or such boundaries as an M.B.A. association or alumni groups by year of graduation.

Opportunistic networks are created when the possibility of payoff appears. By definition, they are intense, interesting, sporadic and usually short-lived.

Establishing useful networks involves common sense strategies and a careful weighing of the value of one's time. Here are some questions which may help in assessing the potential career value of your networks:

- At work, have I created connections with people in other branches, divisions, and specialties inside my company and outside with individuals in trade, professional and social organizations?
- How active is my networking? How many people do I discuss business matters with? How much time do I spend doing this? What kind of exciting and intellectual programs is the network providing that I cannot get elsewhere?
- How dense is my network; i.e., to what degree do I reach out beyond personal friends, people I know and casual contacts?
- What is the intensity of my network, how frequently do I interact with its members, how do I measure the quantity of the exchanges?

- What do I bring to the table? What do I offer in exchange for what I gain from the networking experience?

A final set of questions will establish a network's value. Is it worth investing the time and energy in order to have this particular net in place for future opportunities when it is needed? Is there time to cultivate key relationships in this network? Can I take the risk of not developing this networking opportunity? How attractive are the members of the network and the organizations they represent? What is the network affiliated with that I value? Does the network provide opportunities that I cannot acquire elsewhere?

Building Your Own Brand

Savvy women entrepreneurs and managers work on building their own brand. Too often people take this to mean building a brand only in connection with the products and services that we market or the image we build for our company. But, as Robin Fisher Roffer said in a keynote address to the National Association of Women Business Owners, it means working to create a personal image that brings a positive association in the minds of others. Drawing on her rich and varied background as a branding expert who has worked for Turner Broadcasting's CNN, Headline News, TNT, and TBS, and strategist in launching dozens of brands for clients like 20th Century Fox, Sony, Disney, MTV Networks, Warner Brothers, Verizon and others, she identified the key steps as finding out who you are, defining your dreams, going after a target audience, re-evaluating and developing new skills if your initial strategy doesn't appear to work, getting feedback on how others are branding you and developing a consistent new plan. As she reiterated in her 2009 book, *The Fearless Fish out of Water: How to Succeed When You're the Only One Like You*, in today's crowded marketplace only the branded thrive.

Need inspiration? A second conference keynote speaker, Bonnie St. John, who has been featured on *NBC Nightly News* as one of the five most inspiring women in America, presented another view. With only one leg and very big dreams, she became an Olympic ski medalist, a Harvard honors graduate, a Rhodes Scholar to Oxford and Director for the National Economic Council during the Clinton administration. She is currently CEO of Courageous Spirit, Inc. One key to her success, she says, was not just the willingness to get up again and again after the spill, but to get up quickly: "I was ahead in the slalom. But in the second run, everyone fell on a dangerous spot. I was beaten by a woman that got up faster than I did. I learned that people fall down, winners get up, and gold medal winners just get up faster." Her second key to success was to invest and reinvest in herself. "So many people are afraid to put their own money on the line for their dreams. Spending it on "things" seems safer, but it isn't!"

In a questionnaire completed by a large group of women entrepreneurs at the NAWBO conference, the majority identified their career strategy as that of a Boundarypreneur—one with endless cross-over options. They felt they could be a business owner today but if a better alternative came along tomorrow they would be ready to make that transition.

Such flexibility is the in vogue wave in evolving careers. Being capable and ready to move back and forth by using talents well honed from the private ownership environment to working for someone else under just the right set of conditions can measurably increase the opportunities for success.

There are other changes you can make to build brighter career options. One is to develop a global perspective. Leslie Grossman, co-founder of Women's Leadership Exchange, president of B2Women and author of *SELLsation: How Companies Can Capture Today's Hottest Market: Women Business Owners and Executives,* and former founder and President of Communications/Marketing Action, Inc. (CMA), a New York-based public relations/marketing firm for high-growth companies, pointed out at the NAWBO conference that 97 percent of all exporters are small businesses and two-thirds of them have fewer than 20 employees.

During her 14 years at CMA, Grossman learned quickly that companies attempted to market to businesswomen the very same way they marketed to men and it simply did not work. This led her to the 2000 launch of B2Women, which she established to create marketing and public relations initiatives for corporations, women's business organizations, conferences and leading women-owned firms. Her client base included companies like American Express, Platinum Guild International, MetroPartners, SAAB Cars, Northwestern Mutual Life Insurance, BBC and North Fork Bank. The approach was so successful that in 2002 she and Andrea March co-founded the Women's Leadership Exchange (WLE) to provide women leading established businesses with the tools, connections and resources to grow their businesses. The WLE conferences in New York City, Dallas, Chicago, Southern California and Atlanta have attracted more than 12,000 women.

Another part of building your successful career brand is to take your team along with you and the process begins by listening. You might want to check your listening time by becoming aware of how much of it is spent thinking about your response. The successful image is one you develop rather than the label someone else designs for you, and it begins by being fully present in all your interactions and engagements.

Suzy Spafford

Founder and CEO, Suzy's Zoo

My husband and I were in Japan recently to visit the stores where my licensed products are sold. Seeing the many, many families so happy to meet me because they love my characters brought many happy tears to my eyes, and in my heart, the joy of knowing that my characters have done what I hoped they would from the start: To make people happy. Little did I think from the beginning that this would be possible across borders and in other languages of the world!

Suzy Spafford is still creating her animal characters now known in many countries as Suzy's Zoo. As a college student, she was majoring in art and working her way through school by selling at various outdoor art marts whimsical drawings of animals and animal characters. A vacationing couple stopped by one day, quite by chance, and upon chuckling over the many pastels of turtles, frogs and a whimsical yellow duck-like character, wondered if she would be interested in going into business selling illustrated note cards. This query led to the launch of her Suzy's Zoo greeting card company in 1968 while still an undergraduate at what was then San Diego State College. Her first fully developed animal character, which she describes as a cross between a chicken and a duck, was a cheerful extrovert who later became known as Suzy Ducken. Her often humorous drawings now feature more than 200 animal characters drawn in bright colors, wearing clothes, shoes, and happy expressions. Each has a personality and back-story and they all live in the fictional town of Duckport. In 1999, Suzy developed a subset of characters to be licensed for products for babies and toddlers, called Little Suzy's Zoo.

At first, Suzy had done all of the artistic work herself, "drawing and laughing and creating those characters to make people happy, to share the joy you experience if you don't forget what it is like to be a child." This was because of her labor of love for each of the characters she brought to life. But by 1985 her enterprise had begun to expand into a growing worldwide business and she needed to hire assistants to help her keep up with the demand for more and more art for a rapidly growing product offering, people with "the ability to expand my concept, to add to value." In addition, starting in 1973, Suzy had also begun licensing her art to other companies. One was for cocktail napkins in the US and the other was for greeting cards published in the UK. Through licensing, Suzy's Zoo became visible in even more widely distributed markets. What started as note cards and greeting cards soon expanded to other companies and other markets. This meant an even wider demand for more and more art.

Suzy notes: "I also started to hire illustrators to draw in my hand starting in 1992. In all, there were seven of us in the art department: four illustrators including myself, and three graphic designers. By 1997, our total staff reached 55 employees and our annual retail potential in the U.S. was between $50 and $70 million. That number goes up and down, depending on our licensees and their product offerings. Our core business, the greeting cards and related merchandise, were all low-ticket items. Our licensees' products were things that retailed much higher. Our actual annual gross receipts were more like $6 million, a figure we maintained for about 12 years. Eventually we got out of the warehousing and shipping part of the business, and now everything you see that is Suzy's Zoo is produced through licensing."

"It was not as easy as I first thought. After reanalyzing all the jobs, I discovered that while I had talented people, no one could replace my feelings for the characters." "I have created something that's unique," Spafford says: "These characters come from my own observations of people, and from my childhood memories. I feel I must be the only one who creates each character."

Suzy's smart business decision was, as she says, to let "someone else take care of the accounting, the word processing, legal aspects, and marketing" and tell her artists, "be graphic, have good composition, good words, but let me own the character. I am the little personality."

Over time, the product lines of Suzy's business expanded from boxed notes to cards for all occasions, stationery, calendars, stickers and similar products sold in thousands of stores all over the world. She has written several dozen books for children, starting with *Alphabetical Soup* and *Witzy and Zoom Zoom,* to the *Tales from Duckport Reader* series for early readers and the *Little Suzy's Zoo* board books for babies and toddlers. In 2005, Suzy entered into a licensing partnership with PlazaStyle of Tokyo, Japan, which has since grown into a very successful and popular range of lifestyle products. Most recently, that company has released Suzy's characters in animation form.

In 2010, Suzy's Zoo partnered with Dalmatian Press to develop coloring books, Level 1 Reader Books and Board Books for the Little Suzy's Zoo and Duckport character sets to be offered at Target, Dollar Tree, and other retail locations throughout the US. In February, 2011, Lawless Entertainment, the worldwide representative for animation, licensing and merchandising for Suzy's Zoo, concluded a deal on behalf of Suzy's Zoo with Fun Rugs to develop rugs for the Little Suzy's Zoo and Wags and Whiskers character sets. Today, she has more than 900 designs on the market and export and licensing arrangements worldwide.

For her success, Suzy credits her husband and C.P.A. wizard, Ray Lidstrom, now President of the company, her now retired business partner Mary Jean Hogg, Art Director Doug Schmitt and many others dedicated to the company's mission. About her work, she reflects,

> *It has been amazing to me to see how these characters have survived over the many years they have been in print, and how they have made friends with people from generation to generation. The real secret to the characters' popularity is that people have identified with them and made them their own. Fans wrote to me early on insisting that I tell them the names of the characters. So I named them as I drew them, and began to think of each as having a distinct personality. That led to creating their stories. I have discovered over the 40+ years that Suzy's Zoo has a grassroots appeal that goes beyond the U.S. borders or the English-speaking world.*

Labels Can be Confusing

Consider the term "working mother." Despite advancements in education and financial and business savvy, the clock never stops ticking for women at the end of the business day. Even the best attempts to balance family and work still leave the lion's share of child care, home care and senior care to women. One result is an unrealistic expectation of what a working mother should be.

Partially based on childhood myths, unrealistic expectations lead to unattainable goals and an accompanying guilt for not being able to achieve it all. A resulting, somewhat overstated, so-called "opt-out revolution" thus led many women to leave bad work environments to become stay-at-home moms during their children's preschool years. But this did not alter their drive for creativity, the imperative to make money or the need to measure self-worth by work-related objectives. Collectively, they have become known as mompreneurs, and here is where the labeling problem comes in. The name contradicts the struggle women have faced for credibility.

MarketWatch has just released a statement on what the average annual pay for stay-at-home moms would be if they were actually paid for their work at home: $117,856. For working moms, add $71,186 to the salary they make elsewhere. But women's work at home is not salaried, and that often creates the perception it has less value. An illustration: Suppose you are a member of Mothers and More, a support group for stay-at-home mothers, and have a home-based business that markets products useful to the average consumer. Would a strategy of calling yourself a "mompreneur" lead to capturing the largest market share? What might the label mean for your company growth and development down the road?

Consider also the variance in the definitions. One well understood definition of "mompreneur" is "a female business owner who is actively balancing the role of mom and entrepreneur" (Entrepreneur.com). But MompreneursOnline.com defines the "mompreneurs" as work-at-home mothers.

There is a world of difference between the two definitions. The first consists of those entrepreneurial women who are balancing their business needs and responsibilities at home. The second means women who operate their businesses from home, some of whom, according to statistics on these businesses, are managing home-based firms that gross the stunning total of more than a million dollars a year.

Aliza Sherman, creator of Cybergrrl and an international organization for women in new media called Webgrrls, and more recently Mediaegg, whom I interviewed at a focus session at the Berkley Center of Entrepreneurship at New York University, suggests that the labeling of "mompreneurs" may critically interfere with one's ability to be taken seriously as a successful entrepreneurial woman. The title, she says, "diminishes the very real accomplishments of a woman with kids who works at home on her home-based business … and especially the extremely successful women whose home-based businesses gross over $1 million US per year." As a stay-at-home mother who runs an extremely successful marketing business, she is considered an authority.

Terms can be confusing, and inferences can be misleading. The first definition of "mompreneurs" includes all those who seek the illusive work–life balance. In fact, as most women business owners with family responsibilities will tell you, it is a real struggle to find balance and achieve all the goals. Says one, "I find I can't reach 100 percent in either area, so somehow 85 percent has to be OK—which is not easy. However, at the end of the day I realize how fortunate I am to have success in both career and family. Sometimes I need to step back from the minutiae to see it."

The point is that in categorizing female entrepreneurs, the term "mompreneurs" creates an image that positions them outside the paid workforce. This may become a negative for the entrepreneurial woman. In the business world, the terms "entrepreneur" or "business owner" provide the recognizable description one needs to advance a professional business strategy. So it is always important to be cognizant of the desired long-range outcome in marketing your image.

Women in Organizations

Credentials, Women and Wages

Between 1970 and 2009, according to the Bureau of Labor Statistics, the number of women in the labor force more than doubled. Slightly more than one-third of employed Americans in 1970, women made up almost half of the labor force in 2009. Fewer than one-third held full-time jobs in 1970; more than four in ten did in 2009.

The rise in the educational credentials of women over the same period was simultaneous, equally transforming and not unrelated.

According to U.S. Department of Education statistics, between 1977 and 2008, the number of women earning Associate's and Bachelor's degrees more than doubled. By 2008, women were earning more than half of all Bachelor's, Master's and Doctoral degrees and a fraction less than half of all professional degrees and, according to the 2010 *Chronicle of Higher Education Almanac*, made up well over half of the enrollments in two-year institutions, four-year colleges and graduate programs.

The gains had not come because women were taking the places of men—the number of men earning Bachelor's degrees also rose—it was because women were enrolling in programs of higher education in greater numbers. Many of their fields of study had direct applications in the workplace. In Business, Management and Marketing, women now earned two-thirds of the Associate's degrees, nearly half of the Bachelor's and more than 40 percent of the Master's and Doctoral degrees. Women earned three-quarters of the professional degrees in Veterinary Medicine, two-thirds in Pharmacy, more than half in Optometry and Osteopathic Medicine, not quite half in Medicine, and more than 45 percent in Dentistry and Law. Women earned over 40 percent of the Bachelor's degrees in the fields of Security and Protective Services, Science Technology, Mathematics and Statistics, and the Physical Sciences.

Yet the gender gap in wages persists. The Bureau of Labor Statistics reports that, in 2010, the median wage of the nearly 100 million women working full time was 81 percent of what men earned.

Skeptics of a wage gap contend that disparity exists because women entered many fields only recently. In time, they say, it will disappear. The argument makes some sense when you look back over three decades at occupations like physicians and surgeons, where women earn 71 percent of what men do. It makes less sense in the field where the largest number of women are working full time: registered nursing. Nine out of every ten registered nurses are women. Their annual median income is 87 percent of what the male registered nurses earn.

A pay disparity exists in every single occupational category. Nine of ten medical assistants are women. Their median annual wage is 3.6 percent lower than men's. Eight of ten elementary and middle school teachers are women. They have a median income that is 90 percent of their male colleagues. More than half of all financial managers are women. They earn about two-thirds of what male financial managers make. The six of ten education administrators who are women confront a 23 percent wage gap. The wage gap is equally visible in fields where the numbers of women are low such as computer scientists and system analysts (30 percent women, wage gap 28 percent).

One can look at the numbers and claim progress. The current 81 percent gap in the median annual earnings of women working full time compared to men appears better than the 59 percent gap of 1981 and 71 percent gap in 1998. However, some of that increase was due to a greater decline in men's earnings in the first two years of the current recession, and with more recent employment data showing men's job prospects significantly greater than women's, it is likely that the real wage gap is greater than the latest earnings statistics indicate.

Studies continue to show that higher levels of education translate into greater income, but this is true for both men and women, and there are few data to suggest that education closes the wage gap. Starting salaries and job responsibilities are among the strongest reasons for the continued existence of the gap. According to a recent Catalyst study, men were more likely to start their first post-M.B.A. job at a higher level, received salaries that averaged $4,600 more and took their first assignments at a higher rank with greater levels of responsibilities.

The suggestion for the women with skills: Avoid a lifetime of lower wages and jobs with less future. Before the job interview, research thoroughly to find out what the men in the position are making, their job titles and the responsibilities they have. In the job interview, ask for at least that. Then be prepared to avoid being maneuvered into agreeing that the position you are being offered is "different." It probably isn't.

Her Power

A considerable body of research dismisses stereotypes that women don't want to reach the highest organizational ranks because of gender or because they are less oriented to power or are more submissive than men. Just the opposite. Among other findings, according to a study published in *Industrial Management*, there are no significant differences between male and female managers in the measures of the power difference stereotypes (shy versus venturesome, humble versus assertive, group-dependent versus self-sufficient, conservative versus experimenting, tough-minded versus tender-minded). But women do appear to go after power differently, want it for different reasons, and exercise it in different ways. There is some indication this is because positions of authority in the organizational hierarchy have usually been occupied by men and thus the male model became the norm for the way to behave in organizations.

To compensate for not being able to rely on power that derives from holding a position, many women develop the skills to wield personal power. They project the ability to be credible, reliable, and trustworthy. They prefer to influence rather than command. They view power as a means to promote change by sharing information and empowering others through team-building in an environment that subordinates find empowering. They practice participative management techniques such as involving people who will be affected by the decisions in making the rules. They exercise authority carefully because they have seen men praised despite their incompetence and women who paid a heavy price for the slightest error.

This appears especially true for the entrepreneurs I interviewed. Facing a crossroads with an opportunity to grow significantly, the owner of an investment advisory firm said to her people, "In the beginning I set up the goals, but tomorrow we're all going to sit down. I'm going to say, 'We're getting more and more institutional clients. How are we going to do this, do it well, and make sure we meet the clients' needs as well as our own?'"

Says another entrepreneur, "I see myself as a facilitator of my employees. They know exactly what they're doing. I've trained them. Now they are real good at it. And I'm not about to get in their way. I do call them out in the office about once every week and say, 'Okay. I'm going to be boss for about two minutes and then I'm going back to my office and let you all do your work.' And we just laugh. And that's kind of the camaraderie we have built."

This kind of managing is not easy. Says one CEO, "learning to be able to get the big vision communicated and implemented. I am always repeating the same things over and over. You can't move on until you have the last person on the train or you are forced to leave them behind."

There is considerable evidence that leaders who share power are quite effective. But whether seeking power or exercising it, it is important for women to stand their ground. As Mary Ellen Iskenderian, President and CEO of Women's World Banking, a consortium of microfinance institutions, recently noted, there is "a tendency for men to take over any sector as soon as a profit motive is introduced. This has been happening in the previously woman-dominated microfinance industry, since it has been proven as a profitable business model." She also provided an example at the Forum which was published in *Foreign Policy* of a "group of women in eastern Africa who had traditionally planted, harvested, and processed a particular ground nut. Once Western supermarkets became interested in the nut, the women were shunted aside, and the whole supply chain was co-opted by men in less than a year."

This is nothing new. In a 1994 *Harvard Business Review* article, Robert Schrank described what occurred during a rafting exercise in which the participants took turns at leadership. When men were in control, other men encouraged them. When women were in control, men plotted to protect their power from female encroachment by discouraging them. Schrank concluded that in shrunken job markets similar things might be happening. For women to be successful, he suggested, there must not only be a shift in power but a supportive climate to go along with the shift.

As more women entered management, many worked to create that supportive climate, moving away from the concept identified by Catalyst (2005) of "taking care" to "taking charge." The mission of the National Association of Female Executives is to reduce the gender gap across all corporate functions with the explicit objective of gaining access to the pipeline to the profit and loss positions in large companies, because that is where the power is. Their long-range program includes identifying high-potential women during their first two years, partnering with the good old boys, strengthening high-level connections, and establishing a 10-year program for personal networking.

Aliza Sherman

Founder, Cybergrrl, Conversify and Mediaegg

The dramatic version of my entrepreneurial journey is that I was held up at gunpoint and kidnapped with my boyfriend in 1994. We managed to escape, and then I decided that I needed to pursue my own dreams so started my first company.

Yes, that is a true story, and staring down the barrel of a 9mm handgun shook me to my core and made me realize that I had to face fears that were holding me back in my career. Starting a business seemed terrifying to me, but I did it with no money in the bank and just a straightforward business idea: Help companies and non-profits get a website.

After attending college for four years but not obtaining a degree and deciding between a "cubicle" in a bank or the option of managing three agents in a growing music booking agency in North Carolina, Aliza chose the latter, only to be told after several years they were not ready for a woman agent. She moved on and ended up working for four years in the music industry in New York City overseeing some of the largest heavy metal groups, bands like Metallica and Def Leppard.

"I wanted to manage bands. My bosses at the time said I could but they never approved the bands I wanted to manage, including The Black Crowes. Then I found out the men in the office who I considered to be my peers made twice as much as I did, six figures. I asked my bosses why and was told it was because 'they are married, they have families.' And I was a single female 'without a lot of expenses.'"

Around the same time, Aliza had met a photojournalist who took pictures of rock bands but also documented domestic violence. "I started helping her part time and then quit the music business to run her non-profit organization on domestic violence awareness," says Aliza. "We worked with the Mayor's office and the Governor's office on awareness campaigns, and I spent over a year immersed in domestic violence work. Then I was held up at gunpoint."

She left New York after the incident and headed to Santa Fe, New Mexico, where she learned about the web, took a class in HTML and built her first website. She returned to New York City determined to start her own company building websites for companies and non-profits wanting to reach women online. That was the origin of Cybergrrl, the first full-service woman-owned Internet company. At the time, women made up 10 percent of the Internet population. "I felt so empowered by the internet," she says, "and wanted to help other women learn how to go online, to gain skills as web developers and to break into a decidedly male industry." Soon after, Aliza founded Webgrrls International, the first global internet networking organization for women, which grew to over 100 chapters worldwide and over 30,000 members in the late 1990s.

Leaving Cybergrrl after five years, Aliza embarked on a new internet venture—Eviva.net—a bilingual community and resource for Latina professionals to network and do business online. "Then the internet bubble burst and my business partner and I worked to return the $250,000 funding we received from an angel investor. We could have burned through the money but felt the relationship with our investor was much more important and busted our tails to get the money back to her—even the money we had spent. At that point, I was essentially broke but took part of a book advance and bought an old RV then spent the next year driving around the country by myself." Her travels became an online road diary, RVGirl.com.

Aliza followed her travels with a two-year stint managing public relations and marketing for an economic development agency in Wyoming. In 2003, she founded an internet consultancy that grew into the social media marketing agency Conversify. In 2010, she launched Mediaegg, providing high-level, strategic digital and mobile consulting to companies and non-profit organizations. The company launched an app for iPod, iPhone and iPad called "Girls Can Be Anything Paperdolls," part of a project to create age-appropriate, family-friendly digital and mobile content. "I like to think of myself as a technology tour guide," Aliza says, "I get out and explore, develop some level of knowledge and help develop best practices. Then I work to make it easier for the layperson—usually the non-techie businessperson—to understand. That's kind of my modus operandi—discover, explore, explain, integrate."

As for work–life balance, Aliza admits that she was surprised at how difficult motherhood could be. "The most challenging thing is to split myself appropriately between my work life and home life, between being a career woman and being a wife and mom. Those roles seem to take distinctly different aspects of myself and turning them on and off is a struggle for me. I love my husband and daughter but also know I'm the best wife and mother when I do get 'out of the house' to travel and work on my projects." For Aliza, motherhood is an intense, immersive experience and she says she sometimes feels like she is barely keeping her head above water. "My daughter is very vocal about getting me to stop work or to get off my computer to pay attention to her. I don't think I manage work and home life very well," Aliza says, "and I'm not really sure how anyone does it because, in my experience, if I put a lot of effort toward work, my home life and personal relationships suffer. If I devote more time to family and friends—which I truly believe is the more important part of life—I produce less work. I don't see any hope of balance here but more conscious choices and acceptance as needed."

With regard to the workplace, Aliza says, "women make incredible strides but there is a fundamental problem with the very foundation we all work on top of in our industries. There is still inherent sexism in places, there are still gross inequities in places, and I'm not talking just about third world countries but also here in the US. People are afraid to rock the boat or talk about the prejudices out there for fear of being blacklisted. But I'm getting a little too old now to care what people think. I think you hit middle age and realize 'half my life is over. Have I lived a good and honorable life yet?' Okay, maybe not everyone thinks that, but it is something I'm grappling with now. My mission used to be to help women and girls embrace and benefit from technology. Now I think it is more to speak the unspeakable so others don't feel so alone."

"Action is in order," says Aliza. "I started a project called Chain of Daisies to create not only a pipeline to help business, tech and venture conferences find more qualified female speakers but to also help transform the landscape, tools and resources available to women to help them identify, submit proposals to and land these coveted speaking opportunities. We just have to work together to put virtual jackhammers to the status quo, shake up the foundation, and rebuild it with better ways and attitudes. We need to do something or support those who are doing something positive."

Aliza was named one of the Top 50 People Who Matter Most on the Internet by *Newsweek* in 1995 and one of the Most Powerful People in Their 20's by *Swing* magazine in 1997. An article in the *Wall Street Journal* said of her, "It's a man's world out there in cyberspace—but not if Aliza Sherman has anything to say about it. Her mission: empower women and girls through technology." She has published nine books and produced content for both public radio and public television. In 2009, *Fast Company* recognized her as one of the Most Powerful Women in Technology for her writing and blogging. Her two most recent books are *The Complete Idiot's Guide to Crowdsourcing* and *Mom Incorporated.*

All Minds Needed at the Table

In 1998, Catalyst and the National Foundation for Women Business Owners published a joint study showing that women were leaving corporate and public sector organizations to start businesses of their own because, among other reasons, they continually encountered gender stereotypes that held them back. Much earlier, in the course of my own research, Jill Martin Fugaro, a very successful entrepreneur who had trodden a similar corporate path, put it this way: "I live in San Francisco, and I liken the disillusionment in a corporation to a creeping fog. In the nighttime, the fog slowly comes in from the ocean and goes under the Golden Gate Bridge. You are really not aware of it at first, and eventually you hear the foghorns in the distance, and those foghorns indicate a change in the environment, a slow creeping disillusionment."

In 2004, Catalyst released the results of a study of the experiences of male and female executives of Fortune 1000 Companies. It reported that, while both men and women have similar goals on entering organizations and strategies for reaching them, and that both groups would encounter barriers in their careers, women had the additional problem of encountering harmful gender stereotypes. How that was happening was crisply explained three years later in the title of the 2007 Catalyst study: "The Double-Bind Dilemma for Women in Leadership:

Damned if You Do, Doomed if You Don't." Stereotypes and their harmful paralyzing effects on women's career opportunities and advancement have not gone away. According to a 2010 Catalyst report, gender stereotypes continue, and especially in male-dominated organizations.

We have known for half a decade at least why it makes no sense for companies to tolerate this. A 2004 Catalyst study reported results from an examination of some 353 companies that maintained their Fortune 500 rankings four years out of a five-year period. It showed that companies with the highest percentage of women in top management had a higher return on equity (35 percent) and greater total returns to shareholders (34 percent) than companies with few women top managers. A 2009 Catalyst study suggested an additional reason. The higher return on investment was seen in firms where male managers saw the value of diversity training and then carried out the results in working with members from diverse groups.

Assuming that the point of operating a business is to make a profit, what does this tell us? Volumes. As a 2004 study of the benefits of a climate of diversity said, companies hiring and advancing qualified women access a larger pool of talent and benefit from considering all minds valuable. Where women are given equal (not special) opportunities and bias-free measurements of job performance, it is possible to eliminate or reduce the harmful outcomes of stereotypes. Companies are then able to operate on a higher level and perform better.

It would be more profitable for companies if managers were to set stereotypes aside and follow leadership styles that advance the organization's mission. Unfortunately, far too many major corporations and smaller companies around the globe still use at all levels of the organization outdated styles of management and leadership ill suited to benefiting from employee diversity.

Catalyst (2009) suggests an approach to bring about change is to introduce diversity training programs in ways that men perceive as important. When this happens, organizations become more efficient. Companies that seek success also need to set standards of "no tolerance" for managers who deliberately use stereotypes to avoid appraising and paying women professionals the salaries they deserve.

How new are these ideas? Sixty-five years ago, Peter F. Drucker, probably the most prolific writer and well-respected figure in the field of management, observed that companies would benefit from "solid" human resource practices "that promote workplace diversity" by following impersonal, equal opportunity selection "policies based on a criterion of promotion." "Equal opportunity," he said, "means advancement not be based on external hereditary or other fortuitous factors" but "according to rational and reasonable criteria."

Elsewhere, in organizations where stereotyping is supported or tolerated by top management, aspiring women are learning work styles that enable them to counteract and maneuver around gender stereotypes, and along the way improve the climate for all employees. Not an easy task, but, for many, a strategy that contributes to higher returns on investment and a more positive business climate and culture.

Organizational Career Tips

Managing Up

A quick web search yields some 290 books on managing up, meaning to manage your boss.

The way organizations operate today is a product of the numerous forces that dismantled many old operating systems, particularly those that were dysfunctional. In their place rose the advantage of using the new information sharing technologies to bring together in work teams, either physically or virtually, people with differing resources, perspectives and skills to achieve organizational goals. Much of the organizational work today, particularly the creative work, takes place in teams because, done right, the result is a collective creativity. But work teams are only effective when people buy into the organizational goals in a cooperative endeavor and the organization delegates power to the team to go ahead and solve problems. In settings where team performance is highly valued, a leader who encourages open exchanges, collaborations and collective creativity provides a new culture and becomes an enabler of productivity.

The problem organizations have is that, as they restructured, employee trust eroded. The organizational dilemma was obvious. Companies needed to find team leaders who excelled at bringing people together and motivating them to solve problems, leaders who could create a climate of work team trust and themselves be entrusted with power.

What many firms are finding is that this means they need a new type of leader—one with an interactive, open style of leadership that is based on skilled communication. Because this is exactly the job approach that many women cultivated so their talent, experience, education and work skills would not be brushed aside by gender bias, they are moving into these new positions of leadership in organizations. These women will be instrumental in putting our economy back on track.

What steps can you take to begin cultivating the skills to move into one of the team leadership opportunities in your company? Begin by managing up, building trust one step at a time and then work to hold the trust in place:

- Know your job. Be so good at it that everyone in your work setting understands that you know what you are talking about.
- Figure out what your company needs to be successful. Do your homework.
- Network throughout the organization. Build relationships with people who understand your ability to get things done.
- Go where the action is. Join work teams and contribute in a collaborative way.
- When you feel you are ready and the opportunity presents itself, grab the chance to lead.
- Focus on the task at hand and the goals of your team and organization. Remember it is always professional and

solution oriented, never personal. Avoid getting sidetracked into pushing your own agenda and personal interests.
- Articulate clearly what you and your team need to achieve its goals. Enlist your supervisor, keep him or her informed, leverage his or her strengths and talents in carrying out the team objectives, and make sure that the supervisor knows you appreciate and acknowledge the value he/she adds to the team.
- Be honest and trustworthy.
- Understand your own management style.

It is no accident that women are moving into positions of team and organizational leadership and also that large numbers of them are well positioned to make a leadership difference. Ursula M. Burns, CEO of Xerox, illustrated how important her approach was in turning the company around, "I wanted (Xerox) employees to take more initiative and be more fearless and frank with one another ... We're family, so we can disagree."

A Mentor Should be an Advocate

What kind of mentoring do women need and want on the job? All generations of the women who make up almost half of today's workforce have the same list: a boss to help navigate career paths, straight feedback, advocacy and coaching, sponsorship for formal development programs and flexible schedules.

On the surface, the mentoring news seems good for women. A 2008 Catalyst survey of more than 4,000 high-potentials (women graduating from top M.B.A. programs between 1996 and 2007) shows that more women than men have mentors. But not all mentoring is created equal. These women were paid $4,600 less than men in their first post-M.B.A. jobs, held lower-level positions and felt less career satisfaction.

How did this happen? Among the reasons, as Linda Babcock and Sara Laschever suggest in their book *Women Don't Ask: Negotiation and the Gender Divide,* is that most women simply didn't speak up. They just took the salary that was offered at the outset and didn't bargain. At work, they may still be doing the same, and that could be hurting them.

The hidden key to moving up the ranks, according to Herminia Ibarra, Nancy Carter, and Christine Silva, in an article in the September *Harvard Business Review,* is "sponsorship," meaning having a mentor who does more than give feedback and advice but instead uses his or her position and influence to be your advocate. Compared with their male peers, say the authors, women with the highest potential were actually "overmentored and undersponsored." "Programs that get results clarify and communicate their goals, match sponsors and mentees on the basis of those goals, coordinate corporate and regional efforts, train sponsors, and hold those sponsors accountable."

What does this have to do with your career? You need an advocate who is a mentor and sponsor, because most companies do not assign mentors, and even in companies that do the mentors do not always work out. For this reason, you need to find someone who will have your best interests at heart. Here's how to start:

- Seek out a mentor from someone senior in the organizational hierarchy because advisory relationships usually don't start on their own, especially between men and women, and mentoring develops most rapidly from a structured relationship.
- Keep your mentoring relationships professional and confidential. Plan a monthly agenda and set mutually beneficial appointment times to get together. Give notifications in advance on the topics you want to discuss to gain from the mentor's reflections. Cultivate the ability to take positive and negative feedback. Avoid burning bridges when it is time to move on (some of the most successful mentorships last only one year).
- Make mentoring a proactive process to achieve tangible rewards that are important to you. Don't settle for mentoring as just a tool for better understanding yourself, your

operational style or how you might need to change. This approach can quickly turn off your most potentially valuable mentors. It's about your work life, not your personal life.

- Frame the process to engage your mentor as a public advocate. The difference is between a mentor who says, "I am going to recommend you if a position comes up," and a mentor who says, "I'm going to speak to so-and-so about putting you in charge of that project" and then does it.
- Recognize the existence of a chain of command and use it. Build relationships with influential people who can advocate for you.
- Use a venture capitalist strategy to identify what you and your company need to do to get ahead. Self-diagnostic questions and target areas include aspiration (What do I really want to do and where do I want to be?), core strength (What am I doing really well right now?), critical assessment (What am I not doing that could get me ahead?), time allocation (If it's important, make room for it; if not, cut down) and the company and areas of strength (What does the firm need most and how can I help?).
- Remember the value of face time. You may easily be able to do all of your work on your home computer. But are you missing out on the opportunity to be seen working hard by the people who count?
- If there is a cutting-edge, high-visibility program at your company, get involved. If it requires new skills, get the training.
- Move up from junior-level mentors in your company to more senior managers. Tip: One strategy that has been used quite successfully to get a mentor sensitive to the problems of women in the workplace is to identify men whose wives or daughters have started jobs.
- Remember, while you may own the mentoring relationship(s), the advocacy you need for advancements is not something you own. It is your ability to appreciate, to show that appreciation in tangible ways and to give back that will make the support possible.

Climbing to the Top

Research presented at recent annual meetings of the Academy of Management includes findings relevant to women desiring to move up the ladder and identifies some possible stumbling blocks along the way.

As Konrad, Kramer and Erkut have found, and more recently a Catalyst study has noted, when the number of women on a corporate board reaches critical mass (at least three), there is an observed positive contribution to innovation in the firm. The suggestion is that when an individual woman is no longer seen as a token but as a group member, there is an opportunity to not only open things up but to create workable coalitions for progress.

An Academy of Management presentation of the analysis of data from more than 217 nations around the globe suggests that the important keys to building a power base for women leaders include the involvement of their countries in global marketplaces, international trade and modern technology. While developments in both economic and human health terms and the level of education are important predictors of women's leadership aspirations everywhere, the key to actual progress for women is gender equality. As workforce pay, equity, banking and property rights advance, so does women's personal power. Where there is government support and respect for entrepreneurs, women tend to gravitate toward business leadership.

Networking and information sharing facilitate the rise of women leaders. The informal motto of the global participants—collective, collaborative and connective—is also an excellent description of how this works.

For aspiring female leaders, the suggestion is that if you are the first or second member of a board or work group, it is to your advantage to lower the ladder to help other women up. It takes numbers to get women accepted, and only then do you have the opportunity to get things done.

How might you approach the system? One recommendation is to apply the "alpha female" approach while maintaining your "feminine mystique." It requires a delicate balance and an understanding of the power games. Try these eight steps:

- Begin by approaching every situation as if you are on a level playing field while at the same time fully understanding that no such thing exists.
- Always prepare in advance before you enter the meeting, conference or board room.
- Start out in neutral and coast into the right gear, the place from which you can begin to maneuver.
- In individual and group interactions, remember: It isn't personal, and it can't be about you. It's the agenda on the table and your strategy to advance a position you already have thought about and mapped out.
- It is all right to make concessions as long as they advance your position and are not seen as weakness.
- In meetings, always close on an upbeat note to avoid the impression that you prefer collaborating or just getting along to achieving the best result.
- Given a chance to lead, use interactive leadership and power sharing. It works because both men and women welcome the change from the traditional, top-down way things have been done in the past.
- Develop an inner circle of five or more people with the common mission of building alliances so each of you can advance projects.

None of the above is going to change the world, but that is not what you are trying to do. For women, it is mostly an uphill climb. What you are working toward is making it easier by making the slope more gentle for those who follow in your path.

Kay Koplovitz

Founder and CEO, Koplovitz & Company

It empowered me to think that we could have more than three television networks, that we could have more sources of information, that people in despotic governments could know what was going on in other countries, and the knowledge could set them free.

As her family was preparing to move into a new house, 5-year-old Kay Smith told her father that "it's very nice that we have a new home but I can't live there. I have to graduate with my class." Told that was not an option, she continued, "Okay, but then I have to take the bus to my school and I need an increased allowance so I can pay for the bus fare." This she was allowed to do and Kay finished kindergarten with her classmates at her first elementary school.

After graduating from high school as valedictorian of her class, Kay entered the University of Wisconsin, where she was a Science major studying Biology with a minor in communications. Between her junior and senior years, she took a short break to travel in Europe with a backpack on $5 a day. While in England, she was inspired by a lecture she had heard by science fiction writer Arthur C. Clarke on the power of satellites and how they could change communication. "I was a television producer working my way through college," she says, "and I really saw the structure of television as it was then and could imagine what it could be if you could open up the access to programming." Graduating Phi Beta Kappa with a Bachelor of Science degree, Kay went on to Michigan State University where she earned an M.S. in Communications. Her thesis was on the impact of satellite communications on government and industry. After graduating, Kay set her sights on the satellite industry and landed a job at the Communications Satellite Corporation (Comsat). There she learned the business of satellite communications before moving on to the cable industry working for UA Columbia Cablevision, a nationwide cable operator. Following her stint at UA Columbia, Kay took on a slate of consulting assignments, one of which was Home Box Office, the pay television provider. For HBO, she organized "The Night that Changed the Course of Television History" by demonstrating the power of satellites for commercial television. The event was "The Thrilla from Manila," the third boxing match between Muhammad Ali and Joe Frazier and the event that convinced Washington that satellites could be used to further develop the programming for the cable industry.

In sports, Kay had found her opportunity. In 1977, with partner Bob Rosencrans, Kay launched the Madison Square Garden Sports Network. Striking a deal with New York Yankees owner George Steinbrenner for coverage of the Yankees games, she parlayed that into a deal with Major League Baseball that was followed by carriage deals with the National Basketball Association and the National Hockey League. Said NBA Commissioner David Stern much later, "Our first deal was for $400K for the season. Last year our cable deal called for $225 million. I always knew that Kay knew something that I didn't know." Today, the NBA receives over $2 billion per year in TV license fees.

As Chairman and CEO, Kay added non-sports programming to the network and changed the name to USA in 1980, launched the Sci-Fi channel in 1992, and added USA Network International in 1994. Under her direction, USA Networks challenged the broadcast networks, among other ways by launching new shows in summer, moved into original programming and molded itself as television's first advertiser-supported basic cable network. For 13 straight years, with Kay as Chairman and CEO, the network held the number one ranking in primetime viewership among cable networks.

Kay stepped down from her position in 1998 after the controlling interest in USA Networks changed hands and there were strong indications the network's mix of programming would be changed. She then considered, but did not accept, an overture to become Major League Baseball's Sports Commissioner.

Almost immediately, Kay was appointed by President Bill Clinton to chair the National Women's Business Council, an advisory group for women-owned businesses, a position she held until 2001. In 2000, while at the Council, she co-founded the non-profit firm Springboard Enterprises, a nationwide initiative to match female entrepreneurs with venture capitalists. During the first 10 years, Springboard companies raised more than $5 billion in equity capital. In 2001, Kay co-founded Boldcap Ventures, a venture capital fund designed to invest in early and mid-stage companies in the media, technology and health care fields. The next year she published *Bold Women, Big Ideas: Learning to Play the High Risk Entrepreneurial Game*, an encouragement for women that, in addition to describing itself in the title, stresses being motivated by the need to achieve not by fear of failure.

Kay has received numerous awards, among them being named one of the most influential "men" in sports by *Sports Illustrated* magazine in 1992. To this she responded, "My mom will be thrilled with that. She's quite a sports fan." Kay holds honorary degrees from Emerson College, St. John's University and her alma mater Michigan State, has served on boards of directors of numerous public boards, including General Re, Nabisco, Instinet and Oracle. She serves as Chairman of the Board of Liz Claiborne, Inc., and serves on the board of CA Technologies and ION Media.

Kay currently chairs Koplovitz & Company, which provides investment services to entertainment companies, sports organizations and others and makes investments in early and mid-stage companies in media, technology and related sectors.

Kay's career spirals out across an array of public and private service ventures and provides an illustration of just how creative a 21st century womanpreneur can be when she adopts the motto "Motivation by achievement rather than fear." She is out there creating new pathways for all women. What is so exciting about Kay's endeavors is that she is on the forefront of creating avenues to capital access for women in the technology, media and health care fields who are building sizeable businesses. This is the next frontier for a woman many call a true visionary.

Building the Right Networks

For women in the workforce, networking is not only necessary but advantageous. In its simplest form, networking is an interaction to discover commonalities. The objective of business networking is to create and expand long-lasting relationships for mutual benefits. Referrals generate 80 percent more results than cold calls. Job opportunities and career options result from introductions and recommendations.

A person who thinks highly of you and says the right thing to the right person at just the right time can be behind your promotion. On average, your network contacts may know as many as 200 to 250 people. You may not know any of them.

Networks of trusted and knowledgeable advisors aid in navigating organizational cultures. They are critical to becoming an "insider." This is because networking often leads to becoming a member of a group that meets formally or informally to study or plan or recommend a strategy that draws special attention.

Sometimes, especially if the group is predominantly male, a female member may be designated to take notes. Grab this opportunity if it arises. You gain a special voice as record keeper. Most likely, you will then become the only member of the group who can later say with confidence (based on your carefully recorded notes) that: "What we decided earlier was . . ." or "What (the absent member) said last time was . . ." From committee member to "authority" in one important step.

Networks also aid in problem solving. Dealing with a difficulty in your company? Most likely, the dilemma is new only to you. While you can't talk to your next-door neighbor about the issues and a family member may not have enough inside information to provide the intelligent guidance you need, a sage acquaintance or someone you respect in your immediate network may shed some real light.

Networks require personal involvement and investments. Don't want to talk about the problem to someone in your immediate work group because the conversation may come back to haunt you? Invite the wise acquaintance or someone you respect from another department or division in the company or from an outside similar, non-competitive company to lunch or coffee at your expense. At the least, the small effort can further cultivate your friendship. At best, you find the new perspective you need.

Networks also offer a sanity check to see beyond the current mess or when you feel that nothing good is happening or to rebuild your confidence to face challenges. When something really bothers you, a good support group is critical. Thinking about a career transition? Well-formed networks can provide the initial support and realistic advice.

Some things to keep in mind in building an effective network:

- It may be structured or casual. Some research indicates that informal networks are more important than formal ones.
- Maintaining networks is demanding and requires carefully honed time-management and people skills.
- Working within networks requires paying attention to seemingly little things. Come to the relationship to listen and show empathy. Project a professional image by the way you dress and carry your body. Develop a short and lively personal introduction that provides an open avenue for exchange. Prepare a professional business card and your own name tag to take to meetings.
- Because the most effective networks are built on mutual trust, they evolve over time. Keeping your word when you promise to say or do something builds credibility.
- Construct networks so they are well in place long before you need them.
- Avoid developing superficial networks. Gossip may be fascinating, but participating in it provides few targeted benefits.
- Networks are a two-way street. Support members of your network when they need it. Don't keep score. It is not just when you want something: the goodwill in the bank and the right to request a favor without hooks when you really need help is important.
- Develop networks across generations. Avoid the dilemma of thinking everyone in your network should be your age or younger. You need wisdom and perspective across generations: Silent/Traditional, Baby Boomer, X and Millennials.

References

Profile: Ruth Ann Menutis

The draft profile corrected and approved by the entrepreneur drew from New Orleans CityBusiness (2000, Feb. 28). Women of the Year: Ruth Ann Menutis. Retrieved from http://www.allbusiness.com/north-america/united-states-louisiana/908850.html and the *Independent Weekly* (2008). Women Who Mean Business. Retrieved from 2008 http://www.theind.com/index.php?option=com_content&task=view&id=2881&Itemid=10-1

The Job

Job Hunting

Crispin, G. (2011). The staffing strategy connection. Retrieved from http://www.careerxroads.com/about/index.asp

King, D. J. (2011). The business case for career development. Retrieved from http://www.careerfirm.com/bizcase.htm. See also: Desperate worklives at http://www.careerfirm.com/articles.htm; and Defining a generation: Tips for uniting our multi-generational workforce at http://www.careerfirm.com/generations.htm

Myers, F. R. President, Career Potential (2011). Q&A with Ford R. Myers—Parts 1 and 2. Retrieved from http://www.quintcareers.com/QuintZine. See also: http://www.careerpotential.com/corp/ford_myers.htm

O'Connor, J. (2011). Individual outplacement solutions—Building personal brands. Retrieved from http://www.careerproinc.com/

Palmer, C. (2011). Executive online and offline job search strategies at call to career. Retrieved from http://www.calltocareer.com/about/

Robinson, K. (2011). Turning point—Enjoy your work. Enjoy your life. Retrieved from http://www.turningpointboston.com/about_us.shtml

Safani, B. (2011). Exclusive Q&A with Barbara Safani—Resume writer and author. Retrieved from http://www.careersolvers.com/about_us.html

Retooling

Massachusetts Institute of Technology Career Reengineering Program (MIT). Cover for *Professional Education.* Retrieved from http://web.mit.edu/professional/pdf/crp_brochure.pdf. (Cited material on the brochure cover.) Also while there, see: Career Development Center. Retrieved from http://web.mit.edu/career/www. See also *Career development handbook* (2009–2010) and *Going global—Visit on careerbridge.*

Answering Key Questions

Moore, D. P. (2000). *Careerpreneurs.* (Rebecca Smith quote at pp. 179–180.)

Career Networking

Haller-Jorden, E. T. (2006). Women working together: What networks can do for women and the workplace. *Corporate Alumni Networks: Leveraging Intangible Assets, XING Think Tank, Panel & Discussion White Paper,* 134 pages. (Cite at p. 70.) Retrieved from http://www.corporate-alumni.info/survey_corporate_alumni_networks_summary_english.pdf

Other Useful Resources:

Donnellon, A. & Langowitz, N. (2009). Leveraging women's networks for strategic value. *Strategy & Leadership, 37*(3), 29–36.

Durbin, S. (2011). Creating knowledge through networks: A gender perspective. *Gender, Work & Organization, 18*(1), 90–112.

Greve, A., & Salaff, J. W. (2003). Social networks and entrepreneurship. *Entrepreneurship: Theory & Practice, 28*(1), 1–22.

Hersby, M. D., Ryan, M. K., & Jolanda, J. (2009). Getting together to get ahead: The impact of social structure on women's networking. *British Journal of Management, 20,* 415–430.

Moore, D. P. (2000). *Careerpreneurs.* (See Networks, pp. 61–87.)

Pollet, T. V., Roberts, S. G. B., & Dunbar, R. I. M. (2011). Use of social network sites and instant messaging does not lead to increased offline social network size or to emotionally closer relationships with offline network members. *CyberPsychology, Behavior & Social Networking, 14*(4), 253–258. doi: 10.1089/cyber.2010.0161

Roomi, M. A. (2009). Impact of social capital development and use in the growth process of women-owned firms. *Journal of Enterprising Culture, 17*(4), 475–495.

Building Your Own Brand

Grossman, L. Co-founder of Women's Leadership Exchange (WLE). *SELLsation: How companies can capture today's hottest market—Women business owners and executives.* Retrieved from http://www.sellsationbook.com/about.php. Notes referenced from session, NAWBO Mid-Year Conference Feb. 9, 2002, Tempe, AZ.

Roffer. R. F. (2009). *The fearless fish out of water: How to succeed when you're the only one like you.* Hoboken, NJ: John Wiley & Sons, Inc., See also Roffer. (2000). *Make a name for yourself—8 steps every woman needs to create a personal brand strategy for success.* New York, NY: Random House, Inc. Also referenced: Moore, D. P. Notes from Roffer's keynote presentation, NAWBO Mid-Year Conference (Feb. 9, 2002), Tempe, AZ.

St. John, B. Author, International Speaker and Management Coach. Retrieved from http://www.bonniestjohn.com/AboutBonnie.aspx; and http://cms.careerexposure.com/upclose/upclose_detail.jsp?

siteid=2&DS=uupclos-bonnie. (Cite at p. 1 of profile.) Moore, D. P. Notes from keynote presentation, NAWBO Mid-Year Conference (Feb. 9, 2002), Tempe, AZ.

Profile: Suzy Spafford

Final approved profile developed from interviews with entrepreneur, website materials, and additional information furnished by the entrepreneur. See history and product line at Suzy's Zoo at www.suzyszoo.com/

Labels Can be Confusing

Market Watch. (2010). Salary.com's 10th annual mom salary survey. Retrieved from http://www.marketwatch.com/story/salarycoms-10th-annual-mom-salary-survey-reveals-stay-at-home-moms-would-earn-us117856-2010-05-05?reflink=MW_news_stmp

Sherman, A. (June 19, 2008). What's a Mompreneur ... really? [Blog post]. Retrieved from http://shine.yahoo.com/channel/life/whats-a-mom preneur-really-189355/

Women in Organizations

Credentials, Women and Wages

BLS (Dec., 2010). *Women in the labor force: A databook* (Report 1026, 2010 Edition). Washington, DC: U.S. Government Printing Office.

BLS, XPC (2010). *Median weekly earnings of full-time wage and salary workers by detailed occupation and sex.* Household Data Annual Averages, Table 39.

Catalyst (Aug., 2011). Quick Takes: Women MBAs: Women's enrollment and degrees around the world. Retrieved from http://www.catalyst.org/publication/250/women-mbas

Chronicle of Higher Education Almanac Issue 2010–2011 (Aug. 27, 2010). LVII, 1, 26–31.

U.S. Department of Commerce, Census Bureau, Current Population Survey. (2010). Annual social and economic supplement (Prepared March, 2010). Tables 3, 9.

U.S. Department of Education, National Center for Educational Statistics. Tables 278, 285, 288, 291, 292, 294. Retrieved from http://nces.ed.gov/programs/digest/2009menu_tables.asp

U.S. Department of Labor. Bureau of Labor Statistics (BLS). (Dec., 2010). Women in the labor force: A databook (Report 1026, 2010 Edition. BLS (2011). Household data annual averages median weekly earnings of full-time and salary workers by detailed occupation and sex, Table 39; BLS (2011). Employment status of the civilian non institutional population, 1940 to date; BLS (2010). Median earnings of full-time workers 16 years and older by detailed occupation and sex; BLS (2010). Current population survey, Employment status of the civilian non institutional population by age, sex and race. Retrieved from BLS web sites http://www.bls.gov/eps/wlf-databook2010.htm; http://www.bls.gov/cps/tables.htmhttp://www.bls.gov/data/;http://data.bls.gov/cgi-bin/surveymost?In

Her Power

Catalyst (2005). Women "take care," men "take charge." Retrieved from http://www.catalyst.org/publication/94/women-take-care-men-take-charge-stereotyping-of-us-business-leaders-exposed

Cook, S. H., & Mendleson, J. L. (1984). The power wielders: Men and/or women managers? *Industrial Management, 26*(2), 22–27.

Schrank, R. (May–June, 1994). What really happened to Raft No. 4 on an outward bound trip down the Rogue River, *Harvard Business Review*, 68–76. (See p. 76.)

SHE-POWER: The impact of women in society (2010). *Foreign Policy*, 181, 12–13. Retrieved from EBSCOhost. (Cited material from M. E. Iskenderian at p. 12.)

Spence, B. (Winter 2010/2011). National Association of Female Executives (NAFE) Women's Leadership Roundtable—Why P&L jobs matter, *NAFE Magazine*, 16–22.

Profile: Aliza Sherman

The draft profile corrected and approved by the entrepreneur incorporates as the opening quotation a paraphrase of her reply to a May 4, 2011 interview on the entrepreneurial blog Boss Start, "10 Q's With . . . Aliza Sherman" and incorporates other material from the interview. Retrieved from the entrepreneur's website http://alizasherman.wordpress.com/2011/05/10/my-interview-on-boss-start/and from http://www.bossstart.com/featured/10-qs-with-alizasherman/.

All Minds Needed at the Table

Catalyst (Jan., 2010). Women in male-dominated industries and occupations in US and Canada. Retrieved from http://www.catalyst.org/file/461/.pdf

Catalyst (2007). The double-bind dilemma for women in leadership: Damned if you do, doomed if you don't. Retrieved from http://www.catalyst.org/file/45/.pdf

Catalyst (June, 2004). Women and men in U.S. corporate leadership: Same workplace, different realities. Retrieved from http://www.catalyst.org/publication/145/women-and-men-in-us-corporate-leadership-same-workplace-different-realities.

Catalyst (Jan., 2004). The bottom line: connecting corporate performance and gender diversity. Retrieved from http://www.catalyst.org/file/44/.pdf

Catalyst (Jan., 2004). Catalyst study reveals financial performance is higher for companies with more women at the top. Retrieved from http://www.catalyst.org/press-release/2/catalyst

Catalyst, The National Foundation for Women Business Owners (NFWBO), with support of the Committee 200 Foundation. (1998). Women entrepreneurs: Why companies lose female talent and what they can do about it. NY, NY. Catalyst. 43 pp. (Cites @ pp. 13, 22.)

Moore, D. P., & Buttner, E. H. (1997). *Women entrepreneurs.* (Cite at p. 6.)

Prime, J., Moss-Racusin, C. A., & Foust-Cummings, H. (2009). Engaging men in gender initiatives: Stacking the deck for success. Retrieved from http://www.catalyst.org/publication/273

Virick, M., Goswami, R. M., & Anieszka C. (2004). Diversity climate: A reality check, *Academy of Management Proceedings,* H1–H6. doi: 10.5465/AMBPP.2004.13863029

Wright, P. M., McMahan, G. C., & Williams, A. (1994). Human resources and sustained competitive advantage: A resource-based perspective. *International Journal of Human Resource Management, 5*(2), 301–326. (Cite at p. 304.) While Drucker (1946) introduced the reader to different elements of staffing, appraising and compensation, a more contemporary conceptualization of human resource practices include planning, staffing, appraising, compensating, and training and development. Human resource practices are defined as "the organizational activities directed at managing the pool of human capital and ensuring that the capital is employed towards the fulfillment of organizational goals."

Organizational Career Tips

Managing Up

Bryant, A. (2010, Feb. 20). Xerox's new chief tries to redefine its culture. *New York Times* business section. Retrieved from http://www.nytimes.com

A Mentor Should be an Advocate

Babcock, L., & Laschever, S. (2003). *Women don't ask: Negotiation and the gender divide.* Princeton, NJ: Princeton University Press.

Ibarra, H., Carter, N. M., & Silva, C. (Sept., 2010). Why men still get more promotions than women. *Harvard Business Review, 88*(9), 80–126. Retrieved from EBSCO*host.* Catalyst Report (2008) by Ibarra, Carter, & Silva. Retrieved from http://www.scribd.com/doc/38433210/Why-Men-Still-Get-More-Promotions-Than-Women. (Cited items at second page in online copy.)

Climbing to the Top

Bullough, A., Kroeck, K. G, Newburry, W., Lowe, K. B., & Sumit, K. K. (2010). Women's participation in leadership around the globe: An institutional analysis, Academy of Management symposium paper. Montreal, Canada.

Catalyst Report (Dec. 13, 2010). *Women on boards* (pp. 1–16). Cited in Tarr-Whelan, L. & Zehner, J. (Aug. 27, 2010). Womenomics, a slow road. Retrieved from http://www.financialexpress.com/news/womenomics-a-slowroad/672634/0

Globewomen issue 80 (Dec. 17, 2010). Retrieved from http://globewomen.org

Konrad, A. M., Kramer, V., & Erkut, S. (2008). Critical mass: The impact of three or more women on corporate boards. *Organizational Dynamics, 37*(2), 145–164.

Nanivadekar, M. (2010). Overview: Women's leadership in the global context. In Karen O'Connor (Ed.), *Gender and women's leadership: A reference handbook* (pp. 293–303). Thousand Oaks, CA, London and Singapore: Sage Publications. (Using the political system to advance women.)

Profile: Kay Koplovitz

Final approved profile developed from entrepreneurs website materials at http://www.koplovitz.com/About.html; site postings and references at The Alliance of Women Entrepreneurs http://www.winwomen.org/mc/page.do?sitePageId=125137); Businessweek.com; and additional information furnished by the entrepreneur.

Building the Right Networks

In-depth References for Further Reading:

Donnellon. A., & Langowitz, N. (2009). Leveraging women's networks for strategic advantage. *Strategy and Leadership, 37*(3), 29–36. (Approaches to focusing networks to advance women up the pipeline.)

Durbin, S. (2011). Creating knowledge through networks: A gender perspective. *Gender, Work & Organization, 18*(1), 90–112.

Hersby, M., Ryan, M. K., & Jetten, J. (2009). Getting together to get ahead: The impact of social structure on women's networking. *British Journal of Management, 20*(4), 415–430. (A collective strategy to address barriers to promotion through network collective terms.)

Moore, D. P. (2000). *Careerpreneurs.* (See pp. 61–87.)

Moore, D. P., & Buttner, E. H. (1997). *Women entrepreneurs.* (See pp. 116–151.)

Redien-Collot, R. (2009). Female entrepreneurs' authority: Is the creative aspect of authority a masculine fiction in managerial and entrepreneurial paradigms? *Journal of Enterprising Culture, 17*(4), 419–441. (Examines role of authority and exercise thereof in developing social capital.)

4

ON THE ROAD TO ENTREPRENEURSHIP

Introduction

Career jolts, lack of satisfaction, inequitable wages, new value sets and changing organizational environments inspire many women to evaluate their options. A 1998 Catalyst and National Foundation for Women Business Owners study revealed that the major reasons women entrepreneurs had left jobs in corporate America to found a business were lack of flexibility (51 percent in private firms and 44 percent in non-private), glass ceiling issues (29 percent in private and 16 percent in non-private), unhappiness with the environment (28 percent private and 17 percent non-private) and lack of challenge (22 percent private and 19 percent non-private). The percentage of women leaving because they had an entrepreneurial idea diminished from 50 percent to 35 percent in the previous 20 years. In the same period, the percentage of women leaving because they were unfulfilled, downsized, or victims of a glass ceiling rose from 25 percent to 46 percent.

Thinking about going into business for yourself? There is no clear consensus on what it takes to prepare for the important transition from a corporate environment to becoming an entrepreneur beyond the toolkit of transferable and broad-based skills. But it is first important to determine whether you wish to be a small business owner or an entrepreneur. The two are not the same.

To be an entrepreneur is to be creative, one who focuses on a new product, something that has not been on the market, or the revival of an old product idea in a new market. Being entrepreneurial, in short, means spotting opportunities that others miss. (Think Levi Strauss, who viewed the California Gold Rush and saw gold in supplying prospectors with rugged jeans.) While success is never guaranteed, substantial amounts of case data suggest entrepreneurs have a better chance of survival if they get into a business field they know a good deal about.

A small business owner, by contrast, travels a more familiar path, often replicating the general patterns of other small businesses in the industry group while adding something unique. (Think specialty restaurant.)

Whichever it is, there are some important benchmarks in the transition process. First among these is a self-assessment. What skills do I have? What do I need? Where can I get resources and support? What is my detailed business plan? Can I afford the risk that the business may not be profitable for some time; i.e., do I have funds or an income to support myself until the business begins turning a profit, up to two years on average?

When the first glamor of owning a business wears off, can I keep momentum and the shine going? Am I willing to do a lot of everything, to sell myself and the business constantly, to be involved in nonstop networking and, if necessary, wait for success? How do I react to continuous pressure? Can I balance all the pressure with a healthy lifestyle?

It may not appear possible in the early days of your business, but later it will be important to remember that there is more to life than the business. There is no downtime when you own a business of your own. You will bring it home at night and pack it with you on vacations, if you are fortunate enough to have these. And you don't really have a choice. Without some downtime you will not be able to continue to be creative and entrepreneurial, the very reasons you opened the business in the first place.

Before going into a business you should determine your strengths and weaknesses and identify the resources you need and alternative courses of action. Once in business, you will most likely not have enough time or schedule flexibility to do this.

Deborah Szekely

Founder, The Golden Door; Co-Founder (with Edmond Szekely), Rancho La Puerta

The daughter of Jewish immigrants, Deborah Szekely (pronounced "Say-kay") was born in Brooklyn in 1922, and spent her early years in New York City, Tahiti and Mexico. From the time she was 4, her mother, who served as the Vice President of the New York Vegetarian Society, and her father, a garment manufacturer, raised their children on what would now be called a vegan diet that consisted entirely of fresh fruits, vegetables, and nuts. When the Great Depression hit in 1929, fresh produce not only became expensive, it was simply unavailable. Rather than compromise her principles, Deborah's mom announced one morning that the family would soon leave New York—relocating from a comfortable home in Brooklyn to a grass hut in Tahiti.

It was in Tahiti that Deborah first met the man who would ultimately chart the course of her entire adult life—the "Professor" as he was known, Edmond Szekely, a gifted philosopher and teacher who traveled the world advocating what he called "the simple life" and expounding principles of the ancient Essene tradition. Eventually, Deborah became Edmond's secretary and, a year later, his wife. In 1940, when war broke out in Europe, Edmond received a letter ordering him to return to Romania at once and report to duty as a soldier in the army of Hitler's ally. Of course, as a Jew, this was tantamount to a death sentence, and the two simply ignored the summons. Then another letter arrived that forever altered their destiny: a notice from the Department of U.S. Immigration and Naturalization advising Edmond that if he were found in the United States after June 1, 1940 he would be arrested as a deserter and deported to Romania. Thus, Deborah's husband became a refugee, a man without a country, and the two had no choice but to leave the United States.

The professor, 35, and Deborah, barely 18, packed all their worldly possessions into a silver-painted wooden box mounted on the rear of the 1928 Cadillac they'd received as a wedding present and crossed the border into Mexico, which welcomed them with open arms. And, although this was to be but a temporary home until the two could return to England, where Edmond would resume his position as the Director of the British Health and Education Center, the Szekelys lived and worked in Mexico as undocumented aliens for almost a decade when Edmond was granted Mexican citizenship.

Virtually penniless, with a nest egg that consisted of £1,000 and periodic contributions from Deborah's father, the two set about finding a suitable location to host the students who would soon arrive to attend Edmond's annual summer camp, which had been relocated by necessity from Lake Elsinore, California. Tecate—a remote Mexican village of just 400 inhabitants—was selected for its perfect year-round climate.

The couple settled into a small adobe shack which had only a dirt floor, holes for windows, kerosene lanterns and two buckets beside a sink that had no running water. As to the threshold that nearly every new bride dreams of one day being carried over, there was none. Yet Deborah's one-of-a-kind background had perfectly prepared her for the challenge: she'd already lived a third of her life without running water or electricity; she'd gardened, baked bread, kept chickens, milked a cow and survived the painstaking apprenticeship of learning how to cook on a wood stove. To survive, the couple planted an organic garden, bought goats and began putting their combined knowledge of healthy living to the test, experimenting with every health and diet theory, new or old, that found its way on to their radar: Tai Chi and yoga; massage and meditation; bean sprouts and acidophilus. Under Deborah's guidance, what began in 1940 as the Essene School of Life—charging $17.50 a week to pitch one's own tent in the middle of nowhere—is now the internationally acclaimed health and fitness spa Rancho La Puerta, a 3,000-acre spa and eco-resort with a staff of nearly 400, awarded World's Best *Overall* Destination Spa two years in a row by *Travel + Leisure* magazine's Reader's Poll.

In 1940, when Deborah and her husband started the Ranch, the only compass to guide them was their desire to remain true to the healing Essene traditions, which advocated living in harmony with nature; in other words, they flew in large part by the seat of their pants. In contrast, in 1958, when Deborah launched the Golden Door in Escondido, California, she knew exactly what she was doing. Smaller and more personalized than Rancho La Puerta, the Door was built to be a luxurious accommodation as pleasing as nature and her efforts could make it. Like Rancho La Puerta, it soon became world-renowned as a sanctuary and a healing retreat where guests learned to, as Deborah would say, "relax, renew and redirect their lives."

Known as a pioneer of the modern fitness movement and the forerunner of the global spa revolution, Deborah is responsible for launching significant innovations in the industry, many of which were years or even decades ahead of national trends. She is credited with the creation of the "spa schedule"—an agenda which includes yoga, Tai Chi, hiking, aerobics, dance, stretching, weight training, massage, and meditation—that lends rhythm and structure to the spa guest's daily routine and is still used by virtually every fitness spa from coast to coast and across the seas. An early pioneer of the mainstream acceptance of vegetarianism, she used the menus of her two Doors to demonstrate that artful, creative cuisine was achievable without meat and poultry, and—in the process—coined the term "spa cuisine." During these years, she was selected by Presidents Nixon, Ford, and Reagan to serve on their Councils of Physical Fitness and Sports.

When she turned 60, Deborah's perspective widened from seeking to improve the lives of individuals to aspiring to change the lives of millions. In 1982, she ran for Congress and, although she lost in the Primary, she discovered in the process that what Congress really needed was not another Congressperson but a system of management. Thus, she conceived and created "Setting

Course," the first management manual for Congressional staff in both the House and Senate. Now in its 12th edition, the manual serves today as a primary training tool for Congressional staff.

During the 17 years she remained in our nation's capital, Deborah served for six years as the President and CEO of the Inter-American Foundation, an independent agency of the United States Government which was tasked to work to improve the lives of the poor throughout Latin America and the Caribbean. Later, she founded Eureka Communities, dedicated to mentoring and financing the dreams of entrepreneurs. Of this accomplishment she is particularly proud, for it has become a model recognized and emulated worldwide for enhancing the leadership skills of non-profit CEOs. She founded the Combined Education Council of San Diego County, which raised over $25 million to support 21 cultural and art organizations, and has served for over 15 years on the boards of Claremont Graduate University, National Council de la Raza, the Ford Theatre in Washington, DC, and the Menninger Foundation.

Following precepts instilled in her by her mother, Deborah believes that to give is to receive, for one cannot give with a closed hand. In this spirit, since its earliest days, the Ranch has donated a goodly percentage of every penny earned to the service of others, particularly those involving children, and—more recently—the environment. Fundación La Puerta founded in 1978 and now under the direction of Deborah's daughter, Sarah Livia Brightwood, actively supports environmental, social and educational projects in the Tecate and border area. Their focus includes the preservation of endangered native plant and wildlife habitat within the region. When asked "How did you do it?" Deborah simply replies, "I see a need, share the dream, and persuade others to join in to make it happen."

Deborah has received two honorary Doctorates: one from the California School of Professional Psychology, the second from the Trustees of the California State University. A San Diegan most of her adult life, she enjoys the title "Mrs. San Diego," given to her by the San Diego Rotary Club.

The Rise of Modern Women Entrepreneurs

Intrapreneurs

Until recently, career planning was relatively straightforward. For both the organizational and professional careers, the most trodden path to success begins with general education or specific training that opens a place somewhere on the visible job ladders.

In the universe described above, the distinction between working for others and owning your own business—the entrepreneurial career—was clear. Until the 1990s, the gap between the two was viewed as a chasm, primarily because it was thought that the behavior of people in organizations was governed by one set of values, acquired as one developed the skill to accommodate and cope with a bureaucratic hierarchy, and the behavior of the self-employed by another, with the internal motivation to be independent and in control at the core. In this universe, the word "career" meant a sequential set of jobs or positions, held together by the subjective sense of where one was going, to be reinvented as the person or the environment changed.

In the modern era of technological change and evolving organization structures, the burden of career planning has shifted to the individual.

As Rosabeth Moss Kanter observed some time ago, any definition of entrepreneurship restricted to an independent business venture or with ownership of a small business is too narrow. Her definition is that entrepreneurship is any activity that produces something, adds value or capacity to an organization.

The change from an organization-based career to an individual-based career reflects the modern environment of rapidly changing technology and a global economy, a landscape where job security is measured in the skills you control and have at your command rather than a position you hold now. Continuous learning and recognizing and using one's talents to the fullest are required. In this job universe, people follow less predictable, discontinuous, and even zigzagging career paths, often extending beyond retirement. Today's savvy career woman must be a social entrepreneur, constantly managing her pre- and post-retirement strategies and everything in between. The most successful careers are molded and developed by people who have a personal vision of how all the parts might fit together and develop a path. They may become an entrepreneur by establishing a new firm. They may remain inside an organization and, by creating something new, become an intrapreneur.

Today's career dynamics fit neatly with organizational needs. Insightful companies evolve from entrepreneurial ideas, but after a while, as they grow, they develop policies and procedures that often become restrictive. The once-innovative business models conceived by their entrepreneurial founders may now be outdated. What the organization needs now are intrapreneurs to look at things differently, question, cultivate and develop new concepts. This is not easy. The process requires firms to provide intrapreneurs with the trust and freedom they need to reinvent, transform, and push the organization up to new heights. It also requires firms to allow people to challenge the status quo and accommodate those who don't fit neatly into the embedded organizational culture.

The paradox is this: Firms need intrapreneurs. But the creative implementers, the mavericks with intrapreneurial streaks, may exhibit traits that may not be compatible with the status quo and may be viewed as creating turbulence. In static firms, would-be intrapreneurs end up not asking for permission to implement their initiatives because experience has taught them that any creative ideas will be zapped before they can get off the drawing board.

Having trouble getting your organization to accept intrapreneurial initiatives? Here are some suggestions that build on points suggested by Carla King, who has written on the subject:

- Encourage others to take your ideas and make them their own. (Especially higher-ups.)
- Don't let your passion for an idea overshadow your ideas. (Sell it, don't insist.)

- Get involved in situations that put you in front of key partners. (They may be more interested in a solution than the policy manual.)

Jennet Robinson Alterman

Executive Director, Center for Women

Though Afghanistan and Swaziland are so apparently different on the surface, with Afghan women covered head to toe in a veil and in Swaziland a ceremony every year where bare-breasted young women dance for the king, even though they appear to be 180 degrees apart, there were a lot of commonalities, including women not being able to get an education, to vote, to own property, not being able to have control of their own bank accounts. I was starting to get this big message about the absence of women's rights from two different sections of the world.

When Jennet Robinson Alterman became the Executive Director of the Charleston, South Carolina Center for Women in 2001, the non-profit organization was small, loosely organized and without funds. Today, the Center has over 1,000 members and an operating budget in excess of $400,000. With a five-person full-time staff and more than 200 volunteers, the Center provides coaching, counseling, peer support groups and educational programs that address issues important to women. In an average year, the Center conducts well over 100 professional and personal development events that directly reach over 6,000 women in the Lowcountry of South Carolina. In September, 2011, The Center received a five year grant from the U.S. Small Business Administration to develop and build the South Carolina Women's Business Center.

While still a student at Mary Baldwin College, Jennet participated in a joint program with Davidson College, then single-sex, to see if women could handle the academic load. "We were the test drivers," she says. (Davidson became co-ed the following year.) After completing college in three years, Jennet took a job "answering the phones" at a local television station "and then, after rotating in several temp positions, I ended up on air and spent the next three years as a full-time TV news reporter" and anchor. "I left that job because I found out that my male colleagues who had the same job description and not nearly the same performance track record as mine were making almost twice what I was. And when I went in to my boss and asked for a raise, I was told that I would never get a raise because 'I would always be a secondary income' and he didn't have to pay me as much as the men because I would get married and be supported by my spouse. I was shocked, but instead of having a meltdown (it was 1975 after all) I went back to my office and wrote my letter of resignation."

Jennet had learned the important lesson of responsibility and giving back from her parents. When she returned from college, her father had told her she had two weeks to acquire a job. So that decision to leave her anchor job "took a lot of nerve on my part and real guts as I had no other job lurking in the wings but I couldn't stay under those conditions, so I did it and I have never regretted it." Charleston was the city where she grew up, with parents who had both given generously to the community through the gift of theater. She heard from her father, Emmet Robinson, on a daily basis how important it was to give back. She has taken it to heart.

Jennet spent the next two years as a health education consultant and Peace Corps volunteer in Afghanistan, learning Farsi so she could communicate with the mostly illiterate women in rural villages. Returning to the United States, she spent a year as the Producer/Director of the Health Communications network for the Medical University of South Carolina and then, at Lieutenant Governor Nancy Stephenson's request, served as Press Secretary for the first woman ever elected statewide. "I saw the equal rights amendment debated and soundly defeated," she remembers. "It was a stark lesson in the suppression of women's rights in South Carolina and it had a profound effect on me."

After spending three more years in state government, the last as the first Press Secretary to the State Budget and Control

Board, Jennet returned to the Peace Corps, serving as Country Director in Swaziland for two and a half years and the Interagency Coordinator on the Peace Corps Senior Executive Staff for the next six. In that capacity, she developed, implemented and managed international collaborative programs that involved major government agencies and over 20 private voluntary organizations in 40 countries, including community development and micro-enterprise development.

It is this rich background of international and national experience in management, financial administration, project development and implementation in non-profit organizations and governmental agencies that have provided the underpinnings of the intrapreneurial spirit which has led to her mission at the Center for Women. Creating and providing programs to empower, educate and motivate women is Jennet's primary and immediate goal. "The Center provides a model for awareness programs in our state and at the national level that is highly replicable," she says. "It is my ongoing challenge to continue to develop this model as an attitude change agent while at the same time empowering women to be successful in their own right."

Jennet's long-range objective is to create a sustainable process for addressing the indigenous needs of women across our geographic footprint. This objective engages technology for the transfer of information to enable women to make informed decisions about their options. Lofty objective? For Jennet, it is a return to her base, her roots, as she summarizes vivid reflections of service across her professional career. "As a Peace Corps Volunteer in Afghanistan I worked with women who had no rights at all. Returning to my hometown of Charleston, I was appalled to learn that women here still had significant barriers to achieving equality. I realize that it is through learning new approaches to age-old problems, engaging with those who are inspired that sustainable positive change can secure equality and equal pay for women, lowering the ladder to be sure the next one can climb up as well."

In 2005, the Center for Women was the winner of the Award for Excellence in Non-Profit Management by the South Carolina Association of Non-Profit Organizations. Oprah Winfrey honored the Center in 2006 for its outreach and diversity programs with an Oprah's Angel Network grant of $25,000. The Charleston Metro Chamber of Commerce recognized the Center with their prestigious 1773 Award in the Public/Non-profit category in 2009. The Family Circle Cup Tennis Tournament has selected the Center as their charity of choice for six straight years. Jennet's own awards include an Honorary Doctorate of Humane Letters from the College of Charleston (2008) and recognition as Entrepreneur of the Year by the United States Association of Small Business and Entrepreneurship (2011). Serving on numerous boards in the Lowcountry, Jennet has become a representative of the voice of women and their rights to be taken seriously for the intellect and perspectives they bring to the table.

Women Entrepreneurs and Corporate Exits

In a study of women owners who had formerly worked in corporate environments, I reported in my first book (co-authored) that more than one-fifth of the women started businesses of their own because they wanted a different organizational climate. "I think I just wanted a chance to work and to be the best I could be," said one. "What I found in the corporate environment was that they didn't encourage you to be the best you could be. They encouraged you to fit into a niche or slot to meet their expectations."

As ambitious and talented organizational women, these entrepreneurs had focused on superior performance, often bringing them into conflict with bureaucratic, political and stereotypical organizational standards. Many of the entrepreneurs interviewed pointed to former bosses who simply did not know what to do with competent, capable women seeking more responsibility and autonomy. There were also problems of hostile or uncaring organizational environments or a bad manager taking over. As Robert Sutton says in "How to be a Good

Boss in a Bad Economy," those in authority often become less mindful of the feelings or needs of their employees. A California entrepreneur remembered that after a management change "The new leader cut all the programs and killed all the things he had not created. The old power structure was left powerless or replaced."

Research suggests that women are more sensitive to environments where success is based more on *who* employees know than on *what* they know. The most deadly organizational combinations are produced by managers who hoard power, establish a suppressive environment, follow rigid rules (unless he or she changes them) and hand out rewards on the basis of favoritism, creating the impression those who don't fit the mold are not qualified.

Time and again, successful women entrepreneurs who exited bad environments voiced these causes. Said one, "It was politics pure and simple. People who did not do a good job were rewarded in spite of their poor performance. People who did not fit the manager's prescription were left out." "What I was best at doing," says a Philadelphia businesswoman, "bringing an organized and thoughtful sense of inquiry into a corporate situation, was not very highly prized the higher I got in the management ranks." A woman, who later started her own high-tech company, observed of her former corporate environment, "A lack of vision—the mundane approach to operations ... No one took accountability for his or her work. Responsibility was passed onto someone else."

Often women found themselves in the uncomfortable situation of being female pioneers in male-created environments still dominated by men and the culture which that entailed. These organizational settings resulted in "frustration and discontent with corporate life and opportunities for advancement." The continuing difficulties of always being an outsider are such a common phenomenon that researchers often describe women in these environments as "Tokens." One entrepreneur, who formerly had been a top manager, found the token experience educational. After observing the interactions of the senior executives in her company, she changed her mind about the attraction of a top management position: "Being in there and feeling like what it felt like to be there and seeing how they operated didn't make me want to be there." For others, adjusting to the culture exacted too high a price. "I could have stayed if I had swallowed my self-respect and swallowed my self-esteem, but I wasn't willing to do that," explained a Chicago entrepreneur. Such sentiments are typical of women who leave an organization to start their own businesses.

Other entrepreneurs remembered hostile environments but good bosses and the difference they made. A Dallas businesswoman recalled, "We moved into a new building. The men in every office had a big desk. The assistants—some male, some female—had a smaller desk. My mentor took one look at our new office and he shoved the small desk out and down the hall. He then went down the hall and got me a big desk. And all hell broke loose. Men at my mentor's level in the organization just couldn't stand the symbolism of my having a desk the same size as theirs. With clients, I had a professional position rather than a subservient role. That's one of the things that helped me when I later became an entrepreneur. I had been given self-confidence. It was a wonderful example of mentorship. But I also saw the kind of organizational symbolism that is intended to keep women in their place."

Some women remembered much better organizational environments. A Philadelphia entrepreneur formerly in sales management for a large pharmaceutical company recalls, "I got a lot of support from a lot of great guys ... It really was very rewarding." A Chicago entrepreneur remembers that "The company wanted me to stay because they are a big corporation and they wanted female managers. My boss kept saying that in five years he would probably be working for me because they are really putting a push on to increase the female roles in the corporation. They offered me just about anything I wanted, international assignments, anywhere I wanted to go. I liked the work, which is why I decided to start my own business." Sometimes a positive experience developed out of what looked at first like a bad start. A Charleston entrepreneur remembers, "When I first went to work, the first thing my boss said to me was, 'You can be replaced.' I was horrified; I was young, and innocent. Then he turned out to be a wonderful mentor, a wonderful teacher. He had just expected that there was no way I could produce."

Bad bosses or good, the management lessons these entrepreneurs learned have stayed with them. "Because of my experience in the corporate environment I know the political things to do to survive, but I will not run my business that way," says a California entrepreneur. "I realize that people in the trenches get it done." Entrepreneurs with bad experiences uniformly vowed not to repeat the pattern. "I had been in an environment that was very hierarchical, very male oriented, not much personal feedback, not much opportunity for females to advance," says a Dallas entrepreneur. "I was determined that was not going to happen in any business I created."

Working for others is a good way to start a business career because it is a learning experience. But as these entrepreneurs testify, the education may not always be a happy experience.

Intentional Entrepreneurs and Corporate Climbers

In my books *Women Entrepreneurs* (co-authored) and *Careerpreneurs*, I have stated that two main types of female entrepreneurs emerge from corporate backgrounds. One is the intentional entrepreneur. Members of this group always knew they would start their own business. For them, working for someone else was an important and necessary educational stepping-stone. The second group, the corporate climbers, entered companies with goals of reaching the top, or at least getting up high. But somewhere along the line, for a variety of reasons ranging from systematic discrimination to the lack of opportunity to advance to gaining the expertise that made them ready for other opportunities, they launched businesses of their own.

More recent studies say that from the beginning the two groups approach their organizational life differently. In particular, corporate climbers tend to consider their managerial experience more important than do the intentional entrepreneurs. Reflecting on her corporate life, Janet McCann, founder of Janet McCann Associates Inc., an interior design firm in Wilmette, Illinois, said, "If I had planned on having my own business, I would have watched the financial, the marketing, but I didn't. I just liked what I was doing. I was learning my particular skill and I had no thoughts about the rest of it." Today one of Chicago's most respected interior designers and a longtime leader in the field, she is the recipient of numerous awards and serves as a guest teacher and lecturer at the Art Institute of Chicago, the Harrington Institute of Interior Design, the University of Illinois, Northern Illinois University, and The Merchandise Mart. Her observation on founding a business? "I think that tremendous drive is probably the universal characteristic among business founders. It wasn't being the entrepreneur. It wasn't running the business. It was the drive for doing what you wanted to do under your own terms. And that burning desire puts you in a situation where you can't fail."

Corporate climbers may be less likely to be aware that one of the key advantages of entrepreneurial firms competing with much larger rivals is the ability to identify and serve a specific market niche in a superior fashion. One corporate climber, who had risen successfully in her organization over a 15-year period, discovered this when opportunity knocked. She had done a video feature on Arabian horses and later had been asked to do a very large horse show in Arizona. "The Arabian horse owner said, 'Why don't you put yourself on an airplane and come out here and be our guest for a week.'" Said L. Elaine Green, later, "That airplane ride was probably the most important ride in my life. I thought, this is what I want to do—to be in video arts."

By contrast, during their organizational tenure, the intentional entrepreneurs tended to value marketing and technical training more highly than people skills. Said one, "I own my own business. I have always wanted to do this since being a senior in high school. I have really never wavered. I really like what I do. I want to make buildings. It fascinates me endlessly."

Once in business for themselves, however, whether having traveled the intentional or corporate climber route, and suddenly confronted with the people-related problems of sales and management, many entrepreneurs had to learn new skills quickly. As the CEO of a Dallas-based market, consulting and seminar firm pointed out, "You can build a better mousetrap, but if you don't have a way to let people know about it, you're going to starve to death." Said a Midwestern entrepreneur, "I have worked with a lot of start-ups. When you start talking about selling, they say, 'What do you mean about selling? All I want to do is do the work.' If you don't want to sell yourself, then go work for somebody."

For aspiring entrepreneurs, the lessons are to take advantage of the invaluable experience offered in an organizational setting, but don't burrow in too narrowly, too early. Get a balanced organizational education that includes product, market, finance, people skills, sales and management. While entrepreneurial success is heavily correlated with extensive managerial and start-up experience, it is the ability to react quickly to environmental change and to identify new opportunities in a competitive market that becomes crucial.

There are some lessons here for corporate climbers, too. Avoid a career path of management-only experiences that can be a mile wide and an inch deep. Even if you are not currently interested in going into business for yourself, remember that no one knows what the future holds. Recent research shows that there are no significant differences between the two groups in career or personal goals or later success as entrepreneurs.

Women Entrepreneurs and Success

The Incubator Effect

The correlation between organizational experiences and the types of businesses entrepreneurs create is fairly well established.

In our cross-country study, my co-author and I discovered that 71 percent of the entrepreneurs we surveyed had previously worked in a field very similar to their current business. Nearly 90 percent said they used the information and experience they had gained from their former organization. This finding is also supported by more recent research.

Leveraging knowledge, skills, relationships and networks provides a sound approach for women ex-corporate managers when starting and growing new ventures. One researcher refers to this as "embedded career capital." Entrepreneurs with prior corporate experience benefit because the organization, in effect, functioned as a laboratory where it was possible to learn the ins and outs of a field of business, acquire skills to deal successfully with problems and people, gain managerial savvy, and acquire confidence in their abilities—a real-world education.

Corporate experience confers other advantages too, such as extensive and expensive training.

Taking advantage of every educational and training opportunity broadens horizons and addresses niches. Deborah L. Hueppeler, a Wharton School M.B.A., now an independent business owner in Dallas, mapped out a career on Wall Street with an ultimate goal of landing in the Sunbelt. "Here I started with financial services to gain the financial background and familiarity with a lot of different companies and industries. This would provide an important building block for the company I later created."

One advantage of using the organizational experience as a springboard is the security it provides while preparing for a new venture launch. "I began by developing a clientele and working insane hours for about three years prior to striking out on my own as an architect," said Julie Coulter, AIA, LEED AP, who is currently Principal of Coulter Building Consultants, LLC, "so when I left, I had a client base." For another entrepreneur, the new business allowed incubator skills to be used in a setting free from organizational headaches. "In a nutshell," she said, "we design licensed apparel. Requests from licensers allowed us the opportunity to spin ourselves off from the company. It also got us out of the loop of the manufacturing and its frustrations and so forth." Still another entrepreneur started her business while fully employed. "I received telephone calls from attorneys in the state who I had worked with. They said, you know, could you help us out? This led me to starting a business."

A number of women business owners had not thought of entrepreneurship initially, but after accumulating knowledge and expertise through an array of organizational experiences they saw opportunity. Says Elizabeth Morris, CEO/Chief Economist of Insight Research Corporation in Dallas, a firm that has completed over 7,000 economic analyses for a wide range of public and private sector clients, "I think the business kind of came and got me. It developed out of the previous work I had done. I spent seven years in city management. We were responsible to everyone. Everything we said, everything we did was screened through different filters to be sure it conveyed accurate information. I had moved from that position into real estate brokerage where I saw a totally different business pace but very little research to accompany it. So on one side we had extraordinary levels of research and on the other side we had none. I moved to a corporation that developed office buildings, warehouses, and apartment complexes. I was in on the ground floor. Inside three years I had an opportunity to build an office building, a shopping center and a 120 unit condominium complex virtually unsupervised because the company was growing so fast. I got a real quick education as a developer. Because I did an extraordinary amount of research on my projects, people kept asking me if I would help with theirs."

In case after case, women entrepreneurs reported that their organizational experience allowed them to accumulate a wealth of knowledge of irreplaceable value. Findings support a generalization that a major role of the incubator is its importance in gaining survival skills, learning to cope with setbacks, and dealing with special challenges. After corporate life, said one entrepreneur, "I had the experience and the confidence to be able to go out and really market myself. I had a lot to sell and I had a very strong network." Reported another, "The biggest thing I gained was credibility. I can go into an important client and say I have done this for an industry leader. Then they listen." A Cincinnati entrepreneur flatly says that she gained the self-confidence she needed from her organizational incubator. "I felt that the company had been a wonderful training ground; I started seeing that I wasn't helpless."

Other entrepreneurs took a different path. Michele Jacob today owns Michaul's Live Cajun Music Restaurant, on St. Charles, a nationally recognized restaurant and catering service. Disney World schedules parties in her establishment, and there are long lines to get on her list for Sugar Bowl parties. She has been honored as both a New Orleans and a State of Louisiana Entrepreneur of the Year. She came to entrepreneurship via a route of training and experience on the job without the advantages offered by a college degree. "I thought it would be wonderful to go to college," she says. "When I did go, I was older. I sat there in the classroom and all I could think about was how I needed to be out working and making money. I asked the professor if I could get what she was saying on my own. She said, 'Yes, you have worked all your life. You can take the book and learn what I am teaching in this class.' It was such a relief. It would have been a luxury to sit in the class and learn, but I decided that I would take the book and learn on my own. So I brought the book back to the restaurant. Every day I got my employees together and we had a lesson from the book. We all learned the material together. All of my new employees have college degrees, especially in sales and management." Michele's story lies at the heart of preparing for entrepreneurship with all the tools one can muster. Her best wisdom is to get the most out of your education and to realize that you are going to have to work extremely hard if you want to succeed. Know the financial and managerial aspects of the business before you start, she recommends; "Luck is nothing more than labor under controlled knowledge."

The education and experience to be gained from an organizational experience are portable commodities, useful to corporate advancement, entrepreneurship, or a transition to public service. The organizational experience at someone else's expense becomes a great training ground, an incubator, for opening the business of one's dreams. The roads to the dream are many. For those currently in organizations, it is important to recognize the company attributes that enable you to accomplish career objectives, whether it is in owning your own business or advancing in the corporation.

Carol E. Farren

Founder and President, Facility Management Worldwide, Ltd.

I had a teaching assignment in Dubai and another one in Kuwait. When I got to the Kuwait hotel they said you have to go up to another floor to register. What a wonderful surprise! They put me up in the Executive Suite and showered me with baskets of fruit and flowers—I was treated like a queen! That was a fantastic acknowledgement of my worth.

Carol Farren was a dean's list and honors student in Interior Design at Cornell University, spent a year at Parsons School of Design, worked in architectural design, entered corporate life as chief designer combined with purchasing agent for an expanding entertainment conglomerate, jumped to independent design work in her own business after a career block, performed freelance work for her former employer while studying for her M.B.A. at the New York University Stern School of Business, graduating in the top 10 percent, and was then recruited back to corporate life. She spent nine years at Time Warner, where, as Director of Facilities with a $3 million operating budget and a $12.5 million capital projects budget, she managed operations and renovation projects for the one-half-million square foot headquarters and another half-million square feet of office space in the greater New York area. She also managed operations for the Franklin Mint, a five-building manufacturing subsidiary set on 25 acres, built an earth station and head end in Brooklyn for Time Warner Cable, and was responsible for the design work for the 975,000 square foot expansion of Time Warner Cable across the United States.

Observing that smaller companies could not afford their own planning and facilities department but badly needed the services when they became involved in a major construction, renovation, or relocation project, she started Facility Management World Wide, Ltd. (FMWW) to fill the niche. Her firm provides recommendations and customized solutions to streamline project management, maximize the value of physical assets while minimizing the costs, increase employee productivity and acceptance of change, and promote green building design and management.

Her entrepreneurial journey had its own learning curve as she reached out to network across gender lines in a male dominated field. She quickly learned about embedded barriers to women. "I was in the Building Owners and Managers Association for a number of years," she recalls, "but irrespective of my contributions to the organization I found there were no reciprocal business benefits."

With more than 40 years of experience in interior project management, Carol has directed a number of high-profile design and relocation projects. She most recently managed a New York City governmental agency relocation of 3,800 people. A Certified Facility Manager (CFM), she is past President of the Greater New York Chapter and past President of the Consultants' Council of the International Facility Management Association (IFMA), and an IFMA Fellow.

Carol's book *Planning and Managing Interior Projects,* currently in its second edition, is a comprehensive text that addresses the ins and outs of downsizing, company mergers, information technology and how they affect workspace design, and provides valuable insider information on how private and public sector organizations can save money. She is on the Advisory Committee for Pratt Institute's Master's Degree Program in Facility Management and initially formed an IFMA committee to develop the curriculum. Her managerial style is not complex. "I tell people what I need them to do but not how to do it—unless they ask," she says. "When I put people on staff I like to hire experienced people who already know how to perform project and operations management. They may not work exactly the way I do, but as long as the end result is good and the job gets done on time and in budget and the clients are happy, that is what is really important."

Carol got into management consulting when Sterling Drug asked her to figure out why the carpet was already getting stained and the reception glass doors had fingerprints but the 450,000 square foot building renovation was only half complete. Also, the architect wanted the mail room in the basement and the Office Services Manager said it couldn't be there, but no one could make a good case for where it really should be. She joined the Institute of Management Consultants (IMC) and became a CMC (Certified Management Consultant). She was asked to be on a panel for the US Navy to determine why 67 percent of Navy facilities were in fair to poor condition and to recommend how to fix the problem. The final report, delivered to the Secretary of the Navy, was accepted.

She was asked to jump in as Senior Project Manager for MortgageIT, a subsidiary of Deutsche Bank, for a three-month full-time assignment until the facility manager recovered from a stroke, and ended up there for almost three years. This brought up a new challenge—how to restart FMWW after being out of the network and doing no marketing for three years? The dilemma ended when she was asked to help a construction management firm get into facility management in the Middle East, which is an ongoing effort.

Facility management, including many of its subsets such as architecture, engineering, construction management, and operations and maintenance, is still frequently thought of as a male profession. How does a woman compete and get ahead of her male competition, especially in New York City, which is one of the toughest places to succeed in the world? She must develop exceptional skills, earn superior credentials, provide excellent results, be reliable, keep her word, and be honest and ethical in a field that is often marred by corruption and kickbacks. Says Carol, "She must be steadfast, persistent, optimistic, and never give up."

Building Customer Loyalty—Minding the Gap

All business owners, executive officers and career oriented managers recognize that the most important survival tool is building and maintaining customer loyalty. It is the lifeblood of the business because, irrespective of competitor advertising, promotions and price cuts, repeat customers keep the business in the black. Findings from Weinstein's study of customer retention suggest there are seven important cornerstones in building a positive customer and employee working base:

- It costs five times as much to win a new customer as retain one.
- On average, US corporations lose half of their customers in five years.
- A 5 percent improvement in customer loyalty leads to over 25 percent in profit improvements.
- Satisfied customers help build the business through positive referrals.
- Loyal customers are less price sensitive, more understanding if prices must rise and easier to interest in a new product or service.
- Treat customers in a professional, friendly and patient manner. If costs are involved, balance between potential gain and loss.
- Build a climate of trust with your employees. You need the candid and informative feedback they can give.

Customers make their assessments of services and products based on performances which, according to Berry, Wall, and Carbone, are based on numerous clues. These are embedded in technical performance (functional clues), the tangibles associated with service (mechanic clues) and the behavior and appearance of service providers (humanic clues). According to marketing experts, it becomes the responsibility of management to consistently design and orchestrate the clues in job descriptions. In practical terms, as recent research in the *Academy of Management Journal* indicates, it becomes a matter of building trust with both customers and employees. This is not always easy to do. Here are some guidelines for creating a wider and more loyal customer base while retaining your present clientele through trust and consistency:

Create, deliver and communicate your inspirational trust story. Answer the question most people never ask directly: Why should I trust you? Be specific. Include the information in your brochures and on your website. Be results oriented. Above all, avoid promising what you may not be able to deliver.

Remember that a business deals with individuals. Avoid turning people off with the electronic barriers of robot messages, endless menus and deadly wait times punctuated by the recorded voice that keeps saying "your business is important to us" while communicating the message that as a person you aren't.

Be reliable. Recognize that your word is all you have. Avoid making promises you can't or don't intend to keep. Once lost, trust is almost impossible to regain.

Learn to really listen to your customers and clients. It is about them, not you. If you are all caught up in your personal story and problems or go on and on with an unwanted sales pitch, they may appear to listen and even be compassionate. But you have given your customer a window into your business they don't need and information that at best adds little or no value to your product or service and at most turns people away.

Be especially careful about your passions, whatever they are. Don't get caught up in this age of us-or-them politics, insult humor, me-first web posting or useless twitter. Why take the chance of offending the customer you really don't know that well with a rant about your political beliefs? The offended customer will not likely recommend your business to others even though you provide valuable services or products. That customer may also think seriously about whether they wish to continue doing business with you. Whatever your product or service, it is unlikely you have a total corner on the market. Why take the risk?

Carefully train yourself and all who work for you to be cognizant of all of these guidelines. There are few business owners who can afford to drive customers away—employees become the representative voice of the entrepreneur/owner.

Listen to your employees. The things they tell you may be vital to your business.

Value your employees. Customer rudeness is on the rise. There is a direct relationship between mistreatment of employees by customers, negative employee treatment of customers and employee job satisfaction. As Fred Bendaña, Executive Director of Client Services, Maritz Loyalty and Motivation, says, "Employee loyalty should be thought of as a parallel counterpart to consumer loyalty." "Apply the same successful strategies to attracting, retaining, and motivating talented employees as to building brand and segmentation strategies."

Figure out in advance how to handle problems. Can the first person the customer speaks to put the problem to rest? The customer is looking for a solution, not the frontline employee who can only say, "I don't know," or "So-and-so will be back at ..." or, even worse, the impersonal statement that "Company policy/the computer/the system won't let us do that." Complaints need to be dealt with professionally. Most of the time there is a solid reason someone is unhappy, and the issue may reveal something the business needs to change. Always remember the delicate balance between winning the argument and retaining the customer.

Understand the downside of blogs and such social network websites as Twitter, Facebook, LinkedIn, and other types of shortcut communication methods and social media. Every single thing you post is going to be viewed. If you are charming in person with a customer and something else online, your good work is undone. The starting point: No one should send a message or make a posting without first writing it out, thinking it through from the perspective of the customer and completing a thorough audit and edit. Once out there, the message is your permanent representative.

As the London tube (subway) signs say, “Mind the gap.” In the beginning, you may have paid a lot of attention to what your individual customers needed. Are you now addressing them as a faceless group or are you continuing to cultivate these important relationships?

Patterns and the Future in a Changing World

Development of Women Entrepreneurs Globally

Worldwide, one woman in 11 is an entrepreneur and women-owned firms comprise more than one-third of all entrepreneurial activity. Their numbers are growing. It is part of the broad pattern of change that includes among other things the restructuring of organizational environments in the wake of competitive globalization and the increasing numbers of potential (I see an opportunity), emergent (we just started this business), neophyte (been going for a year now) and nascent (just at the point where we can start growing) women-owned businesses.

Who these female entrepreneurs are depends on the local culture, educational opportunities and social perceptions of what is appropriate for women. The reasons why they start businesses are diverse, ranging from the absence of other choices in some low- and middle-income countries, reported by half of the entrepreneurs, perhaps because of reduced access to labor markets and lower levels of education, to the series of factors that have been observed in middle- and high-income nations where women have a higher level of education, greater access to resources and are raised with a strong sense of independence and a high degree of self-confidence.

Researchers also note in the 2006 and 2007 reports of the *Global Entrepreneurship Monitor* (GEM) that, while the increase in the numbers of entrepreneurial women varies across nations, growth is higher in middle-income than in high-income countries. The difference can be attributed to the fact that in areas of the world where educational levels are lower, women's entrepreneurial activity can be driven by necessity. In the high-income countries, by contrast, opportunity and balance are major motivational forces.

Differences among opportunities for women vary from country to country for a variety of reasons: socialization ("You can be anything you want" versus "Women don't do that"), education ("Equal opportunity for all" versus "Girls do not get a formal education"), educational fields and attainment (Are the numbers of women who major in science, technology, engineering, math and business large or small?), push and pull economic factors and traditional attitudes. The last is the most important. No matter how individually talented, capable and motivated an individual woman is, the choices she makes are inevitably set within circumstances that range from restrictive to supportive. Her success is dependent on whether that environment enabled her to gain the right educational and business experience and the ability to take advantage of the opportunity. Not surprisingly, as noted in the GEM 2007 Report, the highest ratios of women entrepreneurs are found in Western Europe, in Belgium and Switzerland, and in the United States.

Changes have been coming fast and more of them are on the way. Over the next decade, two movements will combine to transform the global economic landscape even more. The first is that small businesses will be formed and run by a new and more diverse group of entrepreneurs. The second is that the largest of these entrepreneurial groups will consist of women: some influenced by the desire to escape the limitations of the glass and steel ceilings; others, immigrant entrepreneurs, migrating to societies that offer them the freedom they need.

Women Entrepreneurs and the Innovation Driven Economies

Two current developments are interacting worldwide simultaneously. One is characterized in the special task force on women in the economy published in the *Wall Street Journal* (April, 2011), which reports that half of the global growth in women entrepreneurs comes from the developing world. The second is highlighted in the 2006 and 2007 reports of the Global Economic Monitor (GEM) which lists the 24 high-income, innovation-driven economies.

Here is how they fit together. Innovation-driven economies have the advantages of a base of ongoing research and development, a knowledge intensity and an expanding service sector that provides a great potential for innovative entrepreneurial opportunity. This does not mean that the effects on women and men are equal. The proportion of women entrepreneurs within the GEM group is not high overall. Socialization, fields of educational attainment and push and pull economic factors all play a role. The highest ratios of female entrepreneurial participation are in Belgium and Switzerland, with ratios of around 80 women to 100 men, and in the United States with a ratio of 85 to 100.

The current U.S. ratio is heavily influenced by the bleak corporate picture. As a result, the two most distinct groups of women entrepreneurs consist of the careerpreneurs and the mompreneurs. Careerpreneurs are the women with corporate experience and ambition, predominantly mid-career, who are most likely to succeed in starting and running a business. The mompreneur group is made up of the more than 72 percent of mothers participating in the U.S. workforce for whom technological innovations have made possible the part-time, private business ownership that gives them the flexibility they need to balance work and family.

Norway is representative of the change underway in Europe. Norwegian women constitute three out of five students in the universities, but the majority of them major in education and social sciences and enter the public rather than the private sector, many on a part-time basis. Consequently, Norwegian women are an entrepreneurial minority. In 2007, only 4 percent of the women versus 9 percent of men were involved in early stage entrepreneurial activities. Women represented fewer than one-third of the new business start-ups of sole enterprises and constituted only one-sixth of entrepreneurs in private limited companies. Only 26 percent of owners of sole enterprises and 27 percent of owners of private limited companies were women. As a result of the low numbers, the Norwegian government formulated an action plan with the objective that women would represent at least 40 percent of all entrepreneurs by 2013. The initiatives put in place include enhanced rights to maternity leave, parents' relief for self-employed persons, increased grants to micro credit-projects and support for a research program to improve the understanding of entrepreneurship among women.

In 2009, the European Commission helped establish the European Network of Female Entrepreneurship Ambassadors. Originally launched in Stockholm, the network is designed to inspire and assist women to set up their own businesses. Some 150 ambassadors of female entrepreneurship, from 10 European countries selected via the Commission's call, met to network and attend the inaugural ceremony. Following a second call for entrepreneurial ambassadors, 12 new countries joined the network, bringing the number of ambassadors to 250. This was followed by a networking event on December 8, 2010, co-organized by the Commission and the Belgian Presidency of the European Council.

The European formation of networks to aid the development of opportunities for women owners followed a pattern that had emerged much earlier in the United States. As more women became business owners, private organizations arose to facilitate their common aims. Among the most influential is the National

Association of Women Business Owners (NAWBO), currently comprising more than 80 chapters and 9,000 dues-paying members and representing every industry, and through affiliations in 33 countries around the world. NAWBO concentrates on building social capital with the objective of creating and developing strategic alliances, coalitions, and networks to positively affect the business landscape for women owners. In 1980, NAWBO began seed funding for the Committee 200, today one of the most powerful groups of women entrepreneurs in the nation. In 1987, NAWBO was influential in opening up local Rotary Clubs with its informal business networks to women's memberships. Under the auspices of NAWBO, the National Foundation for Women Business Owners (renamed the Center for Women's Business Research in 2001) became active as a research organization. Continuing to focus on research, in 1998, the NFWBO began connecting women owners to public policymakers to improve business opportunities. The same year, the Association of Women's Business Centers, created as a national non-profit organization to represent women business owners through a network of women's business centers, became instrumental in establishing education, training, mentoring, business development, and financing opportunities. The Women's Business Enterprise National Council, a coalition created in 1997 in partnership with women's business organizations, today provides access to a national standard of certification and facilitates the flow of information.

Julie R. Weeks

Founder, President and CEO, Womenable

Bricks do not a building make: there are a growing number of initiatives, programs, and organizations springing up around the world aimed at economically empowering women, but they are still scattered and not yet assembled into a structure that is both sturdy and inclusive. Until that happens, the gaps we see in entrepreneurship rates between women and men and in the relative size and growth of women- and men-owned firms will continue.

Perhaps no one has done as much to provide factual information about women-owned businesses over the past two decades as Julie Weeks, first as the Managing Director and Director of Research at the non-profit Center for Women's Business Research (1993–2002), then as the Executive Director of the National Women's Business Council, the federally funded bipartisan policy advisory body created to serve as an independent voice of women's entrepreneurship (2002–2005) and most recently as the President and Chief Executive Officer of her for profit firm Womenable (2005–present). She gives the reason why these data are important in the first sentence of her recently completed comprehensive study, *The American Express OPEN State of Women-Owned Businesses Report, A Summary of Important Trends, 1997–2011:* "It is frequently stated that one cannot manage what one cannot measure."

Perhaps more important to those concerned with the empowerment of women entrepreneurs, without the measurements Julie has made and continues to produce, no one could begin fact-based discussions of important issues. Some recent facts from her 2009 Womenabler blogpost "The State of Women's Enterprise: Talking Bout a Revolution":

- Women continue to start businesses at twice the national average rate in the US and account for between one-quarter and one-third of all formal sector enterprises worldwide.
- Loan repayment rates from women are higher than those from men; moreover, the more money lent to women, the higher the rate of return.
- International donor agencies are finding that the amount of investment in business development assistance given to women correlates directly with healthier families and communities.
- The World Bank has found a strong statistical evidence that the amount of corruption in government drops in direct proportion to the increase of women in government; more women, less corruption in the country.

"But facts, as integral as they are to facilitating progress in women's enterprise development, can't stand alone," according to Weeks. "They can be thought of as the foundation of a 'three-legged stool' for the women's enterprise movement—with the legs being comprised of women-focused public policy actions and actors, intermediary and service delivery organizations (such as educators, training programs, and business associations), and women business owners themselves, playing a visible and vocal role."

Julie has played a role in each of these sectors. She holds a Bachelor of Arts in Political Science and a Master's in Political Science with a concentration in research methodology, both from the University of Michigan, and has done additional course work at the Inter-University Consortium on Political and Social Research. Before helping to grow the Center for Women's Business Research, she had more than a decade of market opinion research experience in politics and public policy, and served at the U.S. Small Business Administration as Deputy Chief Council for Statistics and Research (1990–1993). Thus, she's been directly involved in initiatives for the development of women's enterprise both in government and the private sector—not only in the US but internationally as well. Currently, she serves on the board of the Global Banking Alliance for Women, chairs the Board of the Association of Women's Business Centers and is on the editorial advisory boards of *Enterprising Women* magazine and the *International Journal of Gender and Entrepreneurship.*

Julie established Womenable in 2005 as a research, program and policy development consultancy whose mission is to work with a variety of organizations to enable women's entrepreneurship worldwide. What do we need to do next? "Build an escalator," says Julie. "While the interest in supporting women's enterprise development is growing, it is still largely concentrated on either end of the business spectrum—economically empowering the very poor or helping businesses to get started, or at nurturing fast-growth or 'high potential' businesses—leaving out the vast majority of women-owned firms, the so-called 'missing middle.'

That's going to be the 'sweet spot' for women's enterprise development for the next decade or more. In addition, there needs to be much more connectivity across the world—sharing good practices, knowledge, and networks."

Trends in Women's Entrepreneurship

Two major forces have influenced the rise of women entrepreneurs. The first was an era of social transformation (1960–1979) when women, minorities, immigrants and the disabled entered into the mainstream. The second was the era of technological disruption (1980–2000) driven by the introduction of personal computers, the internet and increasingly sophisticated software that reduced the costs of starting and running a business.

According to Intuit predictions, the next decade will see these two movements combine to transform the economic landscape and begin an era of economic decentralization. By 2017, small businesses will be formed and run by a new and more diverse group of entrepreneurs, as further supported by the international research of Wood, Davidson, and Fielden. The largest numbers will consist of women exiting corporate life and immigrant entrepreneurs. Women-owned businesses in the US will create one-third of the 15.3 million new jobs anticipated by the Bureau of Labor Statistics by 2018, according to research cited from the Guardian Life Small Business Research Institute survey.

The rapid growth in women entrepreneurs who found businesses with different goals may be another shaping force. As noted by Sharon Hadary, in the past, men tended to start businesses to be the boss and aimed to grow them as big as possible. Women started businesses to be personally challenged and to integrate work and family, and they wanted them to stay at a size where they personally could oversee all aspects of the business.

There are at least three distinct groups of women entrepreneurs. At one end of the spectrum are the aspiring entrepreneurs and the large majority of women-owned firms that have no employees. They need ready access to survival skills in finance, accounting, banking, management, leadership, access to funding and training in such things as how to negotiate successfully. At the other end of the spectrum are the women-owned firms in the million-dollar range and up. Like male business owners with large, high-volume firms, they have resources available in the form of networks, although often less extensive. Weeks and Riebe note that the largest group of women entrepreneurs is the "missing middle."

Few of these "missing middle" firms have easy access to the up-to-date technological and educational knowledge they need. In a review of more than 300 college and university entrepreneurship programs, I found variations in content ranging from a focus on the traditional types of male oriented entrepreneurship offerings that have been in place since the early 1970s to such women oriented topics as leadership, networks, mentorships, stereotypes, getting along in male oriented environments, and the like. In essence, while these entrepreneurship programs may address the needs of aspiring, neophyte, and start-up micro-business owners and the typical college student, they come up short in addressing the real needs of women entrepreneurs and small business owners in the missing middle. They need information on women's capabilities as leaders, owners and managers; growth opportunities at the various stages of entrepreneurial development; concrete information on the best techniques for financing a new venture; market plan development; negotiation approaches; strategic planning; human resource requirements; high-tech best practices; and suggestions for utilizing social capital and dealing with setbacks in the economy. G. Dale Meyer and I have developed a proposal for a program to initiate the beginning of this mission in a program we have labeled "Women in Transition to Advancement of Entrepreneurial Careers" (WITAEC).

If the key information and venture backing is more readily available, today's "missing middle" will become a powerful force in economic growth and development.

References

Introduction

Catalyst, the National Foundation for Women Business Owners (NFWBO), with support of the Committee 200 Foundation (1998). Women entrepreneurs: Why companies lose female talent and what they can do about it. New York, NY: Catalyst, 43 pages. (Cited references on pp. 13, 22.)

Moore, D. P. (2000). *Careerpreneurs.* (Referenced material on pp. 43–48).

Profile: Deborah Szekely

Final approved profile developed from featured Academy of Management Panel Presentation, follow-up interview, entrepreneur's website biography at RanchoLAPuerta (http://www.rancholapuerta.com/home/history-vision/deborahs-life.html) and the Golden Door Spa (http://www.goldendoor.com/about_golden_door/); featured news stories, and clarifying information furnished by the entrepreneur.

The Rise of Modern Women Entrepreneurs

Intrapreneurs

Kanter, R. M. (1989). Careers and the wealth of nations: A macro-perspective on the structure and implications of career forms. In M. B. Arthur, D. T. Hall, & B. S. Lawrence, *Handbook of career theory* (pp. 506–521). Cambridge, England: Cambridge University Press.

King, C. (March 1, 2004). Intrapreneurship: From incubation to spin out. Sun Developer Network, http://developers.sun.com/toolkits/articles/intrapreneur2.html

Profile: Jennet Robinson Alterman

The draft profile corrected and approved by Jennet incorporates materials from her interview on South Carolina ETV/Radio. (Jan. 21, 2011.) Walter Edgar's Journal. The Center for Women. Retrieved from http://www.scetv.org/index.php/walter_edgars_journal/show/the_center_for_women

Women Entrepreneurs and Corporate Exits

Moore, D. P., & Buttner, E. H. (1999). *Women entrepreneurs.* (See pp. 31–46.)

Sutton, R. I. (2009). How to be a good boss in a bad economy. *Harvard Business Review, 87*(6), 42–50.

Additional Research on Women & Corporate Exits:

Heilman, M. E., & Chen, J. J. (2003). Entrepreneurship as a solution: The allure of self-employment for women and minorities. *Human Resource Management Review, 13*(2), 347–365.

Litzky, B. E., Eddleston, K. A., & Kidder, D. (2006). The good, the bad, and the misguided: How managers inadvertently encourage deviant behaviors. *Academy of Management Perspectives, 20*(1), 91–103. (See Model of Deviant Behavior on p. 92.)

Mainiero, L. A., & Sullivan, S. E. (2006). *The opt-out revolt.*

Mainiero, L. A., & Sullivan, S. E. (2005). Kaleidoscope careers: An alternate explanation for the "opt-out" revolution. *Academy of Management Executive, 19*(1), 106–123.

Mallon, M., & Cohen, L. (2001). Time for a change? Women's accounts of the move from organizational careers to self-employment, *British Journal of Management, 12,* 217–230. (References at 221–226.) Retrieved from EBSCOhost.

Intentional Entrepreneurs and Corporate Climbers

DeMartino, R., Barbato, R., & Jacques, P. H. (2006). Exploring the career/achievement and personal life orientation differences between entrepreneurs and non-entrepreneurs: The impact of sex and dependents. *Journal of Small Business Management, 44*(3), 350–368. (Cite at 350.)

Lyness, K. S., & Thompson, D. E. (2000). Climbing the corporate ladder: Do female and male executives follow the same route? *Journal of Applied Psychology, 85*(1), 86–101. (Cite at p. 36.)

McCann, J. Janet McCann Associates, Inc. Interior Designers Website Description (2011). Update to former interview. Retrieved from http://www.janetmccanndesign.com/site/epage/54810_686.htm

Moore, D. P. (2000). *Careerpreneurs.* (See pp. 5–35; Cited material at pp. 5, 13.)

Wilson, F., Kickul, J., & Marlino, D. (2007). Gender, entrepreneurial self-efficacy, and entrepreneurial career intentions: Implications for entrepreneurship education. *Entrepreneurship Theory and Practice, 31*(3), 387–406.

Women Entrepreneurs and Success

The Incubator Effect

Anonymous (2005). Senior women managers' transition to entrepreneurship: Leveraging embedded career capital. *Career Development International, 10*(3), 246–259. (Cite at abstract, p. 246.)

Coulter, J., AIA, LEED AP, Coulter Building Consultants, LLC (2011). Update to former interview. Retrieved from http://www.linkedin.com/in/juliecoulter

Jacob, M. Owner, Michaul's Live Cajun Music and Restaurant (Babineaux Entertainment Facility Inc., Michaul's on St. Charles). New Orleans, LA (2011). Update to former interview. Retrieved from http://www.michauls.com/ or http://www.manta.com/c/mm59syv/michaul-s-live-cajun-music

Moore, D. P., & Buttner, E. H. (1997). *Women entrepreneurs.* (See pp. 31–36.)

Morris, E. CEO/Chief Economist, Insight Research Corporation (2011). Update to former interview. Retrieved from http://www.getinsight.com

Profile: Carol E. Farren

Final approved profile developed from group and individual interviews with entrepreneur, website materials at http://www.facilitymanagementworldwide.com/about.htm, online reference to *Planning and Managing Interior Projects* (www.amazon.com) and additional information furnished by the entrepreneur.

Building Customer Loyalty—Minding the Gap

Bendaña, F. (April, 2011). Applying consumer marketing best practices to employee loyalty. *Loyalty & Motivation White Paper,* Maritz Loyalty and Motivation, Canada. Retrieved from http://www.maritz.com/~/media/Files/MaritzDotCom/Whitepaper.ashx

Berry, L. L., Wall, E. A., & Carbone, L. P. (2006). Service clues and customer assessment of the service experience: Lessons from marketing. *Academy of Management Perspectives, 20*(2), 43–57. (Cited terms at p. 43.)

Wang, M., Liao, H., Zhan, Y., & Shi, J. (2011). Daily customer mistreatment and employee sabotage against customers: Examining emotion and resource perspectives. *Academy of Management Journal, 54*(2), 312–334.

Weinstein, A. (2002). Customer retention: A usage segmentation and customer value approach. *Journal of Targeting, Measurement and Analysis for Marketing, 10*(3) 259–268. Retrieved from EBSCOhost

Patterns and the Future in a Changing World

Development of Women Entrepreneurs Globally

Minniti, M., Allen, I. E., & Langowitz, N. (2006). *Global entrepreneurship monitor (GEM) 2005 report on women and entrepreneurship.* The Center for Women's Leadership at Babson and Baruch College. Also see: Allen, E. I., Langowitz, N., Élan, A., & Dean, M. R. (2007). *GEM 2007 report on women and entrepreneurship* (published May, 2008). Both sources retrieved from http://www.babson.edu/cwl/upload/GEMWomen07.pdf

Moore, D. P. (Feb. 24, 2011). Evolving research on women entrepreneurs—organizational connections—what we know and what we don't. Presentation, Department of Innovation and Entrepreneurship, BI

Norwegian School of Management, BI, Oslo, Norway. (PDF document and PowerPoint slides.)

Global Growth Resource

Brush, C. G., de Bruin, A., Gatewood, E. J., & Henry, C. (Co-editors) (2011). *Women entrepreneurs and the global environment for growth: A research perspective.* Cheltenham and Camberley, UK, and Northampton, MA: Edward Elgar Publishing.

Women Entrepreneurs and the Innovation-Driven Economies

Allen, E. I., Langowitz, N., Élan, A., & Dean, M. R. (2008). *The global entrepreneurship monitor (GEM) 2007 report on women and entrepreneurship.* The Center for Women's Leadership at Babson and Baruch College [Online]. Retrieved from http://www.babson.edu/cwl/upload/GEMWomen07.pdf. Findings: The innovation-driven, high-income country cluster is made up of Australia, Austria, Belgium, Canada, Denmark, Finland, France, Germany, Greece, Iceland, Ireland, Italy, Japan, the Netherlands, New Zealand, Norway, Singapore, Spain, Sweden, Switzerland, the United Kingdom, and the United States. See also: European Network to Promote Women's Entrepreneurship (WES). Activity Report (2008). Retrieved from http://www.invanor.no and Spotlight on Women Entrepreneurs around the World The Suitcase Entrepreneur. Retrieved from http://womanzworld.com/entrepreneurs/spotlight-on-women-entrepreneurs-around-the-world/#ixzz1O3lIkStX. For statistics Norway: Ministry of Trade and Industry (Trond Giske), 2010. Promoting entrepreneurship. See specifically statistics on female entrepreneurship; Action plan to promote entrepreneurship amongst women; and Increased focus on entrepreneurship in education. Retrieved from http://www.regjeringen.no/en/dep/nhd/selected-topics/innovation/promoting-entrepreneurship.html?id=582899

Alsos, G. A., Kovalainen, A., & Rouvinen, P. (2011). Gender and entrepreneurship: Revealing contractions and underlying processes—the case of Norway. In C. G. Brush, A. de Bruin, E. J. Gatewood, & C. Henry (Co-eds.), *Women entrepreneurs and the global environment for growth: A research perspective* (pp. 40–56).

Christianson, W. S. (April 12, 2011). Half of global growth comes from the developing world. Women in the economy, an executive task force post. *The Wall Street Journal.* Retrieved from http://womenentrepreneurs growglobal.org/

Kelley, D. J., Niels, B., & Amorós, J. E. (2011). *Global entrepreneurship monitor 2010 global report.* Babson College, Babson Park, MA, United States, Lead Sponsoring Institution and Founding Institution; Universidad del Desarrollo, Santiago, Chile, Sponsoring Institution; London Business School, London, United Kingdom, Founding Institution. 82 pp. Retrieved from http://www.gemconsortium.org

Moore, D. P. (Feb. 28, 2011). *Research review and future directions on women entrepreneurs—organizational connections.* Presentation, Department of Innovation and Entrepreneurship, BI Norwegian School of Management, BI, Oslo, Norway. (PDF document and PowerPoint slides of development of NAWBO, Center for Women's Business Research and Centers and research on women entrepreneurs.)

Profile: Julie R. Weeks

Final approved profile developed from national and international conference presentations, work as Executive Director of the National Women's Business Council and Center for Women's Research Directorship, website personal data and accomplishments posted at http://www.womenable.com and information furnished by the entrepreneur.

Trends in Women's Entrepreneurship

Becker-Blease, J. R., & Sohl, J. E. (2011). The effect of gender diversity on angel group investment. *Entrepreneurship Theory and Practice, 35*(4), 709–733.

Guardian Life Small Business Research Institute (Dec., 2009). Special report: Women small business owners will create 5+ million new jobs by 2018, transforming the workplace for millions of Americans. Retrieved from http://www.smallbizdom.com/Research/ResearchMonoraphs/index.htm

Hadary, S. G. (May 17, 2010). Why are women-owned firms smaller than men-owned ones? *Wall Street Journal.* Retrieved from http://online.wsj.com/articles

Intuit (Oct. 2011). The Intuit 2020 Report—Twenty trends that will shape the next decade. Retrieved from //http.Intuit.com/http.intuit/CMO/intuit/futureofsmallbusiness/.pdf

Intuit Future of Small Business Series (Jan., 2007). SR-1037Awww.iftf.org

Moore, D. P., & Meyer, G. D. (2008). WITEC—A flexible college entrepreneurship certification program for women in transition. Symposium Paper, Academy of Management, Anaheim, California, August. (Continued development in 2009; renamed to WITEAC, 2011.)

Weeks, J., & Riebe, M. (May, 2007). Mapping the "missing middle": Determining the desire and dimensions of second-stage women business owners. A Womenable Research in Brief. Retrieved from http://www.womenable.com/userfiles/downloads/ResearchinBrief_Missing_Middle.pdf

Wood, G. J., Davidson, M. J., & Fielden, S. L. (2012). *Minorities in entrepreneurship: An international review.* Cheltenham, UK: Edward Elgar.

5
PREPARING FOR THE FUTURE

Introduction

In the early 1990s, economist Robert Avery, then a professor at Cornell University, estimated that $10 trillion in assets would be transferred from the older generation to the Baby Boomers over the next 15 or 20 years. Estimates today go even higher. As a result of the tremendous wealth generated in the latter 20th century, says a Community Foundation Market Research study, "America, at the turn of the century, [was] home to 276 billionaires, 350,000 deca-millionaires and more than five million millionaires." According to the Center: "The most conservative estimates indicate that $41 trillion will be transferred among the generations over the next 50 years with $12 trillion transferred by 2020."

No matter how you define it, and even discounting the estimated $8 trillion in assets lost after the market collapse in 2008, the greatest intergenerational transfer of wealth in history is already under way.

Most of the assets of the approximately 35 million Traditionalists, also called the Matures, born before 1946, have already been passed on. The defining events of their lives were the Great Depression and World War II (or the immediate family stories), the Korean Conflict, and the golden ages of radio and the silver screen. They experienced the rise of an activist government in New Deal programs such as Social Security and the Federal Deposit Insurance Corporation, which provide a measure of protection from events beyond one's control, and most of them were active participants in the struggle that saved Western civilization.

Wealth in the hands of the next group, the Baby Boomers, born between 1946 and 1964, is now beginning to be turned over. Born in an America atop a mountain of power and growing more prosperous, they lived through the Cold War, the civil rights movement and Vietnam, and all that has happened since. Often maligned—the notion that Boomers claim much of the world by right of inheritance is a negative statement repeated over and over and not a fact of research—they found themselves pitched about by social changes such as the shift in private life, from the traditional family of male at work and mom at home with children to the world of dual career couples and single parenting and economic changes such as the declining expectation of lifelong employment and retirement with pension benefits.

Readying themselves and beginning to take over are the Generation Xers, born between 1965 and 1980, and the Yers or Millennials, born after 1980. Their memories of life-changing events range from Watergate and the resignation of a President to 9/11 to the onset of what is increasingly referred to as the Great Recession. They have grown up in a media-saturated world that is more diverse and interconnected than that of their predecessors.

What can the arriving generations do to best position themselves for the inevitable changes? And how can the older generations help to facilitate the process? The task is the same as it has always been, to recognize the common values, accept any cultural gaps and by reaching across them provide a smooth passing of the torch. Think of it as an Olympic generational victory lap.

Anita Zucker

Chairman and CEO, The InterTech Group

It is critical that we get girls working in STEM (Science, Technology, Engineering and Math). We have to make major pushes in that area, getting girls out into the world of work, hands on work, getting them out to have shadowing opportunities. We are starting early now—at the middle school level—starting to make them think about their future. If people have STEM training in their background, they can fall into any field, work anywhere. If you don't have technology training today you are not going to make it in any field.

In 2010, the *Financial Times* named Anita Zucker one of the 50 most prominent businesswomen in the world. She had become Chairman and CEO of InterTech just two years earlier, on the death of her husband, Jerry. Together, they had raised a family and built the company Jerry had founded, the InterTech Group, into a worldwide operation of more than 100 businesses and one of the largest privately held firms in the United States.

Both Anita and Jerry Zucker's parents were Holocaust survivors. Though Anita's mother was conscripted to work crews in Poland and stayed on the run for much of the war, often hiding in cellars, she cared for and saved her mother, her two youngest brothers and her 18-month-old niece. The risk was considerable and omnipresent. Many who otherwise would have sheltered the family said no because they were afraid the baby would cry and give them away. Anita's father fought with the Partisans. They passed on to their children this legacy of the time of terror: "They taught us about goodness and people who were kind, and who saved their lives," Anita says.

Anita married her husband Jerry when she was 18 and he was 21. "I met his dad when I was 10 and his mom when I was 12. They taught me and brought me home one day and introduced me to Jerry and that is where it all began." "Jerry had been getting patents for his inventions from the time he was in high school, that was his life," Anita says, "He was always inventing, discovering, playing with things, destroying his parents' home while growing up, doing all these fun things, and then he did this with us, and when we started having kids it was even more fun because he could do it with the kids." At the time of his death, Jerry Zucker held over 350 patents.

From the start, Anita and Jerry were copreneurs, operating their restaurant and a record store in college at the University of Florida. Jerry graduated with a Bachelor of Science, with a triple major in Mathematics, Chemistry and Physics, and would go on to earn a Master of Science in Electrical Engineering. Anita graduated with a Bachelor of Arts in Education and would go on to earn a Master of Education from the University of North Florida. Getting their first "real jobs," in the early 1970s, Anita began teaching, and soon became a working mom. She would continue teaching for 11 years. Jerry worked in a paper mill as the head of research and development.

Jerry and a colleague founded InterTech in 1982 with the purchase of a division of the manufacturer where they then worked. The investment became a springboard for a series of increasingly larger manufacturing acquisitions in the 1980s, including several divisions spun off by E. I. du Pont de Nemours & Co. Other acquisitions that followed included the South Carolina Stingrays hockey team, in 1995, which, according to friends, was partly inspired by Jerry's and his youngest son's passion for the sport, and, in 2006, the addition of Canada's historic trading company (and later department store chain), the Hudson Bay Company. The oldest operating business in North America, it had been founded in 1670, the same year the Lords Proprietors established a small Carolina colony at a protected site near today's Charleston harbor.

Anita became the Director of Community Relations for InterTech, a position, she says, "that allowed me the opportunity to work in this community—often." Also serving in this role, "I became the face of our company," she says, "and ended up in many leadership roles. I chaired the Board of the United Way, the Charleston Metro Chamber of Commerce and the Community Foundation." By this time, the InterTech Group, with headquarters in North Charleston, South Carolina, was growing into an interwoven conglomerate of technology-driven manufacturing businesses, business activities such as image marketing and financial transaction services, entertainment and real estate holdings and much more. Always active in the business, after Jerry's death, in addition to becoming InterTech's CEO with their son Jonathan becoming President, Anita succeeded her husband to become the Hudson Bay Company's first female Governor. For the fiscal year ending December 31, 2009, independent financial reporting firms estimated the sales of InterTech at $3.2 billion and, in the teeth of the most severe recession in decades, a one-year growth of 15.8 percent.

"One of the legacies that Jerry left me with and our families taught us," Anita says, "was the principle of *tikkun olam*." The phrase, found in a Jewish prayer, is Hebrew for "repair of the world" and inseparable from the phrase *tikun hanefish*, "repair of the soul." "We use the power behind the products we make and the kinds of companies we have to do repair of the world," Anita says, "whether it is products that save lives or through products that provide entertainment." In "giving back," wrote interviewer Thomas McQueeney, "the Zuckers have been at the very forefront of every major initiative to improve education, industry and social programs in the Lowcountry. Nobody did it better, more often or with as much." Their charitable works include a major role in the initiative to place a Holocaust Memorial at Marion Square in the heart of downtown Charleston, funding the Jewish Studies Program at the College of Charleston, and donations such as that in 2009 that allocated $2 million for the establishment of the Jerry Zucker Endowed Chair in Brain Tumor Research at the Medical University of South Carolina and a similar amount to support spinal cord research and provide neurological care and training to the people of Tanzania, Africa. The work continues through the charities around the world administered by the Zucker Give Team of the couple's three children.

Jerry and Anita Zucker have both been awarded The Order of the Palmetto, the highest honor bestowed by the State of South Carolina. Anita's numerous other awards include honorary doctorates from The Citadel, Johnson and Wales University, the Medical University of South Carolina, the College of Charleston, the Book of Golden Deeds Award presented by the

Exchange Club of Charleston and the Education Foundation's Champions of Education Award, which was renamed The Zucker Champions of Education Award.

With talent, hard work, family values, and a strong sense of ethics, Anita and her husband Jerry followed a lifelong path of working and supportive partner relationships. Their commitment to giving through philanthropy makes them role models of self-made successful entrepreneurship.

Getting What You Deserve

Framing Negotiations

In the business world, difficult negotiations are inescapable. People negotiate for jobs, for promotions and salary increases, for business opportunities, for support—the list is endless. For this reason, learning how to negotiate is a must.

If the issue under negotiation is important to you, the upcoming interaction requires research. This is necessary for two reasons. Obviously, you want a solution ideal from your point of view. But you seldom get everything you ask for. Therefore, you need to decide what a minimally acceptable solution is and understand that this is the point where you will walk away rather than take anything less.

The most important component in negotiation is power. Who has power and chooses to use it influences the outcome, even when the choice is to compromise or accommodate. Assess negotiating situations carefully. Make a realistic appraisal of where the power lies. An example: Suppose you are a skilled, hard-working and valued employee, but fed up with something and feel ready to tell the boss you are leaving if you can't get anyone to understand that it must be fixed. Run through your mind the scene where, after hearing you out, the boss stands up, offers a hand, and wishes you good luck in whatever you do next. Without another job, are you ready for this outcome now? Or would you be better off lining up a new job first and then having the conversation? In addition to power, successful negotiation requires knowledge, self-confidence and perseverance, not necessarily always in that order. It is important to know when to take advice or act on information provided by others and when to trust your judgment. In emotionally charged situations, it can be important to back away before reaching a settlement, to take time to reflect on what is happening.

How issues are framed have powerful effects on the bargaining process. As noted by Jamie L. Moore in *Careerpreneurs*:

> *Framing the negotiation is the art of defining issues in terms that are advantageous to you. Much like placing a painting in a frame helps to accentuate its features, making it easier to sell, framing your side of the issue in a negotiation makes it more marketable. Assume a beautiful painting done by an artist who is competent but not outstanding. The painting has been placed in an elegantly gilded frame and hung in the Louvre Museum with guards all around and precautions taken for its safety. Now think of that same painting in a beaten wooden frame hanging over a cold, darkened fireplace in a run-down tavern on a dirt road on the outskirts of Paris. Are the images anything alike? Does the painting have the same mystique and appeal in both settings? Whose frame is accepted as the foundation for the negotiation is critical to the outcome.*

Much like placing a painting in a frame helps to accentuate its beauty, making it easier to sell, framing your side of the issue in a negotiation makes it more marketable. Work on the frame. It should be well in place prior to entering the negotiation. The person whose frame is accepted as the foundation for the negotiation is already in a position to strongly influence the outcome.

During the negotiation, remember that frames can be directly related to immediate events and therefore can change. As a rule of thumb, the greater the difference in how the parties to the dispute frame the issues in the beginning, the more likely the two frames will converge as the negotiations go on.

Understand that the process itself is a subject of continuous negotiation. In a complex negotiation, new information, the influence of the other party, any ineffectiveness of your strategy, an opponent's change in style or any number of other things can require a reevaluation. If the original frame is not working, step back and review. Reframing may be necessary.

Finally, throughout the negotiation, remember to walk in the shoes of the other party as well as your own. To put it another way, you want the advantages of three perspectives: An impassioned advocate of your position, an objective observer of what is taking place and someone constantly evaluating when it is beneficial to shift strategies.

Negotiating Strategies for Career Success

Changes in company structures over the last two decades have removed layers of managerial authority. The old reporting relationships disappeared and the buffers, rules, policies and procedures that kept interactions structured went with them. People in organizations now relate to each other in new and different ways.

In today's flatter organizations, people find themselves dealing with others who occupy a variety of organizational positions and work at varying distances, real and virtual. Many of the interactions that take place are what Deborah M. Kolb and Judith Williams call "shadow negotiations." By this the authors mean situations where the other person sees no compelling reason to negotiate. They often occur where there are power differences between individuals because of race, age, gender or organizational titles. The key to moving things forward, say the authors, is to begin by creating a value and making it visible. In other words, frame the issue to your advantage in a way that doesn't leave the other person free to sort through the possibilities. This means that the upcoming interaction requires prior research, an evaluation of an acceptable outcome, and a decision on the point where you will walk away rather than take anything less. As Diane Harris, CEO of Hypotenuse Enterprises, advises, "Better to lose a deal than have a bad deal. It's as important to be able to walk away from a deal as do a deal."

While women do not prove to be nicer, softer or less effective negotiators than men, the sex-role stereotype of the American woman as passive and compliant can create a dilemma for women handling complex business negotiations, as can a "feminine" approach to business dealings. Laura Kay, author of "Leading through Negotiation: Harnessing the Power of Gender Stereotypes," cites two important research findings in the difference gender makes in negotiating to solve conflicts. "First," she says, "on average, men's behavior is more competitive, or self-serving, than that of women." "Second, men reap more favorable outcomes on average than do women," and "although these differences may be relatively modest in size, the fact that they occur across a variety of contexts with differing populations suggests they are capturing a robust difference between the sexes."

What can you do to develop a more powerful position in the negotiation process that bypasses the gender and sex role stereotypes? Research by Kray, Galinsky, and Thompson suggests that it is possible for women to perform well in negotiations by strengthening the mental link in the other person's mind between stereotypically feminine traits that are seen as positive (such as empathy and communication skills) to make the important point in their mind that, irrespective of the stereotypes, they are dealing with someone who is rational, assertive and has a high regard for her own interests as opposed to them thinking they are interacting with an emotional and passive female.

In their book *Her Place at the Table*, the authors report interview findings from more than 100 women leaders, many of whom say that in negotiations they made these faulty assumptions:

- My choice is either yes or no.
- My appointment speaks for itself.
- I can pick up the slack.

Keep in mind that not just the outcome is under negotiation but the discussion process itself. A powerful beginning requires doing all the homework to make the process and the setting as successful as possible. And keep in mind it may not be winning this time but somewhere down the road.

Diane C. Harris

Founder and CEO, Hypotenuse Enterprises, Inc.

Asked by a Wall Street Journal *reporter why she thought she could be an entrepreneur after 28 years in the corporate world, Diane answered: "You're asking me the wrong question. You should be asking how somebody as entrepreneurial as I am could have survived for 28 years inside a large corporation." The entrepreneurial path is all about being in charge, the excitement of growth and the knowledge that accomplishment doesn't come from just doing the same things repeatedly, comfortable as the rewards might be. Stretching to do the new and challenging has more of a sense of achievement.*

Diane C. Harris is a Phi Beta Kappa graduate of Catholic University, earned an M.S. degree from Rensselaer Polytechnic Institute, and started with Bausch & Lomb. Her first transition was from a research chemist straight out of graduate school to 14 years of operating division life, advancing through the company's technical, marketing and general management areas to become a Vice-President in the Soflens products group, where she orchestrated B&L's successful entry into the contact lens solutions business. This got her into deal-making—"It was kind of fun," she says—and on to her next transition of a 14-year run as B&L's Vice President of Corporate Development reporting to the CEO. Here, Diane became deeply involved in the acquisition and divestiture transactions that transformed the company into a global leader in optics and health care products. Completing 230 transactions (including 47 acquisitions), over 100 licensings and the divestitures of 25 operations that no longer fit corporate strategies, Diane was central to the billion-dollar corporate restructuring program that emphasized global strategies and put B&L into five new business sectors with operations worldwide and provided half of the company's growth every year for over a decade.

She also saw to some lower profile but significant changes to help other women on the way up, co-leading a new Women's Executive Network, at the CEO's request. One of her treasured honors was receiving, from the women of Bausch & Lomb, a plaque of mirrored glass shards entitled "For breaking the glass ceiling and raising the roof." Diane's contributions to the advancement of women were further recognized by receiving the President's 21st Century Leadership Award from the Women's Hall of Fame.

As the first woman President of the 5,000-member Association for Corporate Growth, she noticed that the handful of professional women in attendance were being treated as spouses of "real" members, so she changed the badge color to differentiate Association members, and established special networking for the professional women to overcome their isolation, inviting several onto her Board of Directors.

Taking early retirement from Bausch & Lomb, Diane made her next transition, founding a company, Hypotenuse Enterprises, Inc., to not only provide mergers and acquisitions services and consulting, but with the component of training her clients in this function as well. Her former employer became one of her first clients. After a number of successful transactions with fees of six digits, she earned a $2 million fee in bringing two companies together. "I remember stopping to reflect that it was time for analysis. How much money is enough? Do I just continue and make more money? Do I really retire now? But it had never been a question of money; it was about being successful in a very challenging world, and the thrill of bringing major transactions to successful conclusion." Through Diane's sourcing, negotiating and deal-structuring activities on behalf of Hypotenuse's client companies, she completed more than $500 million in transaction value, and developed the deal training program "The smART of the Deal."™

After 15 years of running her deal-making, consulting and training company, there was yet another transition ahead. "At one point," Diane says, "I had built the business to ten employees (a substantial number for a firm such as this outside the Wall Street area), but I was the business and it was never possible to just walk away. I never stopped enjoying the work and teaching people but I realized there were many people dependent on my bringing in the business, and my doing the crucial parts of the work, which restricted my flexibility for personal growth. And I didn't need to make more deal fees of two million or five million dollars. I didn't want to build the business larger. I was successful. 'Been there, done that,' as the saying goes. I felt I could close 20 or 30 more deals but so what?"

Today Diane is still the principal lecturer at "The smART of the Deal" seminar presented regularly in various cities in the U.S. and Canada. She still conducts business practice surveys, and serves as an expert witness in transaction-related disputes. Instead of the extensive worldwide traveling she had done in the past, most of her consulting with CEOs today can be done by phone or email. She limits her deal projects as CEO to leave room for the new challenges. Diane completed her 16-year term as a Director of Flowserve Corporation, where she served as Chair of its Audit Finance Committee and on its Executive Committee. She describes that board experience as a capstone event of participation with some of the finest people she has ever met in her career.

What has been thematic in Diane's career is noticing the plight of the underdog, especially in abuse of power situations, and taking the initiative to make a difference. It is emerging in a new area. Couldn't she continue to use these gifts to make more deals, and more money? "Yes," she says. "But money isn't enough. It can never be enough."

Diane's focus today is to employ the skills she learned over a lifetime to serve, as best she can, her faith and the people in her church. Beginning in a small, grassroots, rural parish and growing into taking on hierarchical issues, Diane is contributing to an understanding of the use and abuse of power in the church governance context. Through writing, publishing and even blogging, she plans to continue to disseminate her thoughts and concerns in this arena. She identifies six specific skills which, in the language of business, she "leverages" in service; or, in the language of philanthropy, "gives back." These include: long-range planning in which she spent 25 years at Bausch & Lomb, and the ability to "envision;" finance skills especially honed by board service and deal due diligence; pursuit of the "truth," particularly sharpened by her expert witness and survey work, as well as her scientific background; integration skills in the post-deal bringing-together of diverse groups; the ability learned in negotiating to work either collaboratively or in a hostile environment; understanding the abuse of power, which is not limited to the glass ceiling and communications skills, both in writing and public speaking, to express and teach a deeper understanding of the meaning of ideas, values and events. She points out that these skills are only useful when coupled with the gifts such as energy, courage, and faith she has also received from God. "So," she says, "He is my new CEO. I come as a servant."

Work–Life Balance—The Time Warp

Trying to balance the many demands on one's time continues to be a problem and is becoming more insurmountable. Technology means you are never out of reach. The most recent study by the Families and Work Institute, which tracks changes in how Americans work and live, concludes that the "fast-paced, global 24/7 economy, the pressures of competition and technology have blurred the traditional boundaries between work life and home life."

Huge numbers of people are affected by a lack of balance in their lives, the accompanying high stress and the subsequent fallout in home, work and other environments. According to recent research, one-third of all employees feel chronically overworked, somewhere between 30 percent and 40 percent provided special attention or care for someone 65 years old or older in the past year, and slightly more than half have felt overwhelmed at some time during a recent month. For the first time in the recorded statistics, more than half of the women in the United States (52 percent) are not married, a reflection of the graying of America, the struggles of the working woman, the rise in cohabitation, an increasingly prevalent lifestyle among the 30- to 44-year-olds, which has more than doubled since the mid-1990s, the rising number of people who require caregivers, and a sluggish economic recovery in which men have fared better than women. Because women are the predominant nurturers in families, many expect and were expected to take up the additional burdens. Today it is not at all unusual to hear a working mother say she has not one but two or more jobs outside the home in addition to taking care of her children, a sibling, or an aging parent.

Baby Boomers feel more sandwiched than other generation groups because one in five provides 45 percent or more of a parent's financial support, one in three provides 25 percent or more of a grown child's housing costs and slightly less than half (45 percent) provide at least $2,500 per year in financial support to grown children. No wonder that one in four is delaying retirement, one in three plans to or has returned to the job market, and due to parents' longevity few expect any inheritance. The pressures will continue to increase. The numbers of parents who will need support will more than triple, rising to more than 20 percent of the population.

Work–life balance is also elusive. Ideas of balance vary across generations. Women associate balance with giving priority to family. Men report less balance when they have no personal time for themselves. Surveys report balance is very important to workers under 35, far less so for workers over 55. Wives employed full time devote more than three times what men spend in unpaid caregiving and housework and have far less leisure time and higher stress levels than working fathers and singles. One recent study shows that some 2.6 million women have slightly more than a half an hour a day to do as they please. An additional two million have the luxury of 47 minutes to themselves. Working parents spend far less time with each other. Adding the job of primary caregiver can easily marginalize one's opportunities. The fact that 60 percent of divorces occur during key childbearing years is not unrelated.

Given all the pressures and demands in a world that keeps running faster, what steps can you take? The first is to recognize that it is up to you to put up the sign "Not open for business" to create a buffer between your schedule and the world and get the downtime needed for creativity, rest and career and family survival. According to research at the Families and Work Institute, you now need to answer two questions:

- In the past year, how often did you feel that you put your job before your personal and family life?
- In the past year, how often did you feel that you put your personal and family life before your job?

The answers tell you whether you are work-centered, family-centered or dually centered. Feelings of overwork are less for those in the dually-centered group. There are no easy answers to achieving balance. But here are some suggested strategies for the search.

- Get rid of the idea that the bulk of chores in maintaining a home, child and parental care are women's responsibilities, rather than to be shared with spouses or significant others.
- Deep six the myth that somehow a woman can do it all. In sum work–family balance depends on knowing the facts and sharing the burdens.
- Diminish the negative spillovers by not taking family problems to the office and vice versa.

- Avoid marginalizing work opportunities—your work may be crucial to your caregiving.
- Check how you spend your time by keeping a daily diary for a month.
- Establish priorities for your personal out-of-work hours and explain them to everyone involved.

Today and Tomorrow

Women Entrepreneurs, the Recession and Prospects for the Future

In 2008, the United States entered a recession that became, by all measures, the worst economy since the Great Depression of the 1930s. How have women entrepreneurs and their businesses fared? What comes next?

Succeeding in tough times. Using data from the three most recent business census surveys (1997, 2002 and 2007) and other sources to bridge the gaps, a 2010 American Express report on the state of women-owned businesses estimates that, as of 2011, there are over 12.9 million businesses in which women have at least a half-interest (46 percent of all U.S. firms). They employ nearly 15.8 million people (13 percent of the workforce) and have revenues of nearly $2.6 trillion. Between 1997 and 2011, their numbers increased by 50 percent, a rate one and one-half times the national average. The fastest growth took place in education services (up 54 percent), administrative and waste services (47 percent) and construction (41 percent). Industries with the highest concentration of women-owned firms are health care and social assistance (52 percent of firms), educational services (46 percent), other services (41 percent) and administration (37 percent). The study also notes that "women-owned firms have done better than their male counterparts during the past 14 years."

Are Women Entrepreneurs Different from Men? According to a 2010 Kauffman Foundation study, the answer is no and yes. On average, women and men start their companies in their early forties, have similar educational levels, and equally value prior work experience in start-up success. The five financial and psychological factors motivating women to become entrepreneurs (build wealth, capitalize on business ideas, appeal of a start-up culture, long-standing desire to own their own company, little interest in working for someone else) are also listed as important by men. The most important differences include size (women-owned firms tend to be smaller), there are fewer of them among the larger enterprises (100 or more employees, revenues of $1 million or more) and they have lower profits (27 percent less than men-owned firms).

Why Lower Profits and Fewer Large Firms? According to a 2009 Center for Women Business Research Report, many aspects of today's women-owned businesses reflect generational differences in the educational levels, experience, and characteristics of the owners, in particular the relatively recent access to corporate experiences that provide an important training ground for entrepreneurship. A 2011 Kauffman firm survey points the finger at opportunities for financing and the positive connection between start-up capital and performance. Twenty-nine percent of women obtained their main start-up funding from a business partner, compared with 16 percent for men, 62 percent of women started with less than $25,000, versus 55.9 percent of men. Similar findings are confirmed in a 2009 academic study. Sharon G. Hadary, the former Executive Director and Founder of the Center for Women's Business Research, says the twofold problem also results from "women's own self-limiting views of themselves, their businesses and the opportunities available to them" and the pervasive problems of stereotypes, perceptions and expectations of many businesses, bankers and policy makers.

Future Prospects? Predictions suggest that by 2017 small businesses will be formed and run by a new and more diverse group of entrepreneurs. The largest numbers of these emergent entrepreneurs will consist of women exiting corporate life and immigrant entrepreneurs. Of the 15.3 million new jobs anticipated by the Bureau of Labor Statistics by 2018, women-owned businesses will be responsible for creating one-third of them, according to research cited from the Guardian Life Small Business Research Institute survey.

What do these findings suggest if you work in a corporate environment?

- If possible, avoid getting side-tracked into dead-ended jobs without access to a power base. It will be easier to move if you want to or have to.
- Locate the power base in your company and connect to it.
- Prepare for the important jobs in your company by volunteering or by taking additional courses to enhance your skills.

What is the message for the potential woman business owner?

- Treat your organizational experience as an incubator. Some of you already want to create your own business. Others may decide to later.
- Take every opportunity to learn.
- Don't burn bridges. The company you leave behind is your reference and may be your future customer.

If you are a business owner, what are the lessons?

- Change is coming. It always is, so try to be ready.
- Be realistic. Think growth from the beginning.
- Identify potential markets.
- Network with financial institutions and potential business allies before you need them.
- Be ready to invest in yourself.

Technopreneurs

The U.S. Department of Labor projects a 4 percent increase in information sector employment, 118,100 new jobs, by 2018. Computer-related data-processing, hosting and related services such as web and application hosting and streaming services are expected to grow by 53 percent. The growth will take place in companies large and small. The most recent indications are that the largest growth will occur in small companies in budget and staff positions. The 2011 comprehensive job rankings at JobsRated.com indicates that the rise is due to the growing popularity of smartphone applications and cloud-based software. Software engineer ($87,140) and computer systems analyst ($77,153) are both high on the list, with projections of a positive work environment, low physical demands and stress levels and a positive hiring outlook.

Information Technology (IT) covers a wide spectrum of titles, responsibilities, education, and training, with pay scales varying accordingly. Two of the fastest growing areas in IT are information security and, strange as it sounds, information insecurity. Companies desire information security to stay ahead of cybercriminals and hackers and protect privacy. Many also want information insecurity to access and store customer profiles to enhance target marketing. Today's practice of "scraping," for example, consists of data-mining the activity and habits of internet users on a vast scale and analysis of that data by sophisticated algorithms that can even reconstruct the identities of individuals who try to protect their online privacy.

If you qualify for some of the IT career opportunities that are clearly on the horizon, now is the time to make a skill assessment. Keep in mind that developments in the near future will play out against the background of equally rapidly changing technology and responsibilities. Whereas today a local internet-connected firm may hire its own information technology personnel and take their recommendations to pay for and control its hardware, software and other resources and take responsibility for data storage security, in the future envisioned by many of the large internet service providers and information technology manufacturers, the local firm will avoid these capital expenditures by relying on its IT personnel to acquire the software, data storage and other services needed over the internet, the so-called cloud computing, and pay only for the resources it uses. The two approaches differ considerably. In the first model, the IT specialist is mainly concerned with which technologies and support services to recommend. In the second, along with knowing the field and technology, because he or she can save the firm money and recommend how the technology can be used to increase efficiency, the IT specialist is at the center of the firm operations.

Companies are already requesting more of applicants for IT jobs. The broader and more diverse the IT portfolio you have, the more likely you are to land a job with the salary you want. Be ready to combine skill sets that stood alone in the past; i.e., programming, designing web materials, understanding the underlying principles of computer technology and more. With regard to the needs of the firm, be ready to highlight the financial, management, communication and other business skills you have. Be ready to impress an interviewer by saying, "With my skills, here's how I can contribute to your company's bottom line."

For those considering a career switch or the possibility of advancement, think about these proactive questions:

- Am I ready to change my career planning from IT as a mostly technology field to IT as one of the must-have business skills?
- What software certifications might add to my skill set? Will certification as a systems administrator, systems engineer, technology specialist or office specialist make me more marketable?

Starting at the beginning? One option is completing a 1- to 15-week IT skills certification program in areas such as Certified Information Systems Security Professional, Certified Wireless Network Administrator, Certified Ethical Hacker or Cisco Certified Network Associate.

Here are some important questions to consider if you are an entrepreneur or small business owner:

- What strategy do I have to handle growth by employing technology to maintain a competitive edge?

- Am I sinking into a black hole in terms of the global market if I am not using web-based technology to advance my business?
- Have I identified the best IT resource advisor to keep my company up to date?
- Do men and women employ different IT strategies? (There is evidence that women owners are personally involved in the evaluation and selection of technology more than men are.)
- Can I afford to do business by the old business model, i.e., heavy reliance on the storefront? Or do I need to consider the new technologies? (The Center for Women's Business Research suggests that 76 percent of women business owners can improve their business performance by the better use of technology.)
- Will web-based technologies, the "cloud computing" approaches, have an impact on my customers, market, etc.? Can they help my bottom line?

Exploring IT—Where Are the Women?

Information technology is a huge field. Consider just one aspect of it, the internet. In the web-enabled world, there are bright networks and dark spaces and a gender divide.

How might you prepare for a career in this field for your future best job prospects? Here are some approaches to consider.

According to the most recent Pew Research Center Report, 79 percent of all adults use the internet. Millennials (ages 18–33) are the biggest users (95 percent of them), followed by 86 percent of Generation X (ages 30–45), 81 percent of the Younger Boomers (45–55), 76 percent of the Older Boomers (56–64), 30 percent of the Silent Generation (65–73) and 30 percent of the G.I. Generation (age 74 and older).

Internet shopping and scouting for products and bargains is proving to be a business highway to the future. During the past five years, technology and web-based marketing have created a virtual street fair with an endless line of booths. While it is highly unlikely online shopping will replace storefronts, as some in IT recently have predicted, the technology already is driving the way stores do business. For example, Gen X (30–45) and older cohorts are more likely than Millennials to visit websites and obtain financial information online. The most popular internet activities across all age groups are email, search engine use, seeking health information, getting news, buying products, travel reservations or purchases, online banking, looking at religious information, rating products, services, or people, making charitable donations and downloading podcasts. Older adult participation in entertainment and social networks has increased. Currently, nearly half (47 percent) of internet users and one in four age 50 to 64 (26 percent) participate in sites such as Facebook and LinkedIn.

Businesses like customers who come to stores because they do more impulse buying. Handing out coupons online for special in-store discounts for a given day has been a recent success. Giving discounts in the form of a rebate that requires filling out a form online (perfectly) and a lengthy wait is cost-effective and popular with stores, but much less so with customers.

With more than one million computer-related jobs expected to be created by 2018, a 34 percent increase in the field, according to the U.S. Department of Labor, information technology represents one of the fastest growing career opportunities. Employment in data-processing, hosting, and related services is expected to grow by 53 percent, and software publishing by 30 percent. Many high-paying jobs are expected to be found in IT. According to PayScale.com, the Bureau of Labor Statistics and MONEY research, the current salary range for Software Architects is $72,000 to $146,845, with a top pay level of $162,000 for Senior Software Architects, all along the line additional bonuses running from $2,027 to $20,592 and profit-sharing incentives ranging from $715 to $10,380.

Studies of IT professionals (2007) and gender diversity in the field (2009) raise an important question: Given all this opportunity, where are the women? Presently 96 percent of all software architects are male. Only 4 percent are women and they are paid less than men. This has been trending for some time. A 2009 study of the business dimensions of increasing gender diversity reported that between 1983 and 2008 the IT workforce doubled, but the number of females working in the field dropped from 43 percent to 26 percent. According to a 2005 Bureau of Labor Statics report, female participation in the U.S. labor force has held steady over the past several decades, with women accounting for approximately 40 to 47 percent of the labor force. Yet, as Trauth and Quesenberry have noted, the share of women in IT employment has dropped sharply in recent years, falling from 29 percent in 2000 to 26 percent in 2006. The statistics for 2006 are particularly alarming because it was a year in which overall IT employment hit a record high of nearly 3.47 million employees but female employee participation had fallen 8 percent from 2000.

The trend is counterintuitive. As many women use the internet as men. But somehow, is programming software different? A recent Center for Women's Business Research study shows that women business owners are on a par with their male peers in using technology in their firms to improve quality, efficiency and profits. Relatively few of these women own IT companies or provide venture capital for the technology transfer of information, however.

What's with the decision of young women to miss out on the opportunity to land one of these high-paying jobs? Data from the National Center for Women and Information Technology show an 80 percent decline in the number of female first-year college students who chose to major in Computer Science. In their 2010 study, Morganson, Jones and Major reference a National Science Foundation study showing that in 1985 women constituted 37 percent of the students in Computer Science classes but today make up only 19 percent of the enrollment.

The decline in the numbers of women entering the STEM fields (Science, Technology, Engineering and Math), along with retention problems, raise serious concerns. For those women who do major in these fields, retention in the actual field is also a problem. Among the results, say Wentling and Thomas in a recent study, "is a male-dominated perspective in the development and design of technology," the absence of different perspectives, a lack of diversity in innovations leading to the design of products, "a loss of opportunities for corporations and individuals" and "a loss of talent and creativity for the workforce."

The gender imbalance in IT is attributed to factors such as the lack of encouragement girls receive from parents to study mathematics and science and, until recently, the fact that K-12 programs did not offer computer science as part of the curriculum. Hopefully, the landscape will change due to new initiatives under way. Women in the IT field are building incentives, scholarships and mentoring programs to engage young women. But more is needed.

Women now account for almost half of the nation's workforce. With the escalating demand for technology-based workers—as many as 20 million new high-skill wage jobs are predicted by 2020—it is essential that women be in a position to participate in innovations and advancements in the field. But without skills in math and science, which are the beginning footsteps into the field, it is not possible to be a viable competitor in information technology. For those who wish to prepare for more lucrative salaries, there are also an array of certification programs that take a relatively short period of time to complete.

Virtual Work Teams

As Mannix and Neale noted in their 2005 study, research strongly suggests that work teams are most effective when members feel their work can make a significant organizational contribution, they care about their tasks, believe they are free to make decisions and are mutually confident in each other's skills, trustworthiness and willingness to collaborate. Teams can produce results by utilizing the new information sharing technologies, and therefore the process brings people together with differing backgrounds, information sets, resources, perspectives and problem-solving approaches to contribute to a collective creativity in environments real or virtual.

A positive climate of trust contributes to higher performance, say Salamon and Robinson, but constructing it is difficult even when all the team members work in the same place. The same kind of trust climate can be developed within virtual and geographically distributed teams. However, the interactions that produce trust develop extremely slowly through electronic media, which is why face-to-face meetings to speed things along are important, as indicated by Kirkman, Rosen, Tesluk, & Gibson.

Teams composed of individuals from separate organizational units bring different goals and approaches to problems. (Think a product design team whose members include a creative artist, an accountant from finance, an engineer from manufacturing and a sales representative.) Teams whose members are racially, nationally and gender diverse can encounter additional difficulties originating with stereotypes and cultural barriers. Several later studies endorse findings in a 2000 chapter in the *Handbook of Trust Research* that the key to work team success is an organizational culture that contains "a high degree of taken-for-grantedness because, in such an environment, trust, shared expectations, and teamwork develop even among employees who have no mutual experience or history of interaction." Avoiding communication breakdowns in virtual teams, say Bjørn and Ngwenyama, appears to be embedded in "shared understandings."

Building an efficient team gets even more difficult when members are geographically or organizationally separated. Members of a virtual team do not have the advantages of regular, topic focused meetings, cannot access the social cues available in face-to-face interactions and are unable to do simple things like stopping by someone's desk or seeking them out at lunch to clarify a point. The potential virtual team technological problems begin with the differing skills of team members and go on to include software systems that may not be standardized, lag time, data fragmentation and other difficulties that arise when information is to be shared among people in different time zones or cultures. Further, unless someone is working hard to see there is a common source of information, it won't exist because critical pieces get unintentionally hidden under different topics and filenames in the numerous emails, personal files and other hard-to-find places. Semi-virtual or hybrid teams, meaning a co-located group with other members linked by technology (think crisis management center linked with first responders), may be prone to additional problems of the insider/outsider variety.

Where to begin to create a positive virtual work team climate? Start with understanding that everyone needs to keep remembering that words do not have precise meanings that are universally understood. (Think directions. People living along the Atlantic coast know Colorado is out west. Californians are equally certain it is "east.") Across cultures, words don't mean the same thing, even when people share the same language, as do citizens of the United States and the United Kingdom. (Football, anyone?) Because many virtual team communications will be written, it will be necessary for all team members to think, edit and read to make sure the message will be understood and the tone of the communication does not offend.

Sometimes all team members are not on the same page. As individuals reach out to examine information, confirmation bias and selective interpretation can lead to differing conclusions. (We do/don't have to consult experts or examine this particular item more closely because I already agree/don't agree with it.) Then again, too many of us may be on the same page. If the page is Groupthink, it can lead to bad team decisions. (I'm not going to bring it up even though I feel there may be a problem; everyone else seems to be in agreement, they're saying what the boss wants and they may be right anyway—I would never want to look like a fool.) Combined with Hive Mind (by golly, we're enthusiastic, smart and all together with the right answer), the potential for going off the cliff becomes more deadly.

As a team leader, or someone who can influence a team leader, what actions do I need to take? Work to build team trust. Your team needs clear goals, expectations and guidelines. This enables a high level of accountability. If possible, recommend increased opportunities for face-to-face time in order to moderate the difficulties of physical separation and enhance opportunities for trust building. Work to see that explicit guidelines for team actions are written, talked about and understood. Remember that perceptions are important. Others may not be responding to you but to what they see in the documents, messages and exchanges you presented. Brief messages have a built-in capacity to be terse and misleading. (I'm doing my best to be crisp, clear and definite on this. Why does she think I'm trying to order her around?)

Three steps for each team member.

Come across as a professional. Project sophistication, intelligence and credibility. It begins by thinking out what you need to say and writing it out. Taking the necessary time to make your communication clear and concise is infinitely better than sending something longer and rambling simply because it's quicker and easier.

Then wait. Before pushing the button to send, review and check again to get the spelling, grammar and word usage right (the spellchecker cannot do this for you). Edit to maintain a professional appearance. Visualize yourself as the recipient of the message. Be especially careful to remove language that might offend. Avoid being too clever. What is momentarily cute to you may be considered sarcastic by another.

Don't think you are too busy to do these things. Just think of how much time it will cost to rectify errors or repair relationships if you send the wrong message, even without intending to destroy someone's trust in you.

Which Way Government?

Early actions of the Federal Government facilitated the rise in women's entrepreneurship. This may no longer be happening.

In addition to the legislation and executive orders that opened the way for women and minorities to compete in the marketplace on more even terms, the actions of the Federal Government include the addition of gender in reporting by the Business Census, in 1977, which for the first time recognized women-owned sole proprietorships as a segment of the economy worth tracking, and the 1979 Executive Order of President Jimmy Carter creating the Office of Women's Business Ownership. This was followed by the 1988 Women Owned Business Act (HR 5050), largely crafted from the work of the National Association of Women Business Owners to bring attention to the importance of women-owned businesses and their vital role in the economy, and created a pilot program that led to the establishment of the Women's Business Centers program. The 1988 Act also amended the civil-rights-inspired Equal Credit Opportunity Act to include business loans, established the National Women's Business Council, tasked initially with identifying barriers to women's businesses and reporting annually to the President and Congress, and directed the Business Census to report on C-Class Corporations that were 51 percent owned by women, a change from 50 percent which increased the accuracy of reporting the number of women-owned firms. The 1997 Small Business Reauthorization Act made the Women's Business Centers program a permanent part of the Small Business Association's entrepreneurial development efforts and changed the method by which they were to be funded to insure more long-term stability.

While the creation of a system of Women's Business Centers and the subsequent legislative initiatives to expand opportunities for the women owners appeared impressive on paper, in practice, administration of the program under the SBA did not fulfill the aims of the legislation. The WBCs were designed to provide training and technical assistance to new and nascent women business owners with a focus on socially and economically disadvantaged populations. Pressure from the Association of Women's Business Centers and the support of Senator John Kerry led to an audit conducted by the SBAs Office of the Inspector General in 2007. Along with hearings before the Senate

Committee on Small Business and Entrepreneurship, the audit revealed the WBCs had been severely hampered by SBA legal interpretations that led to the curtailment of federal funding, delays of nearly a year in the SBA disbursement of specifically targeted funds, which forced 98 of the 113 Centers to lay off staff, and seven straight years of administration recommendations for no increase in the SBA budget from 2002 to 2008.

The 110 Women's Business Centers now administered under the SBA are designed to assist women start and grow small businesses with the mission to "level the playing field" for women entrepreneurs and "especially women who are economically or socially disadvantaged with a comprehensive training and counseling program." The initiative predominantly deals with start-ups, covering such items as writing business plans, coming up with a marketing strategy, basic financial areas of concern in getting the business off the ground, coaching and counseling tailored to the needs of women. As findings from the Center for Women's Business Research (2009) note, "Most of the programming now offered through the public and private sector is dated and focused on individuals who want to start a business. While these programs are important and meet a need, there are few solid programs that actually generate information and knowledge and engage entrepreneurs – especially women and minorities – to grow their businesses. The programs that do exist have little, if any, evaluative research behind their claims." For this reason, the House Small Business Committee has recommended that, because of the duplication of business development services funding for the nation's 110 Women's Business Centers should be eliminated in the fiscal year 2012 budget.

Passage of Time through Generations

The Family Business

As William O'Hara said in his book *Centuries of Success,* "Before the multinational corporation, there was family business. Before the Industrial Revolution, there was family business. Before the enlightenment of Greece and the empire of Rome, there was family business."

Globally, family firms dominate. They also make up a huge slice of the North American economy. The Raymond Institute/MassMutual, American Family Business Survey, the most recent comprehensive study on family businesses, states that between 80 and 90 percent of all U.S. companies are family owned and controlled. Chartered as corporations, partnerships and sole proprietorships, these businesses create more than 78 percent of all American jobs. Most are classified as small businesses, meaning they have fewer than 500 employees, but many are very large. According to testimony presented to the House Committee on Ways and Means, families own 37 percent of the Fortune 500 companies and control 60 percent of all publicly held companies.

Until recently, there was little statistical information on women in family firms. In 2003, the Center for Women's Leadership at Babson and the MassMutual Financial Group compared their survey with others. Among the Center's findings: that, in the five years beginning in 1997, women-owned businesses increased by 14 percent while the number of women owners of family businesses rose by 37 percent; that women-owned firms were 1.7 times as productive as family businesses owned by men and that women-owned firms were more than twice as likely to employ women family members full time, six times as likely to have a woman CEO and more likely to have a gender-balanced board of directors. Reporting data from the MassMutual/Raymond Institute survey, the Center notes that nearly 10 percent of family businesses had a woman CEO, up from 5 percent five years earlier, and more than 34 percent said their next CEO might be a woman, up from 25 percent in 1997. The rise of large numbers of women into positions of leadership in family firms, while relatively new, is a promising phenomenon.

As the Family Business Survey further notes, founders, wives and daughters are now running substantial businesses, with $26.9 million in average annual revenues and some reporting

$1 billion in sales. Taking the pulse of family businesses, Stacy Perman reports that daughter-led firms have a 40 percent lower rate of family-member attrition, tend to be more fiscally conservative, carry less debt than male-owned businesses and are more concerned with succession planning than their predecessors. Among the reasons for the success of daughter-led firms, she continues, citing O'Hara, is that "daughters get along with their fathers better than sons do. There isn't that male competitiveness in those relationships, and more are coming to the forefront."

Challenges in Turning over the Family Business

The American Family Business Survey puts the challenge this way: "Since the birth of America, family-owned businesses have shared a fierce desire to survive." Facing unprecedented challenges today, surviving and thriving "will require family businesses to constructively address the many issues they face in the interest of both business success and family harmony."

Replacing leadership is a critical transition for any business. According to a 2010 study in the journal *Entrepreneurship & Regional Development*, the fact that most family business owners want to pass the firm on to the next generation means the owner is thinking in the long term, which is an important reason family businesses outperform non-family businesses.

But success is often elusive. As studies in *Financial Executive* (2007) and the *Journal of Accountancy* (2008) note, only slightly more than one in three family firms (35 percent) make it into a second generation. Only one in five moves on to a third generation. Only 3 percent are passed down to a fourth. This makes it imperative for a family owner to develop a succession plan. But among owners 55 or older, says G. T. Lumpkin, fewer than half (45 percent) have chosen their replacement. Sometimes the reason is a lack of interest in the next generation. More commonly, it is because family business owners hesitate. One in every four winds up doing nothing besides writing a will, and this can be disastrous. The failure to plan carefully for the business succession, according to the University of Connecticut Family Business Program, accounts for nearly half (47.7 percent) of the failures of family-owned businesses.

Family business owners have a significant investment, sometimes a lifetime, in building a clientele through their knowledge, expertise in the field and experience and also in the trusting relationships that have been forged with employees, the business community and customers. Owners acquire a special sense of responsibility and a sense of accountability. Owner feelings of invulnerability can make it difficult to turn loose. The process of writing an exit prescription is a challenge.

Developing a succession plan and getting it right is difficult for other reasons. Although they share many of the same experiences, members of different generations do not look at things in the same way. The psychological baggage of parent and no-longer-a-child may also be present. Family rivalries and potential succession battles can strengthen the desire of owners to retain control. The potential for a family business to go through a difficult period during succession planning has always been present. Discussion of sensitive matters is unavoidable and critical. Taking time to understand both the different frames of reference and the common ground between generations is a healthy preliminary to developing an effective succession strategy.

The key issue in a family business transition is identifying the potential successor who is up to the challenges. Will that person care as much about the company's values, goals and employees, who have in many cases devoted a major portion of their careers to the family-owned business? In my interviews with successful business owners around the nation, I met many whose most difficult conflict was between the roles of parent and small business owner. Some even had the unpleasant experience of having to fire a son or daughter because the latter was incapable of exercising good judgment or did not have the drive to work hard or the intellectual and people skills the business needed.

The first step can be the most important. The owner needs to identify that special member of the family who has the entrepreneurial spirit to manage and lead the company irrespective of the challenges. This family member must be capable of thinking beyond his or her own personal interest, have a commitment to a high standard of ethics, and most of all have the knowledge, skills and aptitude to continue to develop the business in an ever-changing global marketplace. This first step may also lead to a conclusion that the next owner or interim manager of the business has to be someone outside the family because all the needed skills are not yet in place. The assignment for the second generation, if interested in taking over, is to be a quick study and acquire skills, expertise and the business savvy needed to move the firm forward.

Writing a thorough business plan, the same first step for entrepreneurs starting a business, is also a good idea. A transition business plan can identify the strengths of the existing business, the opportunities that may open up, threats that could undermine the firm in the future and address the company's immediate and long-term needs.

Anne Shybunko-Moore

Owner and President, GSE Dynamics, Inc.

That third generation—we'll see what happens on this end. I would never pressure the boys, or want them to feel pressured. I think the success I have with Dad is because we did not have preconceived expectations. I would encourage the boys to go out into the world and do what they want, gain experience and then make a decision when they are 30ish. There is a lot of maturity that occurs in those 20-something years. Time will tell.

Dan Shybunko studied engineering at the Brooklyn Polytechnic Institute of New York University, worked for Grumman Aircraft in the summer in various skilled jobs of aircraft construction—riveting, wiring, drafting—and after graduation went to work full time in the structural design of aircraft. When Grumman became involved in new manufactured products, he was asked to participate. Though Grumman obtained a substantial number of contracts, the Board of Directors decided not to go ahead with the operations and Dan was asked to be a consultant to help a Long Island manufacturer phase in these products. He immediately enjoyed the environment of a small manufacturing company and, spotting an advertisement of a sheet metal company for sale, went into business with little money by renting the facility and hiring the owner and his people. That was in 1971. In time, he would build the business into GSE Dynamics, which today manufactures structural parts for airplanes, submarines, tanks and more. Exactly three decades after founding his company, he would ask his daughter, the youngest of five siblings, to join GSE as a Vice President.

After earning her Bachelor's degree in Biology at Franklin & Marshall College and a Master's in Physical Therapy at the University of Maryland, Anne Shybunko had worked her way up to Rehab Director for a healthcare facility in Maryland. In early 2001, she made the decision to join her fiancé back in New York and began interviewing for health care management positions. Her father, seeing her success in the business environment, asked if she would have any interest in joining the family business. She made the decision to take the opportunity to work at GSE—and began her career transition. In some ways, she says, "I felt right at home" (she had spent her childhood Saturdays at the company); "in other ways, it was odd and very awkward at first. I had known some of the people since I was seven, and suddenly I'm their boss."

Anne divides her GSE career into three phases. The first consisted of learning the business, modifying the company culture and becoming involved in strategic planning. On her first day, Anne called the employees into a meeting and said, "You know all about this line of business, and I need you to teach me." With the help of long-tenured, (some over 30 years), and loyal employees, Anne learned quickly. The crisis came

14 months after she joined the company when her father underwent a triple bypass surgery and was bedridden. Suddenly in charge, Anne wondered, "Many had known me since I was little, and viewed me as the young daughter. Would they accept my new role? Those six weeks he was out were critical," she says, "and the employees were behind us, and behind me. That gave me the confidence to say, 'I can do this.'" Within three years, GSE had doubled their backlog, began to expand capability, and was recognized for its business growth and performance. The Long Island chapter of the National Association of Women Business Owners (NAWBO) named Anne the 2003 Top Woman Business Owner. As Dan watched GSE grow, he saw his daughter's passion for the business and in investing in the employees. He knew he had found his successor and officially transitioned company ownership to Anne in 2003.

By 2006, Anne had moved into a second phase, implementing a strategic plan, growing the company and developing a stronger management team. It had taken a few years for her to feel comfortable as a woman in the solidly male world of manufacturing military components and selling to the government. Often the only woman in the room, she was able to gain the respect of those men, create her own identity, and utilize it as strength.

GSE was then primarily dealing with metal fabrication for U.S. Air Force parts. An opportunity to diversify into both the U.S. Navy market and composite manufacturing arose when one of the original equipment manufacturers decided to divest one of their divisions. The negotiation began with Anne and her father being informed they would meet with a 12-man negotiation team. The first question they got was where was the GSE team: "Are you the only ones coming?" At one point during the negotiation process her father expressed that this was her deal to make, or not make.

Anne's decision was a critical juncture both in her relationship with her father and for GSE. GSE Composites, and the subsequent start to GSE Southern Composites, in Georgia, would allow the parent company to manage when there was a sharp downturn in Air Force orders only two years later. As other companies in the industry failed during this period, Anne hired key skilled employees to bolster her company. This influx of talent allowed her to redesign her management structure and develop depth and planning for critical roles. The restructuring improved overall production operations and led to the Defense Logistics Agency awarding GSE a prestigious national recognition—Outstanding Readiness Support Award for a Woman Owned Business.

Today in her third phase of sustaining operations and maintaining critical relationships and core capabilities in an expanded marketplace, Anne is the owner and President of GSE. The company has grown from 32 to 48 employees under her leadership and more than tripled its backlog since 2001. Her father remains active in the company as CEO, continues to participate in the sales and bidding phase of the effort—and continues to have the passion and respect for the business he started.

The walls at GSE's 30,000-square-foot building are lined with photos of employees and their families. The company offers comprehensive health care insurance, company recreation facilities, holiday parties, and flexible hours to allow parents to attend to children's needs, something Anne understands well as the mother of four boys. "I always think about how business decisions will impact my employees," she says. "They are the strength of the company, and we spend a lot of time together. It's important they understand how much I appreciate their efforts, and that they're people first, employees second. I believe that's a strategy that works for a successful corporate environment."

As Anne looked to the future and the possibility of passing GSE on to a third generation, she became concerned about how she would replace her highly skilled workforce. There was no pipeline of young machinists, welders, or others with advanced manufacturing and assembly skills. She began to examine the

Long Island community, the resources available to address workforce training and became involved. She became President of NAWBO-Long Island and recognized as a business leader in the manufacturing community, welcoming Hillary Rodham-Clinton, then Senator of New York, to multiple meetings, one of them at GSE to meet with her employees. She has forged a strong relationship with Suffolk County Community College, serves on multiple boards of directors, and was recently appointed to Governor Cuomo's Regional Council to address New York's future economic position—of which manufacturing is critical. In 2011, Long Island Congressman Steve Israel asked Anne to chair a Task Force for Manufacturing with the purpose of providing input on current and pending legislation that impacts the manufacturing community.

As Anne puts it, "Somehow I became a face of manufacturing on the Island and I feel it is my responsibility to support future workforce training and development that will allow not only GSE's third and fourth generations to succeed, but to support the diverse, highly capable Long Island manufacturing community as we look to the future."

References

Introduction

Avery, Robert (1994). The pending intergenerational transfer. *Philanthropy, 8*(1), 5, 28–29. (As cited in Family philanthropy and the intergenerational transfer of wealth, below.) Also see: Avery, R. The ten trillion dollar question: A philanthropic game plan, *Initiatives*.

Community Foundation R&D Incubator (no date). Family philanthropy and the intergenerational transfer of wealth, Tapping into the power of family philanthropy in the 21st century. (Citations at pp. 1, 5.) Retrieved from http://www.cof.org/files/Documents/Family_Foundations/Generational-Succession/Intergenerational-Transfer-of-Wealth.pdf

Profile: Anita Zucker

Final approved profile developed from an interview presentation at the Charleston, S.C. Center for Women. http://c4women.wordpress.com/2011/01/12/c4w-member-profile-anita-zucker/; McQueeney,

T. (2011). Anita Zucker by Heart. Extraordinary Contributions from an Extraordinary Woman. http://lowcountrysun.sc/index.cfm? McKenna, B. (Nov. 5, 2005). Who the heck is Jerry Zucker, anyway? https://secure.globeadvisor.com/servlet/ArticleNews/story/gam/20051105/RCOVER05gy; http://www.forbes.com/profile/anitazucker and http://sb.cofc.edu/officeofthedean/boardofgovernors/spotlight/Zucker.php

Getting What You Deserve

Framing Negotiations

Moore, D. P. (2000). *Careerpreneurs.* (pp. 119–148. See the cited quotation by Moore, J. L. at p. 119.)

Negotiating Strategies for Career Success

Kay, L. (2007). Leading through negotiation: Harnessing the power of gender stereotypes, *California Management Review, 50*(1), 159–173. (Cite at pp. 160, 168.)

Kolb, D. M., & Williams, J. (2001). Breakthrough bargaining. *Harvard Business Review, 79*(2), 88–97. (Cite at p. 89.) Retrieved from EBSCO*host.* See also Kolb & Williams (2001). Shadow negotiation. *Executive Excellence, 18*(4), 9.

Kolb, D., Williams, J., & Frohlinger, C. (2004). *Her place at the table: A woman's guide to negotiating five key challenges to leadership success.* San Francisco, CA: Jossey-Bass.

Kray, L. J., Galinsky, A. D., & Thompson, L. (2002). Reversing the gender gap in negotiations: An exploration of stereotype regeneration. *Organizational Behavior and Human Decision Processes, 87*(2), 386. doi: 10.1006/obhd.2001.2979

Moore, D. P. (2000). *Careerpreneurs.* (Cite to Diane C. Harris at pp. 124–125.)

For additional resources see:

Haines, E. L., & Kray, L. J. (2005). Self-power associations: The possession of power affects women's self-concepts. *European Journal of Social Psychology, 35*(5), 643–662. Retrieved from EBSCO*host.*

Stuhlmacher, A. F., & Walters, A. E. (1999). Gender differences in negotiation outcome: A meta-analysis. *Personnel Psychology, 52*(3), 653–677. Retrieved from EBSCO*host.*

Walters, A. E., Stuhlmacher, A. F., & Meyer, L. L. (1998). Gender and negotiator competitiveness: A meta-analysis. *Organizational Behavior & Human Decision Processes, 76*(1), 1–29. Retrieved from EBSCO*host.*

Profile: Diane C. Harris

Final approved profile developed from featured presentation at Berkley Center of Entrepreneurship and Innovation, NYU Stern, personal interviews, website materials, and additional information furnished by the entrepreneur. See websites for further information: Hypotenuse Enterprises, Inc., *Hypotenuse* and *The smART of the Deal.*

Work–Life Balance—The Time Warp

Galinsky, E., Bond, J. T., Kim, S. S., Backon, L., Brownfield, E., & Sakai, K. (2005). Over work in America—When the way we work becomes too much. Families and Work Institute (54 pp.; see Table 11, pp. 26, 27, 28 for *work-centric, family-centric* or *dually centric* groupings based on indexed responses and potential meanings). Retrieved from http://familiesandwork.org/site/research/summary/overwork2005.pdf

For additional resources see:

Craig, L., & Sawrikar, P. (2009). Work and family: How does the (gender) balance change as children grow? *Gender, Work and Organization, 6*(6), 684–709. (Cite at p. 684.)

Fry, R., & Cohn, D.V. (June 27, 2011). Pew Research Center. Social and demographic trends. Living together: The economics of cohabitation. Retrieved from pewsocial/trends.org. http://pewresearch.org/pubs/2034/cohabitation-rate-doubled-since-mid-90s-only-more-educated-benefit-economically

Kanter, R. M. (2010). Work pray love. *Harvard Business Review, 88*(12), 38. Retrieved from EBSCOhost.

Kochhar, R. (July 6, 2011). In two years of economic recovery, women lost jobs, men found them. Retrieved from http://pewresearch.org/pubs/2049/unemployment-jobs-gender-recession-economic-recovery. See a related analysis: Heather, B. (May 6, 2011). Changing Places: Women continue to lose jobs as economy grows. Center for American Progress. http://www.americanprogress.org/issues/2011/05/changing places.html

MacDonald, M., Phipps, S., & Lethbridge, L. (March, 2005). Taking its toll: The influence of paid and unpaid work on women's well-being. *Feminist Economics, 11*(1), 63–94. See also Sayer, L., & Fine, L. (2011). Racial-ethnic differences in U.S. married women's and men's housework. *Social Indicators Research, 101*(2), 259–265.

Powell, G. N., & Greenhaus, J. H. (2010). Sex, gender, and the work-to-family interface: Exploring negative and positive interdependencies. *Academy of Management Journal, 53*(3), 513–534.

Helpful approach:

Rault, S. (March 28, 2005; Medically updated Nov. 7, 2006). Is your life running you ragged? (WebMD's First of two-part series on achieving better work–life balance). Retrieved from http://www.webmd.com/content/Article/103/106979.htm?pagenumber=3

Today and Tomorrow

Women Entrepreneurs, the Recession and Prospects for the Future

American Express Open state of women-owned businesses report—A summary of important trends, 1997–2011 (March, 2011). American Express Open, openforum.com/women, pp. 1–50. (Cited statistics, pp. 2–6.)

Center for Women's Business Research (Oct., 2009). The economic impact of women-owned businesses in the United States. Retrieved from www.womensbusinessresearch.org (Cite at p. 10.)

Cohoon, J. M., Wadhwa, V., & Mitchell, L. (May, 2010). The anatomy of an entrepreneur—Are successful women entrepreneurs different from men? Kauffman, the foundation of entrepreneurship, Kansas City, Missouri. http://www.kauffman.org/uploadedFiles/successful_women_entrepreneurs_5-10.pdf, 12 pp.

Guardian Life Small Business Research Institute (Dec., 2009). Special Report: Women small business owners will create 5+ million new jobs by 2018, transforming the workplace for millions of Americans. http://www.smallbizdom.com/Research/ResearchMonographs/index.htm

Hadary, S. (2010, Oct.). Launching women-owned businesses onto a high growth trajectory. National Women's Business Council. http://www.nwbc.gov/research/REPORTS.html

Han, H. (Sept. 29, 2010). The National Association of Women Business Owners. The roadmap to 2020 and the missing middle. http://www.nawbo.org/content_2863.cfm

Mitchell, L. (2011). The decade of the woman entrepreneur. Ewing Marion Kauffman Foundation. Retrieved from http://www.kauffman.org/entrepreneurship/the-decade-of-the-woman-entrepreneur.asp

Other studies consulted:

Harvey, A. R. (2011). Women's Business Centers, Office of Women's Business Centers. Small Business Administration. http://www.sba.gov/content/womens-business-centers

Mitchell, L. (May 11, 2011). Women entrepreneurs are trapped within glass walls. http://www.huffingtonpost.com/lesa-mitchell/women-entrepreneurs-trapp_b_860298.html

Technopreneurs

Center for Women's Business Research (2007). Solutions and sophistication technology study, Comparing men and women business owners' use of technology. Retrieved from http://www.womensbusinessresearch.org/

Strieber, A. (2011). Jobs rated 2011: Ranking 200 jobs from best to worst. Retrieved from CareerCast.Local Jobs + National Reach, http://www.careercast.com/jobs-rated/2011-ranking-200-jobs-best-worst

U.S. Department of Labor, Bureau of Labor Statistics (BLS) (2010). *Occupational Outlook Handbook,* 2010–11 Edition (Overview of the 2008–18 Projections). Retrieved from http://www.bls.gov/oco/oco2003.htm

Exploring IT—Where Are the Women?

Bureau of Labor Statistics (2010). *Occupational Outlook Handbook,* 2010–11 Edition, Overview of the 2008–18 projections. Retrieved from http://www.bls.gov/oco/oco2003.htm. See Tables 1 and 2: *Occupations with the fastest growth.*

Center for Women's Business Research (2007). Solutions and sophistication technology study. (Full citation above).

Coder, L., Rosenbloom, J. L., Ash, R. A., & Dupont, B. R. (2009). Economic and business dimensions: Increasing gender diversity in the IT work force. *Communications of the ACM, 52*(5), 25–27.

Madden, M. (Aug. 27, 2010). Pew Internet & American Life Project. Occupations with the fastest growth. http://pewresearch.org/pubs/1711/older-adults-social-networking-facebook-twitter. See Tables 1 and 2: *Occupations with the fastest growth.*

Morganson, V. J., Jones, M. P., & Major, D. A. (Dec., 2010). Understanding women's underrepresentation in science, technology, engineering, and mathematics: The role of social coping. *Career Development Quarterly, 59,* 169–179. Cite at p. 169 to authors: D. A., & Morganson, V. J. (2008). An inclusive IS&T work climate. In M. Khosrow-Pour (Ed.), *Encyclopedia of information science and technology* (2nd ed., pp. 1899–1905). Hershey, PA: Information Science Reference.

National Center for Women and Information Technology. http://ncwit.org/pdf; NCWITScorecard2010_SecondaryEducation.ppt; NCWITScorecard2010_PostSecondaryEducation.ppt; NCWITScorecard2010_Workforce.ppt; NCWITScorecard2010_Entrepreneurship.ppt

PayScale (July 6, 2011). Salary snapshot for software architect jobs. Retrieved from http://www.payscale.com/research/US/Job=Software_Architect/Salary. (The reference to detailed statistics is to Note 4, BLS Occupational Outlook.)

Trauth, E. M., & Quesenberry, J. L. (2007). Gender and the information technology workforce: Issues of theory and practice. In P. Yoong & S. Huff (Eds.), *Managing IT professionals in the internet age.* Hershey, PA: Idea Group Publishing. Retrieved from http://www.personal.psu.edu/gms/cis/old-cis/oldwebiste/05/eileentrauth/researchareasgender.htm

Wentling, R. M., & Thomas, S. (2009). Workplace culture that hinders and assists the career development of women in information technology.

Information Technology, Learning, and Performance Journal, 25(1), 25–42. (Cite at pp. 26, 27.)

Zickuhr, K. (Dec. 16, 2010). Pew Internet & American Life Project. Generations online in 2010. http://pewresearch.org/pubs/1831/generations-online-2010. Full report at pewinternet.org

Additional Resources:

Quesenberry, J. L. (2007). Career values and motivations: A study of women in the information technology workforce (doctoral dissertation). The Pennsylvania State University, Graduate School, College of Information Sciences and Technology. (Cite on the percentage drop of women in IT at p. 4.)

Trauth, E. M., Quesenberry, J. L., & Haiyan, H. (2009). Retaining women in the U.S. IT workforce: Theorizing the influence of organizational factors. *European Journal of Information Systems, 18*(5), 476–497. doi: 10.1057/ejis.2009.31

Trauth, E. M., Quesenberry, L. L., & Haiyan, H. (2008). A multicultural analysis of factors influencing career choice for women in the information technology workforce. *Journal of Global Information Management, 16*(4), 1–23. Retrieved from EBSCO*host.*

Virtual Work Teams

Bjørn, P., & Ngwenyama, O. (2009). Virtual team collaboration: Building shared meaning, resolving breakdowns and creating translucence. *Information Systems Journal, 19*(3), 227–253. Retrieved from doi: 10.1111/j.1365-2575.2007.00281.x

Hewson, H. J. (2005). Hive mind and groupthink: The curse of the perfect IPT. *Defense & AT-L, 34*(6), 32–33. Retrieved from http://www.au.af.mil/au/awc/awcgate/dau/hew_nd05.pdf

Janis, I. L. (1972). *Victims of groupthink.* New York, NY: Houghton Mifflin. Seealso, Janis, I. L. (1982).*Groupthink: Psychological studies of policy decisionsand fiascoes* (2nd ed.). New York, NY: Houghton Mifflin.

Kirkman, B. L., Rosen, B., Tesluk, P. E., & Gibson, C. B. (2004). The impact of team empowerment on virtual team performance: The moderating role of face-to-face interaction. *Academy of Management Journal, 47*(2), 175–192.

Mannix, E., & Neale, M. A. (2005). What differences make a difference? The promise and reality of diverse teams in organizations. *Psychological Science in the Public Interest, 6,* 31–55. doi: 10.1111/j.1529-1006.2005.00022.x

Additional Valuable References:

Kanawattanachai, P., & Yoo, Y. (2007). Impact of knowledge coordination on virtual team performance. *MIS Quarterly, 31*(4), 783–808. (Cite at p. 783.) Retrieved from EBSCOhost.

Möllering, G. (2000) Trust, institutions, agency: Towards a neoinstitutional theory of trust. In R. Bachmann & A. Zaheer (Eds.), *Handbook of trust research* (pp. 355–376). Cheltenham and Northampton: Edward Elgar. (Cite at p. 373.)

Panteli, N., & Tucker, R. (2009). Power and trust in global virtual teams. *Communications of the ACM (CACM), 52*(12), 113–115. Retrieved from EBSCOhost.

Salamon, S. D., & Robinson, S. L. (2008). Trust that builds: The impact of collective felt trust on organizational performance. *Journal of Applied Psychology, 93*(3), 593–601. Retrieved from EBSCOhost.

Webster, J., & Wong, W. K. P. (2008). Comparing traditional and virtual group forms: Identity, communication and trust in naturally occurring project teams. *International Journal of Human Resource Management, 19*(1), 41–62. doi: 10.1080/09585190701763883

Workman, M. (2007). The effects from technology-mediated interaction and openness in virtual team performance measures. *Behaviour & Information Technology, 26*(5), 355-365. doi:10.1080/01449290500402809

Which Way Government?

Center for Women's Business Research (Oct., 2009). The economic impact of women-owned businesses in the United States. Retrieved from http://www.womensbusinessresearch.org. (Cites at p. 10.)

Moore, D. P. (2010). Women as entrepreneurs and business owners. In K. O'Connor (Ed.) *Gender and women's leadership,* (pp. 443–451. Cites at pp. 446–447.)

Whitaker, L. D. (2010). Overview: History of women's public leadership. In K. O'Connor (Ed.), *Gender and women's leadership* (Vol. 1, pp. 61–69) (Cites at p. 66).

Passage of Time through Generations

The Family Business

Allen, E. E., & Langowitz, N. S. (Aug., 2003). Women in family-owned businesses report, Babson College Center for Women's Leadership & Massachusetts Mutual Life Insurance Company, 20 pp. (cite at p.1.) Retrieved from http://www3.babson.edu/CWL/research/Women-in-Family-Owned-Businesses.cfm

Dugan, A. M., Krone, S. P., LeCouvie, K., Pendergast, J. M., & Schuman, D. (2008). A woman's place: The crucial roles of women in family business report. Retrieved from http://www.amazon.com/Womans-Place-Crucial-Family-Business/dp/1891652214#_

O'Hara, W. T., Founder and Executive Director, Institute for Family Enterprise and President Emeritus of Bryant College. The quote is from *Centuries of Success* (2004), Avon, MA: Adams Media. Retrieved from http://thefamilybusinessschool.com/node/60

Perman, S. (Feb. 13, 2006). Taking the pulse of family business. *Business Week* Online in NY. Retrieved from http://www.businessweek.com/smallbiz/content/feb2006/sb20060210_476491.htm)

Challenges in Turning over the Family Business

American Family Business Survey (2003). George and Robin Raymond Family Business Institute, Loyola University, Chicago, Kennesaw State University, Atlanta and Babson College, Boston.

Lumpkin, G. T. (2010). Long-term orientation: Implications for the entrepreneurial orientation and performance of family businesses. *Entrepreneurship & Regional Development, 22*(3/4), 241–264. (Later citation at p. 241.)

Simmonds, R. (2007). The family business: Failing to plan is commonplace. *Financial Executive, 23*(7), 20. Also supported in the March, 2008 article, Family firms lax on succession, management. *Journal of Accountancy, 205*(3), 19.

Sherman, A. J. (no date). Understanding the fundamentals of succession and transition planning (The Kauffman Foundation). Retrieved from http://www.entrepreneurship.org/en/resource-center/understanding-the-fundamentals-of-succession-and-transition-planning.aspx. See also a supporting source: Bareither, K. R. A different model for wealth transfer planning—alarming statistics for family-owned businesses! Retrieved from http://www.fbrsystem.com/families/family-owned-business.html

Profile: Anne Shybunko-Moore

Final approved profile developed from interviews with entrepreneur, website materials, featured presentations, and additional information furnished by the entrepreneur. Also see GSE Dynamics In the News: Long Island Business News; Newsday; CBS Interactive Business Network, Retrieved from http://www.gsedynamics.com/InTheNews.aspx

AFTERWORD

The profiles approved by the women entrepreneurs for this study underscore the desire of so many successful women to make a difference, to add value to our world, to impact other people's lives in positive ways. This is not a surprising discovery; I had seen it before during the interviews I conducted for my earlier books.

Within their industries, these women encourage others, not forgetting how steep the climb up the ladder was. They measure success in the satisfaction of a job well done, a project completed, the respect of their peers and others and their own integrity. They mentor young people and not only watch but delight in their growth and maturity as they prepare for organizational challenges and solutions. They love sharing. They provide scholarships, raise funds for battered women and children's shelters and a long list of other worthwhile causes. They ask themselves, "Did I make a difference today?" And the answer is resoundingly "Yes."

The entrepreneurs presented in special profile cases here and in scenarios throughout the book are making their difference in many ways. Gail Naughton's and Maria Maccecchini's medical research breakthroughs in developing potential cures for skin replacement, cancer and Alzheimer's disease speak of their dedication to producing the bio-technology products to serve people in areas not necessarily designated as high profit, as does Denise Devine's dedication to developing innovative nutritious lines of food products for people of all ages. There are the efforts of Shabnam Rezaei and Suzy Spafford to reach children and communities around the world in imaginative and creative ways beyond stereotypes. The initiatives to better the lot of women and people in the workforce undertaken by Nikki Hardin, Jennet Robinson Alterman, Carol E. Farren, Anne Shybunko-Moore, Eleanor Tabi Haller-Jorden, Aliza Sherman, Julie Weeks, Judith Moore and Kay Koplovitz are many and varied and have a long-range impact. Aliza's Chain of Daisies has opened a special network for women speakers. Jennet's motto and programming to accomplish the message behind "we help women succeed every day" has extended her outreach beyond South Carolina. Aside from joining practically an all-male workforce in handling massive facilities around the world, Carol Farren has created a shelter for cats. The network Tabi has formed on the international front to create opportunities for women at the highest executive levels and on corporate boards has an influence, as does Julie's research outreach to not only educate but to inform beyond borders. From Judith, we have a whole new understanding of a *Surcee*—a word meaning "to care"—a great custom to move beyond Charleston, and also the understanding of just how deep the drive must be to succeed as a small business owner. A word of praise for Anne, who recognized a need greater than that of her own company, the survival of a whole industry in manufacturing technology and set out to develop the alliances to make it happen. There is no way to measure the worth of contributions like the mentoring and coaching of Ruth Ann Menutis, where people every day ask to write business cases on how she helped them in their start-ups or growth ventures, or the focus of Rebecca Smith on making public and community projects environmentally sound. The rededication of Diane Harris to good works starting at the "grassroots level" is an act of renewed faith, as she defines it, because money and success are not enough, but helping others understand and achieve a clearer vision is worth pursuing. As for Deborah Szekely, she is the kind of person you meet once and feel as if you have known for a lifetime. She is a shining beacon of support in numerous cultural, environmental and charitable causes on many fronts in the world and has taught us more about the importance of good health, diet, and exercise than anyone I know. Anita Zucker has reached out to lead the way for young girls in STEM, is an avid community supporter and contributor to a long list of medical and ongoing charitable works, all in the spirit of her family and company motto: "We use the power behind the products we make and the kinds of companies we have to do repair of the world," whether in "products that save lives or through products that provide entertainment." This motto summarizes the approaches used by this set of women entrepreneurs in their companies in a very crystal way.

To the list of entrepreneurs profiled in this book who have been such inspirations and given so much back, I must add two people who stand out in the academic and professional community to advance the knowledge and awareness of the contributions of women leaders and entrepreneurs in university and college environments.

Myra Hart, one of the four founding members of Staples, returned to Harvard to earn her doctorate and then joined the Business School's Entrepreneurial Unit. Inventorying the existing Harvard Business School cases and other teaching materials, which are the "gold standard" in college and university teaching across the country and around the world and are created at the rate of about 700 a year, she discovered that they focused predominantly on men and their accomplishments. To begin rectifying the balance, in 1998 Marjorie Alfus provided a $1 million grant to underwrite collaboration between the School and the Committee 200, an elite group of successful businesswomen, to produce and get into circulation business cases and other materials with women protagonists. With Dr. Hart as the principal research and course development coordinator, the project generated 75 new business cases focused on women during the five-year period of Marjorie's support, and the program continues today.

Women are role models, not just for other women, but for society. The challenge is to move forward, to celebrate the accomplishments of women as well as those of men and to help educate others so the pipelines to success are equally open.

References

Alfus, M. (Feb. 18, 2000). Plenary address: The experiences and lessons of a 20th century entrepreneur: How relevant in the next millennium? United States Association for Small Business and Entrepreneurship. San Antonio, TX. Retrieved from the *USASBE Proceedings* website.

Anonymous (Aug. 6, 2007). Dr. Myra M. Hart—Outstanding at Harvard. Retrieved from http://blog.championboards.com/2007/08/dr-myra-m-hart-outstanding-at-harvard.html. References to this document include http://harvardbusinessonline.hbsp.harvard.edu/b02/en/cases/cases_home.jhtml; http://www3.babson.edu/Newsroom/Releases/MHartCWL2-07.cfm and http://www.hno.harvard.edu/gazette/1998/01.15/NewInitiativeat.html

Moore, D. P. (2000). *Careerpreneurs.* (Referenced material at p. 65.)

ACKNOWLEDGEMENT

The *Post and Courier*, Charleston, South Carolina

The topics in this book contain material that originally appeared in columns I wrote for the Charleston Post and Courier. I express sincere appreciation to the newspaper for their release of all of my columns prior to signing a contract for this book. In cases where columns have been used they have been updated, revised and/or especially written for this book. The material that appears here is based on a continual stream of research in the field of business. For this reason, few of the entries in WomenPreneurs appear in the form originally published in the newspaper.

Moxie Job Coaching Columns Written on Behalf of the Center for Women:

2011 Improve Your Position in Negotiations (7.22)
Recession and the Future (6.24)
Getting What You're Worth (5.27)
Building Virtual Work Teams (4.22)
Women Valuable on Boards (3.25)
New Choices for Women—Female Entrepreneurs Globally . . . (2.25)
Corruption and Complicity—Know When Not to Stand by Your Brand (1.28)

2010 Mentor should be advocate (12.24)
Computer Field Wide Open (10.29)
Copreneurs Have Key Issues (9.24)

Making Climb to the Top (8.27)
Building Customer Loyalty (7.16) (Reprinted by SC Dental Association)
The Need for Networking (6.18)
Mompreneur Label Can Be Confusing (5.21)
Insightful Companies Need Intrapreneurs (4.23)
Generation Differences Pose Challenges (3.26)
Managing Up Builds Trust (2.26)
Gender Stereotypes: All Minds Needed at the Table (1.22)

2009 Women Are Changing Business Landscape (12.11)
Develop Clear Cut Strategies to Land Job in 2010 (11.27)
Create Networks that Mean Something to You (11.13)
Rules Teach Art of Negotiation (10.30)
Take Steps to Retool Skills, Rethink Options (9.18)
Building Relationships: Manager, Leader and Entrepreneur Sustainability (8.17)
Marketing Yourself Gets the Job (7.24)

Business Major Columns under Editorship of Teresa Taylor, *Post and Courier* Business Review. Very special thanks to Teresa for all the wonderful guidance and her editorship of these earlier articles:

2002 Businesses Need to Cultivate Diversity (10.21)
Workplace Generational Differences Noteworthy (5.20)
Succession Plan Important to Family Business Success (3.25)
When Company Actions Veer From Values, Everybody Loses (1.28)

2001 Women Get Short End of Corporate Stick (12.17)
Improving Prospects in a Recession Economy (11.19)
Post-Attack Stress Beginning to Plague Small Businesses (10.15)
How Prepared Are You if Confronted by a Layoff? (9.10)
ADA Makes Positive Impact on Small Business (7.30)
Approaches to Management 101 May Differ (6.11)
Survival May Depend on Changing Style (4.30)
Educators Debate Merits of Teaching Entrepreneurship (3.19)
What's in Vogue for Women Entrepreneurs? (2.26)
Modern Leaders' Resources Plenty (1.29)
Female Entrepreneurs Motivated by Freedom (12.18)
Women Entrepreneurs in Global Transition (11.27)
Higher Education to Play Key Role in Lowcountry Growth (10.16)
Matching Job Alliances to Develop Your Career Goals (9.9)
Job analysis can motivate staff (8.7)
Don't Overlook Job Analysis (7.3)
Anti-discrimination Laws Pose Challenges (6.5)
Stress Builders and Breakers Evaluated (4.10)
Accreditation Key for Business Programs (2.21)
Negotiating Strategies for Career Success (1.17)

1999 Hard Work at Root of Business Success (11.29)
Path is Rarely Well-Marked for Female Entrepreneurs (11.8)
Distressing Business of Hurricane Repairs (10.4)
Book Details Gender Status in Workplace (8.30)
Women's Business Gains Still Impressive (8.9)
Success Reached by Many Routes (6.7)
Decision-Making Skills Key for Managers (4.5)

Career Demands You Plot a Course (3.8)
Corporate Life Stifles Entrepreneurs (2.1)

1998 Inequality Versus Diversity at Work (12.28)
Good and Bad Management Inspire Entrepreneurs (11.30)
Gender-based Management—A Hot Issue (10.26)
Assessing Your Growth Potential (9.28)
Networking Helps Women Build Businesses (8.31)
Women Discover Power of Creating Networks (7.27)
Networking Keeps Entrepreneurs Afloat (6.29)
Men and Women Managers Wield Power Differently (5.25)
Good Bosses Enlist Employees' Help (4.27)
Women Say Glass Ceiling Shatterproof (3.30)
Corporations a Spring Board for Entrepreneurs (3.2)
Entrepreneurs Need Proper Initiatives (1.26)

1997 Methods to Reduce Risk (12.22)
Women Profile Business Success (11.24)
Female Entrepreneurs Enjoy New Clout (10.27)

INDEX